FAMILY REUNION

FAMILY REUNION

Everything You Need to Know to Plan Unforgettable Get-Togethers for Every Kind of Family

❖❖❖

JENNIFER CRICHTON

WORKMAN PUBLISHING · NEW YORK

Dedication

To my great-grandfather, William Crichton,
who left the mines in Scotland at 15,
"came around the Horn in his bare feet"
as a seaman at 16, and jumped ship in
San Francisco Bay at 17—or so they say.
This book is not only for you—it's
because of you.

Library of Congress Cataloging-in-Publication Data

Crichton, Jennifer
Family reunion : everything you need to know to plan unforgettable
get-togethers for every kind of family / by Jennifer Crichton.

p. cm.
Includes index.
ISBN 0-7611-0585-9 (alk. paper)
1. Family reunions—United States—Planning. I. Title.
GT2423.C75 1998
394.2—dc21   97-53256 CIP

Design by Janet Vicario and Natsumi Uda
Catering and Food Consultant: Sarah Stitham

Workman books are available at special discounts when purchased in bulk for
premiums and sales promotions as well as for fund-raising or educational use.
Special editions can also be created to specification. For details, contact the
Special Sales Director at the address below.

Workman Publishing Company, Inc.
708 Broadway
New York, NY 10003-9555

Printed in the United States

First printing July 1998
10 9 8 7 6 5 4 3 2 1

ACKNOWLEDGMENTS

An unexpected benefit to working on this book was the way my research reversed any tendency to slide into cynicism. Reunion organizers are the most good-hearted extroverts to walk the earth, and they peopled much of my world for these past few years. Thanks for drawing me over to the sunny side of the street.

Literally hundreds of people took the time and effort to talk reunions with me. Thanks to all, especially Julie and Lisa Ades, Theresa Bailey, Mary Brockmyre and her cousin, Terry Seacrest, Myndel Cohen, Winifred Coleman, Amanda Dargan, Priscilla Dunhill, Elyse Eisenberg, Maureen Fernandez, Ralph and Debby Gardner, Mary Guterson, Mary Beth Harper, Pete Holste, Blair Hoyt, Bridgid and Winifred Infante, Marita Karlisch at the American Swedish Institute, Katharine King, Dan Leeson, Don LeFevre at the Public Affairs Department of the Church of Latter-Day Saints, Maureen Fernandez, Joyce Little, Dora Loh and Lorraine Loh-Norris, Michele Lovelace, Jenny Lund, Joan McKenna, Nikki Mendoza, Chere Negaard, Dr. Gwen Kennedy Neville, David Novak, Susanne Oberhauser, Susan Pasquini, Kelly Peduzzi, Mike and Becky Porter, Emily Prigot and Shira Rosan of the Fischer family, Rohulamin Quander, Cheryl Reitan, Max Rudin, John Rumely, Helen Russell and Joan Rumely Sparrow, Gale Robinson, Kirk Robinson, Mary Royster, Lanee Slaughter, Llew Smith, Eric Smith, Mrs. Charles P. Stetson, Lindy and Jim Taggart, Marilyn Taylor, Rosemary Toohey, Holly Hollinger Trumbull, Donna Takasuka, Dr. Ione D. Vargus, Ellie von Wellsheim, Randy Williams, Diane Winum, Judy Weiland, Jacqueline and Eugene Withers, Ethel Young, Jenice Ziew, and Dexter and Zoe Lovelace Zimet.

Thanks, too, to the wonderful families who welcomed an outsider into their clan for their reunions: the Sandberg family, especially the lively Lois, Alyson, and Diana Bruu; the Grange family, especially Kitty Goldston, Chris Coleman, and their extraordinarily beautiful mother Jeannie Urquhart; the Davidson crew—thanks for letting me be your fresh-air kid through the years; the Kenney-Austin crew, in particular Nancy Kenney Hays for smoothing the Cotuit Bay waters for me; Lewis Faber and Helen Rubinstein, whose enthusiasm was contagious; Larry Okrent, who knows God is in the details and I am a stumbling acolyte; and the Robinson clan, with many thanks to the generous Doretha Davis.

I am also grateful to the experts who bailed me out at critical points. Evan Imber-Black, Ph.D., and Janine Roberts, Ed.D., were invaluable in their insights as family therapists, as was Elana Katz with her suggestions on easing stepchildren into the extended family. Storyteller Cherie Karo Schwartz and folklorist Steve Zeitlin were inspiring in their suggestions on collecting and valuing family stories. Judith Martin, who could write a book on families and manners (and has!) was the gold standard of graciousness in giving her time. William Raspberry was a richly eloquent source of thinking on families and reunions. I am indebted to my aunt, Margot Feiner Conte, my genealogy genie. And Sarah Stitham was responsible for the accessible recipes for cooking for a crowd.

At Workman, many thanks to Aran Shetterly, for chasing down the flying papers, to Janet Vicario and Natsumi Uda for their artwork, and to my editor Ruth Sullivan, to whom everything matters, who allows nothing to slip by, and who always took my writing where it wanted to go.

And where would I be without my family? Thanks go to my cousin Jean Crichton, who reinvented the wheel when she pulled together our fantastic reunion—and the wheel almost never wobbled. To my cousin John N. (Jack) Crichton and my uncle Andy Crichton, thanks for your support and for being the beacons of openness, energy, and generosity that characterize the Crichtons at their best. To my mother and mentor, Judy Crichton: I hope we always write our books together. To my children, Andrew and Catherine: Thanks for your knowledgeable advice on games and activities, for not touching certain piles of papers, and for shining on. To my husband David Emil: As always, a thousand thanks, and more.

CONTENTS

INTRODUCTION

CELEBRATING FAMILY

We are the people who left home. We left the dirt-poor farms of County Cork for the hardscrabble streets of Brooklyn. We left the mills of New Hampshire for the Oklahoma homestead, and the Oklahoma dust for the wet green of Oregon. We were wrenched from our families in Ghana, dragged in chains to South Carolina, and left the sharecroppers' Mississippi Delta for the automobile factories of Detroit. We left Russian shtetls for the tenements of Manhattan, and Manhattan for the Connecticut hills. And every day we pack up and head for Seattle's quality of life, Tucson's warm weather, Atlanta's professional opportunities, and Montana's breathing room.

As a nation of individualists, we believed in lighting out for the territory, in leaving the family to pursue our destiny. In the great push forward, our forefathers had to keep their minds on the future, not on the past. No other country takes it so in stride when the members of a family scatter across the face of a continent and still presume to call themselves close.

Now, with our relative affluence and assimilation, we have the security to stop, turn around, and look back. How did we get here from there? We feel profoundly grateful to the grandparents and great-grandparents who made this life possible. Reunions are

one way to honor our forebears and that struggle.

In the past, family reunions were about getting back to familiar roots: the old farm or the hometown that shaped us like a third parent. But few of us have that strong a sense of place anymore. We're a nation of mixed cultures, mixed marriages, and ever-changing address books. We believe in movement and the therapeutic benefits of change. Few of us can still return to the homes where we grew up. Retiring parents pack up their golf clubs and head south for dry air, bright sun, and eighteen holes every day. Where is home now?

Today our sense of home is rooted less in a place than in the family spirit itself. Reunions reinvent home, place, and culture. When we walk into a family reunion, we exhale and think, "This is where I belong. This is where I feel right." We fall in sync with familiar conversational rhythms, laughter that sounds like our own, and a deep pool of goodwill.

Holidays used to pull us together, the uncles and cousins and their kids crammed together around the turkey. But who has a living room big enough for all those cousins? And a family with four adult siblings living in Colorado, New York, Washington state, and Idaho can't realistically plan to be together for both Thanksgiving and Christmas. Where would they all stay? What would the airplane tickets cost? What about all the in-laws who must also be visited at holiday time?

A community has always required effort, but the only way for us to feel connected to something bigger than ourselves nowadays is to connect by appointment only. According to anthropologists, there is actually less human contact now than when the country was far less populated. The conveniences created to cope with the huge surge in population—voice mail, E-mail, home offices, cash machines, mail-order shopping—make us ever more isolated. And while many neighborhoods are still lively, others resemble ghost towns during the day. The fabric of our social network has thinned. Cousins

down the block, mothers nearby to baby-sit or to chat with, a town where we're known by sight, if not by name: That's the kind of home we're looking for.

At a family reunion we re-create that home for a day or two, constructing a temporary village of strangers who are somehow familiar, a sense of young and old belonging together, and a sense of belonging, period, from sunup to sundown. Was this how villages used to be in the Old Country? Half the people related to you somehow, the other half married to someone related to you somehow, all sharing a common genetic or cultural pool and a common history?

Kids especially find it reassuring to belong to an extended collection of well-meaning characters. They sense the fragility of their nuclear families. They know enough families in which the parents divorce, die, or move away that they can easily envision such a shattering thing occurring to them. If the high-wire tension of the nuclear family should snap, the presence of an extended family acts as a safety net. While going to a reunion may not be as immediately entertaining as playing a video game, kids still find themselves heaving sighs of relief and satisfaction when they do, even if they're not sure why. The truth is, it's fun—big, deep fun—to belong to something bigger than yourself.

We accept as a given the idea that marriage takes work and that friendships need nurturing, but we resist the idea that family requires work, as well. We're more idealistic—and less realistic—about family than about any other relationship. Family, we feel, should be like a force of nature, continuing on with or without us. But in truth, family is only a system of linked relationships, a network that survives only if we continue to physically and emotionally forge the links and make the effort to be together.

"There was a time when our branch of the family wouldn't speak to our cousins' branch because of the way we felt about the Vietnam War," one woman remembers. Raging arguments about such topics as Vietnam destroyed Thanksgiving dinners and turned New Year's Eves bitter. Unlike the 1970s sitcom *All in the Family,* which showed a father and son-in-law trading zingers on political and racial subjects week after week, the American family was not so indestructible. After a miserable Thanksgiving spent fighting, an uncle and aunt would decide to spend Christmas somewhere else. And then, you just didn't see the cousins anymore.

If the ideologically volatile 1960s taught us anything, it's that families can't talk about everything—a tough realization for a nation brought up paying homage to honesty. At almost every reunion, though, families steer consciously and dutifully away from political topics. Nobody wants to put the family to the test again.

The very act of reuniting heals, pulling and knitting together what was wrenched apart or has slipped away. Often, nothing more is needed to heal a division than simply coming together in good faith. "My mother and her sister had a fight many, many years ago," recounts Gale Robinson, a New York–based filmmaker. "They stopped speaking and my aunt and her family moved away. We pretty much forgot about them. But when my son went to college in St. Louis, he needed a good dentist, and I knew I had a cousin there, so I called her for a referral, and I felt so comfortable talking to this woman I hadn't seen or spoken to in thirty years! That one personal disagreement between my mother and hers had separated an entire family. We knew it was time to come together again." They did, holding a weekend reunion and discovering there's no kin quite like blood kin.

We can love our spouses passionately, and we do. Our friendships may be powerful, and they are. But blood kinship creates an immediate sense of belonging, of being among one's own kind, hard to duplicate elsewhere. When you walk into a reunion and see traces of your father in his cousins, it's more than just the shape of the jaw or the familiar sandy hair that triggers recognition. It's the sound of their laughter, their hand gestures, the rhythm of their speech. It's in what is considered funny enough to laugh about. There's a connection there that is almost tribal: This is how we do things, the little things life is composed of, and we don't even know we're doing them— a convergence of culture and biology.

It's that recognition, that unexpected sense of belonging, that is so moving about reunions, as though you're a piece of a jigsaw puzzle that slips into place without being forced. Part of it may be a DNA-recognition instinct, hardwired into our beings as part of our survival mechanism: We recognize our own people on a subliminal level and feel unusually secure as a result. Reunion goers talk time and time again about an ineffable sense of relief and belonging when they're among family.

That same emotional pull is exerted at weddings, funerals, and holidays, like Christmas, Passover, and Thanksgiving, strengthening a family's sense of identity and continuity. But these are celebrations of the larger culture we share with millions of others. Only family reunions celebrate the fact that this one particular family has gathered. "When you look around at a reunion and you realize that you come from a group of such basically decent, intelligent, good people, it reassures you—not just about yourself but about the world in general," says Diane Winum, who began attending reunions again with her family in Virginia after realizing what she was missing. "You know this family isn't the only one that's so decent. You have a sense of a larger force behind you, operating with goodwill."

Family reunions honor the past, strengthen the future, and bring families together with a keen sense that now is now and will never be just this way, with just these people, again. There's a sense of time having passed, of time passing, of not having all the time in the world. As beloved aunts and uncles begin to falter and beautiful nieces and nephews surge to the fore, there is a clear vision of the fragility and strength of individuals. It's a vision of the family as a stream moving forward into the future, with or without you. At a family reunion you can watch the stream move— and then dive right in, streaming forward with it.

THE RITUAL
OF
REUNION

Why a Family Reunion?
Reunions of the Past
Coming Home

What sets a family reunion apart from other family gatherings or parties? It's a ritual unlike any other—a special time calling ordinary time to a halt, demanding reflection on and celebration of where we've been, who we are, and where we're headed. A big barbecue in the backyard with cousins and neighbors and friends may look from a distance like a reunion. Kids in the pool, chicken on the grill, grown-ups laughing in the dusk at times gone by. But it's not—it's a party. It lacks the common denominator of kinship, and with that, the spoken or unspoken acknowledgment of a shared identity, a mutual past, and vested interest in the future. It's missing the certainty that one belongs to this family, forever and without provisions. Guests attend a barbecue because they've been invited, but a family member attends a reunion on nobody's sufferance.

Thanksgiving and other holidays look like reunions, too—feast days that bring family together and replace ordinary time with a sense of occasion. But holidays place families in a panoramic landscape of other families, reminding us that our family belongs to an even bigger group— a shared history, a shared religion perhaps, the rest of humankind certainly. A reunion appears only on the family's calendar—a holiday about family for family—with a family zealously guarding its uniqueness, sharing the day with no one else. And, for the moment, the rest of the world and its demands and expectations fall away.

Every family approaches ritual differently. For some families, their rituals must be highly structured— their reunion has to be opened with a blessing by a family elder, or it just doesn't feel right. For others, a reunion is a looser affair, with no "liturgy" at all. But no matter how it's structured, when a reunion works as a successful ritual, it manages to make some meaning of our lives, a meaning beyond celebration. Because reunions are about family, and the passages into and out of and through life by the family members, they can never be only unalloyed celebration. What makes a reunion special is the sense of caring about these passages,

FAMILY RITUAL STYLES

It's worth looking at your family's current ritual style—how much ritual it is drawn to and feels comfortable with—before working out what kind of reunion your family might want to hold. In their book *Rituals for Our Times,* family therapists Dr. Evan Imber-Black and Janine Roberts, Ed.D., have defined different ritual styles. Recognizing your family's tendency to minimal or rigid rituals can help reunion organizers move toward the flexible style that families really need and want.

Minimized	Little may be planned for the reunion, with few announcements sent out and few activities scheduled. Affection and warmth may be present, but there may be a lack of cohesion, a sense of never fully coming together, and a lack of closure.
Imbalanced	The reunion may take place at a formal restaurant, where kids have no entertainment, or at Disneyland, where activities are all focused on kids.
Interrupted	After the longtime organizer of a reunion dies, nobody steps in to fill her shoes. Years pass before the family realizes what they've lost.
Rigid/ Obligatory	The reunion is always held in the same place on the same date with the same foods. The structure makes no concessions to newcomers, and everyone is afraid to try something new. Attendance usually dwindles at rigid/ obligatory reunions because in the end, they fill nobody's needs or desires.
Flexible	Families take into account the needs of all those attending, work on ways to include new family members, pay homage to those who have left the family, and organize activities from an intergenerational perspective.

"A *family ritual emphasizes behavior of which a family is proud and of which its members definitely approve. It is what the family sees about itself that it likes and wants formally to continue.* **"**

—*James Bossard and Eleanor Boll*
anthropologists

because everyone in attendance, as family members, will care in a way that others can't. At a reunion, among family, my losses are your losses, your triumphs are mine as well.

The reunion ritual can express, just by existing, the paradoxes of our lives. For example, that while the family may be linked to and strengthened by its past, it still urges itself into the future. Though a family member may belong to the

extended family, he still for the most part goes through the world as a solitary traveler. A family may have one foot in the Old Country but at the same time be fully American. That adults are parents of children as well as children of parents. And that we all want to stay, and we all want to go.

But for reunions to work as rituals, the ritual must be a flexible one, able to adapt to a family's many changes and not become rote. When families march dutifully through the motions, or when the family never celebrates itself, the ritual becomes irrelevant to the family's emotional life, and the hold and rewards of family life dissolve. Rituals don't just happen; they are handcrafted and hand-tooled. Like all one-of-a-kind treasures, the uniqueness of each family's reunion gives it a value beyond reckoning.

A REUNION TOAST

"Mom has always been one for rituals. She's always shown us that it's important to make the effort, to set the table and make a beautiful dinner, to step back from the 9-to-5 grind to see what's special and what matters in life. She always plans some kind of grand event every year, and at first, when she told us about this reunion, we logged it on the calendar as just one

more of those events. But this reunion has already proved to be so much more than I anticipated. Now I want to carry this feeling beyond the reunion, so that the closeness extends into our daily lives, evolves beyond the social graces and the holiday formality. I don't want this feeling to end. I want to make it last, and grow."

—Chris Dunhill, age 29

A SHORT HISTORY OF REUNIONS

Where did the American family reunion come from? According to Dr. Gwen Kennedy Neville, an anthropologist who has studied reunions extensively, these family gatherings make up for what most of us lack in modern life: rural settings, extended family nearby, and a large-scale meal shared by the entire family. Scottish and Scots-Irish Protestants brought over the prototypes for future American reunions when they settled in the South and the mid-Atlantic states.

In 18th-century Scotland, religious gatherings that featured open-air preaching and the taking of sacraments became festive holidays for the newly urbanized Protestants who had been forced to leave rural areas to find work in the cities. For these camp meetings, working people would leave the mills, mines, and factories for a day or two and return to the countryside to reconnect with nature, religion (urban Scots were notoriously indifferent to churchgoing), and the friends and family they'd left behind. It was a temporary respite from the urban, from the secular, and from the isolation that marked the new Industrial Age.

Once they settled in the southern United States, Scottish immigrants continued this tradition, holding outdoor preachings, tent meetings, and "meetings on the hill"—traditions that still survive in some areas today. For many, these religious events served as their only vacations. People traveled for miles, spent the night in rustic surroundings, and engaged in fellowship, prayer meetings, and worship. The belief that unspoiled nature was where people can seek God was an essential component of much mainstream Protestant practice—a spiritual perspective that has caught on among many, if not most, Americans.

As time went on, camp meetings and retreats became more institutionalized, less directly religious, and more infused with the goal of general uplift and self-improvement.

Other gatherings fusing religious observance, family remembrance and elements of holiday festivities contributed to an evolving vision of the American family reunion.

CEMETERY ASSOCIATION DAYS

Families linked by bloodlines or sense of kinship met to maintain the grave sites of ancestors and, later, to picnic on the grounds. (Cemeteries in the South, where this tradition is still honored, continue to provide picnic tables to this end.) Cemetery association days share many features with present-day family reunions. They are occasions on which scattered families come together in a special place to experience a sense of fellowship, honor common ancestors, and share a meal outdoors.

DECORATION DAYS

Known also as dedication days, these gatherings are similar to cemetery association days but are usually limited to a single family returning to a grave site to place flowers and tend to the graves.

CHURCH HOMECOMINGS

Church homecomings draw members of a congregation back to their "home" or "birth" church for a day of preaching, family togetherness, honoring the dead and the founders of the church, and sharing a meal on the grounds. Homecomings are especially important to southern families—Black and white—who have lost many members to industrial opportunities up North. Church homecomings (also called rally days) serve both as family reunions and occasions of spiritual restoration and renewal.

OLD HOME DAY

In the New England states each year, one day was set aside for people to return, mingle, and picnic with old friends, neighbors, and relations in the town parks and greens. These government-sponsored events were created at the turn of the last century as local mills and factories shut down and forced people to move away, looking for jobs elsewhere.

FAMILY CIRCLES

Jewish family networks thrived during the 1930s and 40s, stimulated in large part by growing knowledge of the Holocaust. The sense at the time was "If we don't stick up for ourselves and stick together, who will?" one family-circle member recalls. Siblings, cousins, and their spouses would gather weekly or monthly for a Sunday meal. Some family circles were political—working toward establishing a Jewish state, for instance—while others were chiefly cultural groups in which works of literature were discussed. But most were social, for adults only (membership at age 21 was considered a rite of passage), constructing a reliable network of emotional and financial support for first- and second-generation immigrants. Dues were collected and used to help with burials, family illness, or unemployed members.

COUSINS' CLUBS

Cousins' clubs, which thrived among Jewish families after World War II, were more unabashedly social, typically composed of the sons and daughters of immigrants. Relatives gathered to play cards, eat, and tell jokes. Many cousins' clubs dissolved in the 1960s as the older members headed for balmy southern climates.

FAMILY ASSOCIATIONS

Numbering in the thousands in the United States, these groups are formal structures, with officers, bylaws, membership dues, and newsletters. They are usually composed of genealogists, historians, and family-history buffs interested in a certain family surname or set of original immigrants. The *Genealogical Helper*, a magazine published by Everton Publishers, P.O. Box 368, Logan, UT 84321, publishes an annual issue listing active family associations.

FAMILY REUNIONS

The shape of the family reunion as we know it today really took hold as family members left the rural worlds of the South for the North; the hills of Appalachia for jobs in Ohio, Illinois, and Indiana; and the Midwest of the dust-bowl days for California, Oregon, and Washington. It was this sense of being scattered from an agrarian base, merging with the long American history of religious camp meetings and retreats, that gave the American reunion such a rural image. Today this image has been expanded with reunions held by descendants of those who arrived in America during the great wave of immigration (early 1900s) and have always been, while in America, either urban or suburban.

A Short History of African American Reunions

Since the 1980s African American families have led the way in the changed landscape of American family reunions—held as often at hotels and resorts as at Grandma Mae's farm down South. But African American reunions go back to shortly after the Civil War, when families broken by slavery, scattered by the war, and dislocated by Emancipation (which left many free but homeless) could at last reunite in 1869 during the Great Jubilee year. Later, the Great Migration, which took place during and after World War II, split many fami-

"When my mother was alive, my father used to hold birthday parties for her in Minnesota, which all my brothers and sisters and their children would attend. They were the only time we all came together as a family. After she died we no longer had those gatherings, and at first we weren't aware of what we were missing. Then last year, on the occasion of what would have been my mother's 100th birthday, we all came together in cottages by the lake, and then, boy, did we realize what we'd been missing."
—Susanne Oberhauser
Caroline, Wisconsin

lies right down the middle, with half still in southern hometowns and the other half up North finding opportunity in large industrial centers. Southern homecomings brought together northern and southern siblings and cousins, mingling small-town values and big-city manners in the warm embrace of the supportive, extended family, the hometown church, and down-home cooking.

Meaningful as these celebrations of family and ancestors were, the African American family reunion movement didn't take off as a commercial phenomenon until the 1970s and 80s, when vacation travel opportunities opened up for Black families. "We just would not have felt comfortable booking our family into a

CROSSING THE WATER

THE QUANDER-AMAQUANDOH FAMILY

What: *Old Country reunion*

Who: *Carmen and Rohullamin Quander, a descendant of Henry Quando, who had been a Maryland slave freed in the late 1600s, with probable descendants of Henry Quando's African family*

Where: *The Cape Coast of Ghana, home of the original Quanders, or Amakwandoh*

Number of Participants: *50*

Family Motto: *"We are many, but we are one."*

Family Characteristic: *A belief in the rule of law and justice.*

Quando, a Maryland slave who was set free on the occasion of his owner's death sometime in the late 1600s. (Over the years, the name became "Quander.")

It had long been a matter of family lore among the Quanders, still found for the most part in the Washington, D.C., area, that the first Quando may have come from Ghana. The legend was that his African name, Amkwandoh, had been shortened on arrival in the Colonies. Perhaps someone had asked him his name, and on hearing "Amkwandoh," assumed he was saying, "I'm Quando."

But family lore is one thing; history is another. In

THE QUANDERS UNITED
Tricentennial Celebration
1684-1984

1983, Rohullamin Quander, an administrative law judge and one of his family's historians, decided to take steps to see if he could bring the legend more in line with the rigors of

The Quander family, 2,000 strong, has held annual reunions for about 75 years in Maryland and Virginia. Their roots run deep in this part of the country. The Quanders know how their first ancestor came to America—rare for any family that first arrived in the 1600s, and rarer still for an African American family that arrived in the early days of slavery. But the Quanders can trace their lineage back to Henry

The Amkwandoh family, all sporting the family T-shirt, poses with their American relative, Rohullamin Quander (second row, center).

genealogy. He wrote a letter, for publication, to two Ghana newspapers, requesting any information regarding the Amkwandoh family. He received 200 responses. Amkwandoh was a Fanti tribal name, and a story had been preserved and told through the generations of how one member of the tribe had come to be stolen into slavery. A chief's son, Egya Eduam Amkwandoh, had last been seen at the age of 12 on a certain road beyond his village, en route to another village to sell wares. He never got there

Amkwandoh family members at the Amkwandoh Memorial House.

Rohullamin Quander meets with village elders in Kankan Boom, Ghana.

and was never seen again. The time of his disappearance was traced back, generation by generation, to coincide with the arrival of Quando in Maryland in the 1600s.

To "cross the water" of the Atlantic and link up with African ancestors is the genealogical equivalent of scaling Mt. Everest. The paper trail is thin, with attention paid to the names of slaves by white masters callously cavalier, and oral history tending to get lost in the mists of time.

What made this case different was a number of important elements. The unusual name of Quando was preserved because Quando was released from slavery on the death of his master, and so his descendants did not have to take the name of their owners. His freedom also meant that the family could preserve its strong identity and its family stories.

Finding this link across the Atlantic, Rohullamin Quander felt he had to cross the water himself, to meet his ancestral family in person.

"In Fanti culture, when somebody goes away and doesn't come back, their spirit may be unsettled," Rohullamin explained. When he visited the Amkwandohs in Ghana, they took him to a place on the road where Egya Eduam Amkwandoh had been kidnapped into slavery more than 300 years before. There was a sense of overwhelming grief yet of closure, of connection, of peace, as Amkwandoh's spirit moved that much closer back to his home.

Rohullamin Quander holds a pre-World War I family artifact.

resort unless we knew for a fact that other Black families had gone there and been comfortable," recalls one African American reunion organizer now. "Not being welcome where you're staying—well, it's not a very pleasant way to spend your vacation."

Another incentive to the Black family reunion movement was Alex Haley's *Roots*, which inspired Black families to learn more about their extended families and collective past. Black family genealogy boomed and with it the desire for cousins to meet cousins and to close up and heal divided families.

In the mid-1980s, Dr. Dorothy I. Height, president of the National Council of Negro Women, launched the Black Family Reunion Celebration to fortify and celebrate the historical strengths and traditional values of the Black family. "Dr. Height was reading so much in the media about the so-called disappearing Black family," says Pat Brantley,

the marketing manager for the Black Family Reunion Celebration. "She knew the Black family was far from disappearing and was searching for a way to highlight its already considerable strengths."

African American family reunions now account for half of all American reunions, and they paved the way for the large, highly organized reunion that is a staple of the landscape today. African American reunions are a major economic force, as well—it's estimated that 70 percent of nonbusiness travel by African Americans during the summer is reunion-related. Because many African Americans view reunions more as special vacations than as family obligations, families are ready to make a strong financial commitment toward attending. "You're not just pouring money into some casual amusement," says reunion goer Audrey Walker. "The feeling of strength and togetherness you get out of it pays you back tenfold."

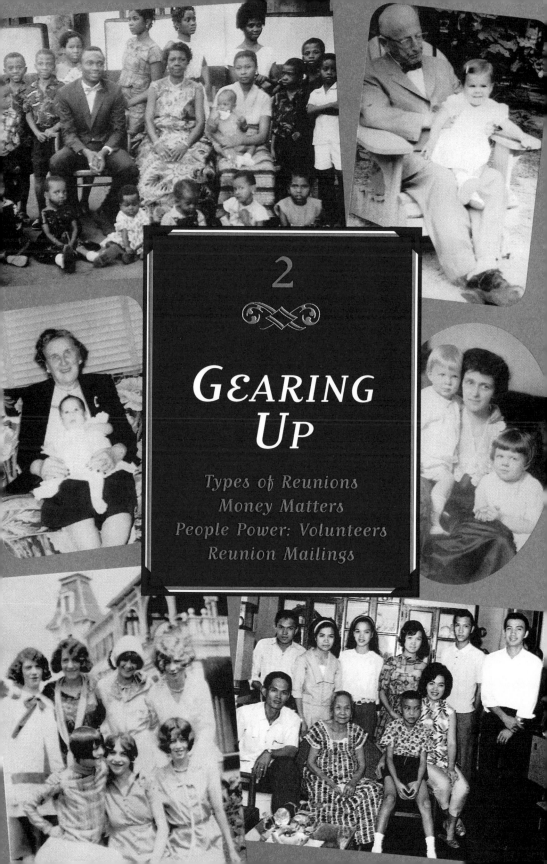

2

GEARING UP

Types of Reunions
Money Matters
People Power: Volunteers
Reunion Mailings

Reunions are connecting rituals, events that pull together families that have changed shape over time, producing bumper crops of babies and spreading out to include prodigious numbers of far-flung cousins. Once upon a time the informal backyard get-together—with the men grilling steaks and hamburgers, the women chatting and watching the children—may have provided ritual enough. But with today's family trees branching out across the country, practical considerations determine, to a great extent, the style and size of your particular family reunion. When cousins come together from Denver, Cincinnati, and New York City, cashing in frequent-flier miles or gassing up the RV for a thousand-mile trek, there had better be something more than a burger at the end of their family-bound journey.

Every family connects in its own way. Some connect by talking, some by competing, others by going fishing together. Some families may have a hard time expressing emotion, but when they're asked to help move furniture or set up a party tent, they're there in a flash to lend a hand. A hundred and fifty years ago they would have appeared at the crack of dawn to help with the barn raising. Now they're waiting for a call to join the family in something just as meaningful.

Organizing a reunion can be a pain—just ask someone who's done it—but there is a huge amount to be gained from making the effort, beyond the satisfaction of creating an event that pulls family together. Reunions offer quality time for folks to get to know one another; for the organizers, that bonding time starts with the planning and continues to build a sense of connection and community way before the reunion ever takes place.

BACK TO BASICS

While a ritual can achieve an organic level of rightness almost unconsciously—a family can often sense when it has enough activities planned or the event has a sufficient aura of an occasion—logistical issues, to a great degree, give the reunion its shape, structure, and sense of scale. How many people will be attending, how many have to travel a good distance to attend, and how much time there is to plan the reunion will determine its basic contours. Families with lots of scattered members will probably need to hold weekend-long reunions to justify the expense and effort of travel, while an event designed to sweep up all the cousins within a 50-mile radius may be planned for just half a day—and extended, spontaneously, when the cousins refuse to go home. See the chart on pages 20–21 for the four basic kinds of reunions.

To determine the scale and extent of your reunion, you need to set some parameters. Decide who is to be included and how wide to cast your reunion net—a siblings reunion, a cousins reunion, an extended family reunion that includes the descendants of your great-grandparents—even an ancestral reunion, with potentially hundreds of attendees.

Reunion Guest of Honor

For first-time reunion planners, the idea of summoning a hundred relatives to a specific place at a specific time may be daunting. Often it helps to have an emotional centerpiece for the event, a pretext for the family to come together. Designating a guest of honor (or subject of commemoration) shifts attention away from the reunion organizers, answers the question "Why is this reunion being held?", and guarantees a certain number of attendees—at the very least, the guest of honor and his or her family will have to show up.

At its best, a commemorative focus accentuates those aspects of ritual crucial to a successful reunion: It sets aside a special time and place to celebrate what's special about this particular family, and it lends an aura of uniqueness, giving the sense that this is an event that should not be missed—it will not occur again.

Here are some occasions that can serve as the focus of a successful reunion:

- relative's 80th birthday
- couple's 50th anniversary
- 100th birthday of a beloved parent who has passed away
- 100th anniversary of the family's arrival in America

For many of us born between 1940 and 1970, our great-grandparents were the first of our family to arrive in the United States, during the peak immigration years at the turn of the

REUNION ROUNDUP: THE FOUR BASIC TYPES

REUNION TYPE	WHO ATTENDS	PLANNING TIME	DURATION
Backyard Barbecue	Siblings and/or cousins (25–60)	2–6 months	Day into evening
Homecoming	Siblings, cousins, possibly extended family (50–100)	6–12 months	Day, with informal get-togethers the day before or after
Weekend Classic	Cousins, extended, or ancestral family (50–300)	1–3 years	Weekend or long weekend (3–4 days)
Family Camp	Siblings, cousins (15–75)	1 year	Week or more

SITE	FOOD	COSTS	DISTINGUISHING CHARACTERISTICS
Backyard or park	Food provided by host family, with potluck contributions	Food and barbecue supplies, park shelter or tent rental	Informal reunion organization; unstructured activities; renews and strengthens existing relationships
Large backyard or town park with tent or other shelter	Potluck or catered	Food and barbecue supplies, park shelter or tent rental, table and chair rentals	Informal reunion organization; somewhat structured activities; strengthens existing relationships and family identity
Hotel, conference center, park lodge, resort, camp	Catered	Transportation, registration fees for directory, T-shirts, meeting room and activities; lodging and food paid for by each family	Formal reunion organization; structured activities; printed materials; time and financial commitment; expands vision of family
Condos, camps, lakeside and seaside cottages	Shared cooking and shopping	Shared rental, food, and housecleaning costs; transportation	Informal reunion organization; structured activities; pitching in with chores; extended time with smaller family group deepens existing relationships

last century. The 100th anniversary of millions of families is fast approaching—the perfect peg on which to hang a reunion.

Connecting

When you plan a reunion, you do a lot of *doing together*. But first, you've got to find everyone. Now is the time to cast a wide net across the family. If the family has held reunions in the past, that shouldn't be difficult. But what if the reunion organizer doesn't know where, how large—or even *who*—the family really is? Putting what you do know down on paper can show at a glance who's missing. And if your family has an amateur genealogist, she can be a tremendous

REUNION NOTEBOOK

Computers are wonderful in a thousand ways, but a three-ring binder with pocket folders can be a model of efficiency in data collection and management. With a three-hole punch, you'll be able to maintain megabytes of data for about $10 —confirmation letters from hotel sales managers (photocopy these, please!), brochures of white-water rafting outfits, and heartfelt letters from the cousins out West who won't be able to attend—all of which you can access with ease wherever you are.

Designate a section for:

◆ Each planned activity, listing items that need to be borrowed or bought, when each part of the activity needs to get done, names and numbers of volunteers, and notes of phone conversations you've held with them.

◆ T-shirt information: Payments received, order numbers, name and numbers of T-shirt company.

◆ Prioritized to-do lists and a calendar of must-do items.

◆ Reunion timetable (see Appendix, pages 238–241).

◆ Notes on location scouting (see Chapter 3).

◆ Menus for catered or potluck meals—even if you're not the potluck coordinator, you may want to maintain some oversight.

◆ Computer printouts of who is attending and who is staying where.

◆ Names and numbers of contact people: tent company, baby-sitters, photographers, musicians or disk jockey, etc.

◆ An abbreviated family tree—to put those cousins giving you a hand back into context.

Whoever is acting as treasurer should keep the account books separate and leave them at home for safekeeping.

resource: At least she'll know where in the world to start looking for those missing cousins.

Telephone directories for the United States are available on CD-ROM and on the World Wide Web, and if your cousins have an unusual last name, these directories can produce them in a minute, complete with ZIP codes. The World Wide Web has a search engine that will help track down names across the nation—www.whowhere.com. Unfortunately, it's far from perfect, and many names listed in the phone books of major cities failed to appear when tested. CD-ROM phone books, with complete listings across the country, are more thorough. Two helpful resources for finding long-lost relatives are the books *Find Anyone Fast,* by Richard S. Johnson, MIE Publishing, P.O. Box 5143, Burlington, NC 27216, and *How to Find Almost Anyone, Anywhere* by Norma Mott Tillman, Rutledge Hill Press, 211 Seventh Avenue North, Nashville, TN 37219.

The phone inquiries to relatives will be the first the family will hear about the proposed reunion. You'll find that calls have a domino effect as one relative passes you on to another. That eases some of the burden on the organizers—and it's great advance publicity.

MAILING LIST 101

A mailing list offers tangible proof that the family really is coming together. Putting the information on

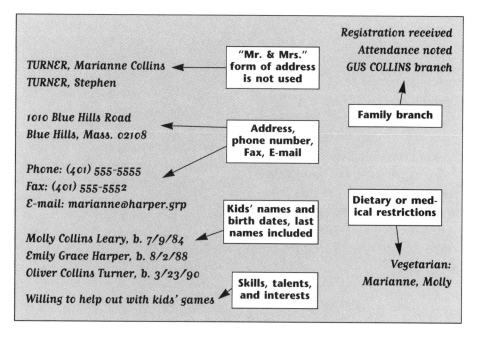

computer obviously makes sense if the family is large and the reunion organizers computer-savvy. But low-tech, low-cost index cards still work; 4-by-6-inch cards give you the most room to work with (see the sample card on page 23). And when the system crashes, you can just pick the cards up off the floor and start all over again.

Begin by listing all members of each branch who will be invited to the reunion. Don't forget widows and widowers of family members—they're still members of the clan. Organize the list by branch: If the reunion catchment includes all the descendants of your great-grandparents, each of the great-grandparents' children is the head of one branch.

Once you've assembled all the names, divide the index cards into two piles: names with addresses, and names without. And then, once

"The first role served by the reunion committee was having their names appear on the letter I sent out. I didn't want cousins I hardly knew receiving it and thinking, 'Who is this Jean Crichton and who does she think she is to start up a reunion?' With my name among three or four others, I felt I could pull it off. And I did."

—Jean Crichton
Summit, New Jersey

you've gotten the addresses, divide again: those family members who've committed to the reunion, those who can't come, and those who haven't yet responded. While you may be tempted to divide the mailing list into family branches, this system allows you to see at a glance where attendance and responses stand.

THE REUNION COMMITTEE

It is the reunion organizer who initiates the idea and sets the timeline for planning the event: How much time do we give the location scouts to find a site? Will the caterers be ready the day the lodge is booked for? The organizer commands an overview of *all* reunion activities and schedules—so she'd better be organized herself, skilled at planning such activities as a PTA fair or a wedding on a budget. She must be responsible, trustworthy, and dependable—a former Girl Scout would be nice.

Some families request that one member from each branch serve on the reunion committee. Committees formed from several family branches have the advantage of knowing, as it were, where the bodies lie. They track down hard-to-find cousins, long-lost uncles, and heretofore unknown great-grandaunts. They canvass the family to find out how long the reunion should be and how much money each member should contribute.

The committee serves as a sounding board for all the preliminary questions: who, where, when, what, how? All members sign the first exploratory letter (see pages 36–37) sent out to the extended family, so that everyone who receives it will know at least one person involved. And the committee continues to send various communiqués—from follow-up letters and registration forms to the final psych-up letter.

Committee members serve as "headhunters" throughout the planning stages, targeting talent and ability from their combined knowledge of the family at large. Who would be willing to scout the reunion site? Who knows every campfire recipe in the book?

While the reunion letters should solicit volunteers, the planning committee shouldn't wait for volunteers to jump up and identify themselves—only the most gung-ho are likely to do so. Think of those who won't put themselves forward: modest cousins who don't know their own strengths, wary types unsure of how much they can commit, in-laws who might perceive the reunion as an insiders' group.

Later on, some committee members may choose to serve in other capacities, while others may bow out of any further commitment. Bring in fresh faces, if only to let everyone know that the reunion belongs to the entire family.

MONEY MATTERS

The committee also deals with the delicate subject of finances. To ensure evenhandedness, make sure the planners represent the full range of economic levels in the family. Any psychologist can tell you that the topic considered the most private and sensitive is not weight, sexual habits, or college-board scores. It's money. And before reunion organizers can decide on a site or style for a

"When my nine siblings and I planned a reunion at three rental houses in South Carolina, it wasn't at all clear how the payments would work. My older brother, who's doing very well in business, supplied the down payment so my other siblings had time to come up with their share. Our father and older sister sat down and figured out what people were able to pay—between them they had a good grasp of where everyone was financially—and put together a sliding scale of payments. None of us knew what anyone else was paying. So, despite a range of income levels, everybody paid what they could and went away happy."

—Ellie von Wellsheim
Menands, New York

AFFORDABILITY CHECKLIST

Despite the difficulties, reunion organizers can keep the reunion accessible to all family members by making affordability a top priority. But they must handle the topic carefully and sensitively. Here are some basic approaches.

❑ The planners involved in the early stages of the reunion should represent a full range of the economic levels in the family, so there will be a built-in system of reality checks.

❑ Include a questionnaire with the first exploratory letter to family members, giving a range of possible expenses based on a realistic assess-ment of what kind of reunion lodgings and activities are available.

❑ Structure the reunion to accommodate a variety of economic capabilities. For example, hold the reunion at a meeting hall or park pavilion with various levels of lodging available nearby: campsites, inexpensive motels, better-level inns.

❑ If reunions are not held frequently, those with fewer financial resources may be more inclined to save up for the special occasion. How often to hold a reunion is an issue to discuss at the end of the event (see pages 232–233).

reunion, there has to be some talk about that tricky subject.

Finances wouldn't be an issue if all members of the family enjoyed the same level of income and the words "affordable" and "too much" held the same meaning for everybody. But what's considered inexpensive (particularly for those who have to add travel expenses to other costs) remains unclear, since the cost of living varies widely across the country. And the question really gets sticky when a family member doesn't want to spend money or vacation time for a reunion but feels pressured by other family members. The organizers' efforts should go toward opening the door to the reunion as wide as possible, and keeping that door open—without forcing anybody across the threshold.

Occasionally one family member with plenty of money (or not so much money as family spirit) picks up the tab for most of the event. Rather than giving Christmas presents to all her brothers and sisters and their kids, one woman in Connecticut springs for the cost of a siblings reunion, which she holds in her backyard every July—and she claims to save money on the deal!

But what happens to the reunion when the family angel can no longer support the event? "I could pay for the whole kit and caboodle, but I don't want to set that precedent," says Joan Sparrow, who organizes the Rumely reunion in Evanston, Illinois. "I want this reunion to go on without me, and the people who have the enthusiasm and interest in taking it over are not necessarily those with a big bank account. So everyone pays their way. I keep a strict accounting and I try to keep costs down."

Helping Hand

Even when the majority of the family can afford to attend the reunion, a few may fall short of the full amount needed. Many families create reunion "scholarships"—a fund to subsidize family members—by adding an

FAMILY FUND RAISING

Families often need to raise extra money not only for reunion scholarships but to underwrite banquets or dances as well. Here are some common fund-raising activities, many of which can be conducted throughout the planning time.

◆ *Group tag sale:* Each participating family gathers all the white elephants it has amassed through the years, advertises throughout the neighborhood, and holds a massive tag sale at a rented meeting hall or church community room—or a good old-fashioned rent-free yard.

◆ *Bake sales and family cookbook sales* can both be handled the same way.

◆ *Raffles:* A 50/50 raffle, in which the winner takes half the pot and the family reunion takes the other half, offers a good incentive to give. Prizes donated by family businesses can also be a nice lure.

◆ *Family auctions and raffles:* Held at the reunion itself, they might feature money prizes, like the 50/50 raffle pot, or family intangibles (time-shares at a condo or professional assistance with computers, for example), or home-made crafts and edibles, such as jams and preserves. These events can give the family a running start on putting money away for the next reunion.

◆ *Family stationery,* created by laser printer, featuring the family logo and packaged in beribboned zip-lock bags, is popular.

◆ *Family quilts:* Each member prepares one square with a design significant to the family. Auctioned off at the reunion, the quilts can raise thousands of dollars—which some families use to start a college scholarship fund for family members.

Note: Many families sell merchandise printed with the family logo or crest—fun, but don't count on these items making much profit, as huge quantities are needed to produce them at affordable levels.

optional surcharge to the general reunion registration fee (often greatly added to by anonymous well-off family members) or by fund-raising efforts such as those mentioned on page 27.

The reunion scholarship fund can be referred to in the explanatory letter, for example: "We have some funds for those who may need help with reunion costs. Our goal is to make the reunion available to all. Requests should be directed to the reunion organizer." If the committee makes the effort to keep the reunion affordable, chances are only one or two families will need to ask for help. And no one but the reunion organizer need ever know who those families are.

SETTING THE DATE

Location may determine when the reunion can be held: That ideal spot may be available only on a certain weekend. But the reunion organizers still need to pick a season and offer the family two or three possible dates to choose from.

Summer is the classic time for holding reunions, with the Fourth of July weekend leading the way. But Memorial Day weekend, the traditional time for visiting and cleaning cemetery plots, is a favorite as well. And the other seasons can work, too. Winter holiday time is good, and autumn, with its shorter days and

"*Every Columbus Day weekend, our family holds a football reunion—we don't play it, we watch. The locale moves from city to city, all along the Eastern Seaboard. Whoever is hosting it gets tickets to a college game and arranges for a giant tailgate party beforehand. The setting seems to make it easier for the men in the family to feel comfortable—sitting together, cheering on the team. After the game there's dinner in a restaurant or hotel banquet room, which is great because sometimes the older family members can't come to the game.*"

—Amity Morrow
New York, New York

tinge of melancholy, strengthens appreciation for family warmth.

No date will be absolutely right for everyone—it may come down to flipping a coin. But once a date is set, *stick with it*. Family members will buy nonrefundable plane tickets based on that date, put in for vacation time, and schedule soccer camp around it. Cancel the reunion, if you must—but don't change the date! If the family just cannot decide between two dates and a coin toss seems too banal, consult *The Farmer's Almanac*. This way, if it rains on July 18 the family has someone—besides the reunion organizer—to blame!

PEOPLE POWER

The next task is to figure out how many hands will be required on deck to create the desired effect. While some roles may be filled by the reunion committee, it's likely that it will have to reach out to other family members to fill all the jobs.

Below are some job descriptions of volunteers needed for a typical weekend classic. In the ideal world, each person would fill one of these roles. But this is real life, and chances are, some people will wear many hats.

Family Correspondent: Known in the old days as the Family Secretary, the family correspondent writes letters, receives and records responses, follows up with phone calls, keeps track of the mailing list, produces the directory, and is the contact person for family members with questions.
Ideal Personality: Anyone with the responsible, outgoing, highly verbal personality of the student council president or yearbook editor—and a willingness to take on multiple tasks.

Reunion Publicist: Writes press releases and places them in local newspapers and magazines; writes to government officials for letters of commendation and keys to the city (see Appendix, pages 244–245). Might start family newsletter.
Ideal Personality: Computer-literate cousin acquainted with writing management reports or p.r. Enjoys por-traying this particular family as an important institution.

Location Scout: Takes location and financial parameters given him by the reunion committee, scopes out possibilities, and reports back. Might also negotiate final deal with location management.
Ideal Personality: Energetic retired person who likes to drive, explore, and solve puzzles.

Set-up People: Fulfill any of a dozen small yet crucial set-up tasks the day before and the day of the reunion.
Ideal Personality: Those who can give an hour or two the day of the reunion; idle youth who are spotted doing nothing; family members who want to contribute in a limited way.

Welcoming Committee: Sit behind the registration table with the guest book and serve as a balm for the soul of the tired traveler.
Ideal Personality: The darling aunts and uncles whose knees are failing but who are the souls of graciousness, kindness, and a warm welcome.

Master of Ceremonies: Makes all public announcements—from the mundane ones about the start of the sack race to announcements of births, marriages, graduations, and deaths. (A card requesting this rite-of-passage information should be included with the reunion schedule when the reunion begins or placed at each place setting at the first dinner).

HANDLING THE VOLUNTEERS

You've lined up a cadre of capable cousins to get the job done. Now what?

◆ Match the person to the job. Assign the most critical tasks to those you know best, or those who can be vouched for by another committee member.

◆ Have a backup plan in case a volunteer turns you down. The volunteer may want to help, but believes that your request is too time-consuming or doesn't match her skills. Offer a less demanding task in place of the original request.

◆ Define the assignment as clearly as possible. You may not know precisely what each job will entail, but give a realistic appraisal of the time, energy, and skill required. And while you may want to support volunteers by assigning them helpers or cochairs, be careful not to undermine their sense of the uniqueness of their role.

◆ Write to each newly enlisted volunteer and repeat what you two have agreed upon: "So glad we can count on you to hire and drive the boat for waterskiing on the after-noon of the reunion." In this way you create a reference point for the volunteer to consult in the future.

◆ Understand why people volunteer. All volunteers want to feel that the tasks they perform contribute to the success of the family venture. The reunion organizer is in charge of making sure the volunteers get paid with those good feelings, and her recognition and approval will be experienced as coming from the family at large.

◆ Keep the recognition coming. One way of doing this is to mention in letters to the family who has decided to help out: "Becky Clarke has agreed to take her well-known culinary talents to the hilt with a special reunion cake for us." List committee members and their tasks in every letter—people like to see their names in print.

◆ If a job isn't getting done and it's critical to the event, you will, in the nicest way possible, have to take it off the volunteer's hands. Assign him another, lesser job so he can save face, rather than relieving him of all duties.

Ideal Personality: You might think it's the family ham or the theater person. But no—it's Ed Sullivan you want, not the Beatles. Someone comfortable wielding authority and secure enough to let others bask in the spotlight.

———

Talent Show Coordinator: Organizes talent show by encouraging participation, arranging order of performances, introducing each performance, and maintaining a sense of fun throughout.

Ideal Personality: Energy, enthusiasm, clear delivery, and humor are more important traits than theater experience—in fact, experienced theater types might prove too intimidating and perfectionistic.

Potluck Coordinator: Asks each family to bring two dishes, keeps track of what is being brought, and reminds people beforehand what they've pledged to bring.
Ideal Personality: The quiet, reliable cousin who is never late with a library book and hates to speak ill of people (qualities you didn't appreciate when you were younger but admire now) is the one to rope in your kinfolk along with their potato salad Dijon.

Kids' Games Coordinator: Organizes morning or afternoon field games or indoor play. Must work in a team with at least one other person. Assembles games kit for freestyle play. Must hold in reserve a well-conceived alternative plan in the event of rain.
Ideal Personality: Parents of young kids (working as a pair) who know what kids can handle and what the hot new games are. Go for those levelheaded yet enthusiastic types who run the PTA spring fair.

Whole-Family Activities Coordinator: Organizes and runs intergenerational games.
Ideal Personality: Should be two volunteers with strong people skills.

Must be able to raise their voices in a pleasant yet firm way—because adults are noisier and less obedient than children.

Crafts Person: Pulls together crafts materials and oversees simple yet interesting crafts projects for kids.
Ideal Personality: The arty cousin who never raises her voice, finds children naturally creative, and can inspire them to make mobiles and God's eyes from popsicle sticks and yarn.

Awards Person: Coordinates raffle items and raffle tickets, creates a door-prize system, assembles jury for nutty awards, and collects a broad array of wacky prizes and awards.
Ideal Personality: A jolly uncle or aunt who has a great sense of fun and enthusiasm.

Family Artist: Creates family-themed decorative material—T-shirt design, family tree mural, banners, centerpieces, logos.
Ideal Personality: The cousin who wanted to be an artist but became a bank officer instead.

Computer Whiz: May work with, or fill in for, Family Artist as well as Family Correspondent. Communicates via E-mail with reunion volunteers and attendees. Designs reunion stationery with a scanned-in logo. Creates family trees and duplicates them. Maintains mailing list and mailing labels. Personalizes form letters sent out to family members.

A Ritual for Every Season

The Dargan-Swink Family

What: Homecoming

Who: Descendants of Evander Ervin and William Edwin Dargan, whose offspring intermarried in the late 1800s

Where: A family farm in South Carolina

Number of Participants: More than 100

Family Traits: Lively respect for family tradition, dedicated pursuit of fun

Family Sport: Pig chase

Checking the chitlins—an acquired taste—for readiness.

The Dargans of Darlington, South Carolina, are a classic southern family, with roots in the soil that go a mile deep. "Everyone in our family has grandparents or parents who were farmers, or they are farmers themselves," says Amanda Dargan, of Hastings, New York. "Our family celebrations have always been linked to seasonal events.

"There's the peanut boil in fall, when peanuts pulled green are boiled until they are soft and delicious in great cast-iron pots that hang from tripods over open fires. You've got to be at least 18 years old to attend, so it's a real rite of passage. Then there's the fish fry when the herring run up the river for three weeks in March. And every Sunday during the summer, my uncle and aunt host an open picnic for anyone passing through Darlington.

"But the Winter Games, are for all the descendants of my grandparents. My parents and their cousins wanted to make sure that their children had the chance to be as close as they were growing up."

The Dargan Winter Games are held the week between Christmas and New Year's—an unusual time to hold a reunion, perhaps, but

The Dargans and Swinks all pull their weight in this classic test of strength and endurance.

Marksmanship is an essential skill in this clan, and the Winter Games' skeet shooting contest puts it to the test.

for the Dargans, it's ideal. They spend Christmas with their nuclear families, then gather afterwards as a clan. It's a cure for the post-Christmas blues, filling that let-down period that often follows the frenzied holiday buildup.

There are the traditional group games: sack races, horseshoes, tug-of-war, and shooting matches, where northern cousins marvel at the South Carolina cousins' dexterity with shotguns.

Then there are the games designed to recapture the farm traditions of the family's past—a corn-shucking contest and a chicken chase. The greased pig chase has become the family sport. About 10 kids, 15 good-humored adults, and one pig

end up in a blur of squealing, slipping, and sliding by all participants—human and porcine.

Catching escaped pigs was once a regular feature of farm life. The greased pig chase re-creates the excitement.

But the rat kill is the real high point of the Dargan Games. In the cool December morning, all the kids pile into the back of pickup trucks and head out to the barns to roust the rats. ("By

the time the noisy kids get out to the barn, whatever rats were there are long gone," Amanda Dargan reports.) In fact, no rats have been spotted in the barns in years.

But a rat is too ideal a villain to be allowed to slide into extinction. Rats used to threaten the sanctity and

Having made the barn safe for another year, a Dargan rat rouster exults in triumph.

health of the family and its grain. Now, in a kind of reenactment of a time when the family had to band together to secure the barn against threats to their livelihood, the kids get to play the heroes.

Walking slowly and methodically, they swat and beat the hay with sticks, connecting to a time when the Dargans cleansed the barn and house in preparation for the coming New Year.

The Dargan family works to stay together, and these gatherings do take work. "As an adult, I can see now how much effort the adults before me put into this event and into making life on the farm so

appealing," says Amanda Dargan. "It's one reason so many of my family have stayed around Darlington. There's always something going on, a square dance, a boat trip, a huge family camp-out with tents as big and colorful as circus tents."

In the South, family time is held sacred and given value above and beyond the labor of the day. "Southerners in general treasure and protect their leisure," says Amanda, who has since moved up North. "Work is not to interfere with family time. It's taboo to talk about it on vacation or at a party. In the homes of some of my relatives, you're forbidden to talk about work in the living room!" She laughs. "It's a foreign concept here in New York, I know, but down South, it's a concept the whole community supports."

She pauses and says, "It's easy to understand why my daughter glanced up at me at the last reunion and said, 'I think heaven must look just like South Carolina.'"

Every ritual needs its period of unstructured fun. Here, Dargan cousins frolic on the trampoline.

Ideal Personality: Relative who may not have an easy way of joining into the flurry of reunion activities—but who has invested thousands of dollars in a computer and is desperate to put the system to productive use before it all turns obsolete.

———

Cleanup Coordinator: Not as odious as it seems. Since this is a family event, everyone should be expected to help with cleanup. The coordinator gets the ball rolling by ordering whole tables of people to dispose of their paper plates, sending idle youths to the 24-hour store for more garbage bags, and hosing down crates of rented china.

Ideal Personality: A kindly but gruff, no-nonsense aunt or uncle, preferably from the Midwest.

———

Special Events Impresario: Makes arrangements for off-site events.

Ideal Personality: Mr. Back to Nature and Ms. Tennis Nut will tend to offer

KID POWER

Kids, especially those between the ages of 10 and 13, can be a great resource. Preteens still want the approval of adults, are desperate to prove their budding competence, and are generally goodwilled. (After the age of 13, they change. A lot.)

Here are a few jobs you can call on kids to perform.

◆ **Run a baby-sitting club.** Preteens are great for amusing toddlers when there's an adult somewhere near. They blow bubbles, talk baby talk, read Berenstain Bears books, put on the radio and dance, and give the parents a break for schmoozing with their peers. Have preteens sign up for baby-sitting stints of no more than half an hour.

◆ **Stuff envelopes, affix stamps, collate papers; assemble reunion** packets. Children under the age of 9 are easily persuaded that these activities are giant fun. (Think of Tom Sawyer's whitewashing party.)

◆ **Sign making, place-card writing,** decorating.

◆ **Table setting.** A hard sell. Bribery with an early taste of dessert is the only hope.

◆ **Selling T-shirts** (for those with at least third-grade math skills). Every kid likes selling things and being in charge of the family store.

◆ **Table service.** Take orders for drinks and desserts. Younger kids may even like a little clipboard with pencil attached. Remind them to move slooowly.

◆ **Job most in demand by 15-year-old nephews:** Valet parking. Here's what you say when the nephews volunteer: "No."

their services in order to be able to (a) pursue their passion at the reunion and (b) create converts out of previously indifferent family members.

Treasurer: Handles all family funds. Pulls together the budget for the reunion at the start and reports about costs at the business meeting. Usually works through his own checking account, which requires scrupulous bookkeeping. Saves all receipts, keeps legible books so that the next reunion treasurer can read them for reference.

Ideal personality: The most literal-minded, fair, trustworthy, organized family member you can draft into service.

REUNION MAILINGS

Letters about reunions are obviously the most functional of communiqués: they give the facts and necessary details and request replies. But more than that, they're a public relations effort. They bang the drum and blow the trumpet to prove that this reunion will be a real *event*, that the family is truly special, and that this occasion is not to be missed. It's economical to send all the information about the reunion in one mailing, but it lacks the drama and excitement of a long, teasing buildup, with four or five letters filling in the details as the reunion nears.

Reunion organizers might be tempted to E-mail communiqués to family members. But it's important

"When we were planning the reunion, we didn't want people to come and just be a "body." We wanted it to be a communal thing. In our letters to the family, we wrote, 'Please let us know if you can help drive people places, which materials you're planning to bring . . .' By making participation a part of attending the reunion, we set the tone right from the start. And people responded!"

—Barbara Winn
New York, New York

to send out highly visible, tangible mailings, ones that get posted on the refrigerator door or bulletin board and are read again and again by more than one person.

Exploratory Letter

An exploratory letter is sent to all prospective reunion goers at least one year before the proposed reunion. It informs everyone that a reunion is being considered and solicits ideas, suggestions, and help. If the exploratory letter is successful, reunion organizers will have a good sense of what area is preferred by the majority of the family, how much the location should cost, an idea of suitable dates, and a handful of enthusiastic volunteers. The reunion organizers can then begin their first main task: a search for a site (see Chapter Three).

Dear Cousins,

Our great-grandparents Sam and Maggie Harper would have celebrated their 100th wedding anniversary next summer, and in honor of that centennial we're considering holding the first Harper family reunion in ten years! Because we're all scattered across the country, we feel the reunion ought to last at least a weekend and be held somewhere in the Pennsylvania-Ohio-West Virginia triangle, otherwise known as Harper Country. We're proposing the July 4th weekend as the date. Anyone got any great, not-too-pricey, spacious location ideas in Harper Country?

We will need YOUR HELP to make this happen. We need a few good Harpers to organize the kids' games, do some kids' crafts, pull together a Saturday-evening talent show, design a T-shirt (a family logo or crest would be nice too, all you artists out there!), and—most important right now—search for the perfect location. Please call one of the reunion committee members to volunteer—we also have plenty of smaller jobs that won't take too much planning and can be done for just a few hours at the reunion. Anyone want to organize a golf tournament for the whole family?

We still don't have addresses for the following Harper cousins: Brian Harper, Ellen London, Brad Harper Maloney. We'd appreciate any leads!

Please fill in the following questionnaire and return to one of the committee members by August 15 so we can get going on planning the best Harper reunion ever!

❑ We would love to come to the Harper reunion next summer.

❑ Not sure yet

❑ Will not be able to attend

❑ The July 4th weekend is fine with us

❑ We can't make it then; a better date would be _____ .

❑ We would be willing to spend this much per adult per day on the reunion excluding transportation:

❑$30–$50 ❑$50–$70 ❑$70–$90 ❑$90–$120

❑ We would be happy to volunteer for the job of _____ .

Your cousins,
The Reunion Committee
(All committee members' names and addresses are listed here.)

Explanatory Letter

As soon as location, date, and price have been fixed, and at least six to eight months before the reunion, a second letter should be sent to all prospective reunion goers. This explanatory letter gives further details about where the reunion will be held, the activities that have been planned, and another call for volunteers.

COUSINS LOST AND FOUND

THE OKRENT FAMILY

What: *Backyard barbecue*

Who: *Okrent cousins from Israel, Canada, Brazil, Argentina, Sweden, and Canada, dispersed by the Holocaust*

Where: *A backyard in suburban Illinois*

Number of Participants: 22

Family Traits: *Mathematical capability, wry sense of humor*

W hen Judy Okrent Simon was growing up in the 1950s, her family was "very nuclear—my mother, father and two brothers. On my mother's side were an uncle and an aunt and three cousins. But there were no other Okrents. We were it. I felt cheated, so jealous of the big families I saw all around us."

Now it's the Fourth of July in suburban Illinois. True to those '50s roots, there's a barbecue going on and corn, still in the husk, cooks on the grill. But flags

Brazil

from Sweden, Brazil, Canada, Israel, and other countries are strung between the trees across the backyard. On a shaded table is a cake with a map of the world frosted onto it. The 20 or so people gathered here chat easily, although they're really strangers—most never having met before this weekend. But they are all Okrent cousins, the family Judy was missing all those years, the family

she once assumed had all perished in the Holocaust.

Cousin Anita Okret from São Paulo (her branch lost the "n" somewhere in transit from Poland to the Americas) stands laughing with Stefa Wajnrib, who was

Argentina

born in Poland after World War II, but was forced out during the 1968 "anti-Zionist campaign." Stefa flew in from Israel for this event. They are the family about

The reunited Okrents chat and laugh easily, as if they'd known each other all their lives.

Under flags from their home countries, the Okrents unite for the first time in Larry Okrent's backyard.

whom Judy's father had said, "If they're out there, I really don't know and I really don't care."

"His father had come to America to escape the Old World and its confining ways," Judy Simon says now. "He was in America to become Americanized and felt there was no place for the past here."

The place for the past is now, in Larry Okrent's backyard. Thanks to Larry's

Israel

efforts, the kin who'd been scattered by war, political, religious and family history, is starting to come together again. Like his sister Judy, Larry had only the vaguest sense that his family might extend beyond his own nuclear one. It wasn't until a young cousin from South America, attending college in Indiana, phoned to introduce himself that the concept of cousins came into focus. Larry then recalled an aerogram that his parents had received many years ago from a cousin in Israel and which he had saved for his stamp collection. He dug it out, had the Yiddish

translated, and found that it was a sort of Rosetta Stone, naming far-flung cousins who also descended from his great-grandfather, who'd been a Hasidic rabbi

Sweden

in the bustling mercantile city of Lodz.

Using the genealogical software *Reunion,* Larry pieced together the family, following one lead after another. He began by putting down everything he knew about the family, iden-

Ancestral grave sites in Poland are the last and . . .

. . . only tangible links to the Okrents' past life in Lodz.

ished in the Holocaust.

In 1993, Larry decided to visit Lodz to find the cemetery where his great-grandparents were buried. It was an unkempt patch of ground, but the gravestones were a tangible and evocative link to his forebears. "That visit was like a drawbridge to the past, lowering so I could walk across it," he remembers. And the impulse to bring the living family together in the present grew stronger.

So in the summer of 1996 Larry invited the cousins to his home in Evanston for an American barbecue, finding rooms at bed-and-breakfasts nearby, and renting large vans to transport people to and from events. That was the

easy part. There was no way of knowing how contrived

Poland

or awkward that first meeting might be. "I thought the reunion might be interesting intellectually," Judy Simon

tifying the gaps in his knowledge, making calls and being passed from one relative to another. Cousins in Sweden (who had relocated there in the early 1970s) passed him on to Polish-

Canada

born cousins who now lived in Israel. They knew of Canadian cousins who passed him on to cousins in Denmark who told him about cousins in Argentina. Larry learned that none of his grandfather's siblings had survived the Holocaust. As the family tree grew in detail, so too did the number of Stars of David that Larry put next to the name of each relative who per-

At the grave of Reb Chaim Mayer Chil Okrent and his wife, Alte Hana, the family reflects on its past and its resurrected future.

recalls. "These people, coming together like pieces of a puzzle. But I never anticipated how profoundly mov-

The Netherlands

ing it would be. I felt as though I'd found the sisters I never had."

"Despite the vast differences in the places we were raised, with access to very different resources," Larry points out, "our similar aptitudes and outcomes are remarkable. While our great-grandfather was a rabbi, few of us are religious, although we all have a strong Jewish identity. We tend to have a great facility with languages, we're mathematical and scientific in our orientation, and many of us are academics."

What was even more surprising was their shared sense of humor. "Wry, ironic," Larry says, "but not cutting." At the reunion, the cousins spoke with surprising ease, describing how their lives had unfolded, what siblings they had lost,

what they had brought with them as they were forced to leave home. They wondered whether the sense of kinship they seemed to share was the result of a common goodwill they felt at the reunion, or the product of genetics, a shared heritage, a family culture that had managed to survive. Separating out the components would be a life's work. The idea of an identity derived from a shared past, so foreign to Larry and Judy when they were growing up, is something the entire family embraces now.

A year after the reunion, the family gathered again—this time in Poland, for the wedding of a young cousin. The Okrents now unite at times

when families traditionally come together—in those rites of passage when the extended family serves as a touchstone of continuity into the future. The Okrents toured the same cemetery that Larry had visited in Lodz, which he and other family members had paid to have restored and maintained. Among the guests was Judy's 26-year-old son. "He is as interested in all this as anyone," she says.

Denmark

"Somehow, this was what he was looking for, too."

A restored extended family of Okrents now regularly assembles for holidays and special events.

Dear Family,

Thanks to cousin Dan Harper Miller, we've reserved the campus of beautiful St. Augusta's School in Brainerd, Pennsylvania, for the July 4th weekend, with meal service in the dining hall from Friday's dinner through Sunday brunch. We will be staying in the dorms—mostly double rooms, with one bathroom for every four rooms. We plan on having a young-women's floor, a young-men's floor, a young-family's floor, and an older-folks floor. The school provides sheets and towels, but no pillows or blankets (or air-conditioning!)—and sorry, folks, no smoking in any of the buildings. The estimated cost for staying at St. Augusta's is $100 per adult, $50 per child for the weekend.

For those who prefer not to rough it, we've reserved a block of 10 rooms at the Lantern Inn in town at a discounted rate; the rooms will be held until May 15. Contact the Inn directly at (222) 555-5555.

Also enclosed is a questionnaire, so that we can include you and your family in our directory. Please fill it in even if you're not planning to come. Our deadline for registering for the reunion is the Ides of March (March 15)—to make final arrangements with St. Augusta's, we MUST have your registration by then.

We still have plenty of openings for volunteers—contact any of the committee members if you want to help out with the kids' junior olympics, running a shuttle service to pick up folks from the airport, or assembling a first-aid kit to bring to St. Augusta's.

We'll be sending you one last letter, a few weeks before the event, with more details. For the time being, think REUNION, and send in your registration form SOON.

Proud to be your cousins,
The Harper Reunion Committee
(All committee members' names, addresses, and phone numbers are listed here.)

Yo, Cuz! Kids' Letter

Some families send out separate letters to each child on the mailing list. The kids are flattered and excited by the attention; the reunion becomes *their* event, not something they're dragged to by their folks, and their enthusiasm is contagious. Make it easy for the younger kids to read their letters independently by double-spacing the lines and, if you're working on a computer, using a larger than average type size.

Request all kids under 12 to bring two riddles or jokes to share in a riddle circle—this gives the kids an active role in the upcoming reunion. Also, cite any events especially planned for them, and request other suggestions—possibly on an enclosed, addressed postcard.

Tell them what they ought to bring—sports equipment, board games, ideas for a talent show and so on. And include a family tree with the kids' names circled or highlighted—it will show in graphic terms what the reunion is all about.

Registration Form

The registration form is the natural extension of the explanatory letter, and for many families it acts as the official reunion invitation. Half the form is sent back to the reunion committee, while each family keeps the other half. Even families who don't need to collect a registration fee may want to make use of a registration form so that the RSVPs are returned in writing.

Many families *will* need a registration fee to cover printing, mailing, and decorating costs, to fund family reunion "scholarships," cost overruns, and other unexpected expenses, and to pay for reunion paraphernalia and entertainment. From 10 to 15 percent of the registration fee is the standard contingency fund. Children under 12 should probably be half-price and babies absolutely free.

The reunion committee should decide on a cancellation policy. If the registration fee covers only postage and copying costs, charcoal and other supplies, the policy might be to refund the entire fee (or at least half of it) if a family isn't able to attend—no matter how late the cancellation. But if a deposit has to be placed for a site or a caterer, the policy may stipulate that no refunds can be given after a certain date; the date should be stated on the registration form. To encourage timely registration and

BUDGET TIPS

When estimating budgets for a family reunion, start with the sample estimating forms in the Appendix, pages 242–243, and follow these two cardinal rules:

◆ *Underestimate attendance if there's a large financial commitment.* When the reunion committee lays out money to accommodate 100 reunion goers but only 60 turn out, a major shortfall occurs. To avoid that kind of jam, think skeptically. Lock in a block of rooms or caterer's services based on the figures you have confidence in—those backed up by checks sent in on deadline. If family members respond later wanting to attend, try to figure out a way. But the entire reunion should not have to assume financial risk for the slow responders.

◆ *Overestimate attendance when attendance is (more or less) free.* If the reunion is held in the backyard or at a park, factor in all possible attendees when arranging for food, drinks, and ice. As long as the financial risk is minimal, the reunion treasurer might as well give others the benefit of the doubt—and drink up all that leftover soda during the rest of the year.

make the organizing that much easier, many families offer discounts for early registration—but other families feel that holding out a financial incentive only commercializes a family event.

The registration form may also include requests for advance meal payments, if the reunion facility does not require that each family send such payments directly to them. With the exception of conference centers that prefer to handle groups through one account, and other slightly unconventional reunion sites, deposits for accommodations and reservations will probably be made directly with the facilities (the reunion organizers will keep in constant touch with the facilities for information on how the reservations are shaping up). Many resorts give reunion organizers registration postcards to be distributed among prospective reunion goers.

The family reunion T-shirt might be listed as an optional expense on the registration form, or the T-shirt organizer can send a separate order form requesting that payment be mailed directly to him.

Final Psych-Up Letter

The psych-up letter should be sent two to four weeks before the reunion. If there are any sluggards who haven't RSVP'd, give the name of the person to call and a "we really mean it" deadline. The letter might detail the reunion schedule and describe activities that had been alluded to in the explanatory letter, tell how many people are signed up to attend and where they're traveling from—evidence that this really is an event. It should list all the items people ought to bring, even if that's all been explained before. Include maps and driving instructions from airports and major arteries, and any newly available brochures. Be chatty, excited, friendly, and useful in content and tone. This is the "voice" the family members will be hearing as they pack their bags for the reunion and head on out.

Cancel or Regroup

It happens. A popular cousin decides to get married the same weekend as the reunion. A relative's death leaves the family too overwhelmed to pull off a jolly reunion. Circumstances arise when you have to consider postponing or canceling a reunion. It shouldn't be a private decision, though—the reunion committee should be consulted as well.

Or sometimes the consensus about a reunion dissipates—turns out there wasn't enough interest in a reunion, after all. Should the reunion be canceled or simply scaled back? Call the relatives who are registered to come and ask them how they feel about attending a smaller event. If there's enough interest to carry on, make a virtue of reduced size. Revel in the intimacy of the smaller group. Cancel the banquet and hold a less

T-shirt as Tribal Symbol

❖❖❖

Every ritual, anthropologists say, has its icons—special objects that hold multiple meanings. And the reunion T-shirt, our version of tribal colors, is our newest anthropological icon. As a symbol, it works on many levels. When we shed our outside clothes and put on the reunion T-shirt, we assume a common identity. Put an investment banker and a supermarket manager side by side in reunion T-shirts, shorts, and running shoes, and what do you have? Cousins.

Aside from blue jeans, what piece of clothing could be more quintessentially American? And the reunion T-shirt is utterly practical. What other social occasion greets you with a fresh piece of clothing on arrival?

Your family members may be so highly evolved that they don't need symbols in their lives. But most of us want a T-shirt to commemorate the event. It's the ultimate souvenir, the tangible, washable memory, becoming more comfortable and well-loved with time. Half a year after the reunion, a cousin can pull on the reunion T-shirt, slip on a sweater, and head out into the cold, thinking, "Not long ago it was summer and I was surrounded by 100

Dour pioneer grandparents stare out from the Grange T-shirt.

people I could call my own. I really belonged."

If you're pressed for time, you can order a standard reunion T-shirt from one of the many companies who produce them. (One good company is Passport International: (800) 606-1383. For more information about the T-shirt business, see Appendix, page 245.)

But if you can find a family artist to design a one-of-a-kind T-shirt that reflects your family personality, you're making symbolic art—and that's even finer. If the T-shirt carries the family name, date, and place of the reunion, you have a collector's item.

Some families color-code their T-shirts by family branch, but most families prefer to throw everyone into the same uniform color and leave the genealogical divisions to the experts.

Ten cousins in Oysterman T-shirts, XX-large.

formal dinner in an interesting restaurant—Dutch treat. Plan a trip to an historic site together. If the event was going to be a potluck meal, splurge on a few special dishes you couldn't have afforded to buy for a crowd. And use the smaller size to be in greater contact before the reunion, planning the activities and games of the day.

THE REUNION STARTS HERE

If the point of a reunion is about connecting with family, then the reunion starts here and now, as family members unite in the process of creating the event. Unlike other events, a reunion is as much about process as product. When a wedding is planned, product is virtually all, as perfection is strived for at any cost—including tension, disputes, and emotional turmoil.

Not so with a reunion, which is more like a family dinner on a very large scale. If the mood in the kitchen is cheerful, with everyone working happily together, but one of the kids is slicing the cucumbers a little too thick—so be it. Thick cukes and a happy family make for a great meal.

Perfection at a family event is never worth tension or ill will, because what you're driving for is emotional happiness, not flawless appearance. A reunion begins with family working with family for family. In the best of all worlds, the reunion starts here. And never ends.

3

LOCATION, LOCATION, LOCATION

Backyard or Local Park
Hotels and Resorts
Family Camps

Why are weekend classics planned a year or more in advance? It's not only that so many people need to be contacted or that family members require lead time to make travel plans. No, it's that the elusive site—pleasant, inexpensive, and easy to get to—needs to be tracked down. And pounced on early, in the form of reservations. The perfect reunion site rarely exists. If it is nice and inexpensive, it is remotely located. Well-priced and convenient? The aesthetics leave a lot to be desired. But a reunion is about family life, and family life is more about trade-offs than perfection. Finding the right reunion site is possible—the place that satisfies most of your requirements, and a few of your desires, and features a couple of significant trade-offs.

So, even if the air-conditioning in the common room is both loud and weak, the family can still hold a wild and wonderful talent show. And relatives can get to know one another on breathtaking hiking trails, even if they return to bunk beds in dorms. And if the carpets are a wretched harvest orange—well, this is family life, after all.

HOMECOMING REUNION

Of course, most families can't accommodate the whole clan in the backyard. But if they plan to gather in a grandparent's hometown, for example, a public park can provide great facilities for a daylong homecoming. A park also works well for relatives who plan to use motels or campsites just as places to crash at night, spending most of their waking hours with the family at the park. (For information about local, state, and national parks, call your local Parks Department, or see Appendix, pages 248–249).

The park should have a pavilion or other shelter to shield the family from the sun and rain. Older and disabled family members will need easy access, and kids will need a play-

Backyard Barbecue

❖❖❖

If the family's not very big but the backyard is, you've got the perfect reunion site. It doesn't seem like home—it *is* home. Requirements are minimal: You need enough room for everyone to sit and eat with space left over where the kids can run around and play. This kind of reunion usually revolves around one meal, with the reunion lasting a half rather than a whole day.

Transform a burgers-on-the-grill scene into a reunion event by stringing a reunion banner from trees, setting aside a table for a guest book, name tags, photo albums, and family keepsakes and for picking up reunion T-shirts.

A rented tent and tables will go far toward creating the atmosphere of an event. When a family gathers under a tent to eat, a sense of physical, social, and emotional cohesion wells up that mirrors the larger sense of family togetherness. And toasts and sharing stories become easier when speakers don't have to struggle to capture the attention of family members scattered across a lawn.

Before deciding to invite the hordes to the backyard, test out the logistics. Is there enough room for everybody you want to invite? How many chairs and tables can fit comfortably in the yard? If there's no tent, visualize the rainy-day alternative of a clean garage or the house itself. For suggestions about preparing for a backyard reunion, see Appendix, page 246.

Walk through the house and picture how many people can fit inside without bursting its seams. If you do opt for a tent, assess the leftover space that can be used for family fun and games. And pray for clear skies. (See Appendix, page 259, for how many tables and what size tents you'll need.)

ground. Check to make sure there are adequate bathroom facilities and sufficient parking nearby. The park should also have electrical power sources, running water, and areas for barbecuing and swimming.

As soon as you find the right spot, contact the Parks Department to reserve the pavilion. And ask about ordinances regarding alcoholic beverages—beer and wine drinkers may have to proceed discreetly, if at all.

Families often hold homecoming reunions at two different sites: a park for daytime activities and a rented space—a church community room, a school or college cafeteria, a country club fieldhouse, the grounds of a historic house, or a conventional restaurant—for a catered or potluck dinner. If the family is renting space and no contract is provided (or the contract is very sketchy), the family

"The early risers would go and stake our claim at the shelter by the Lake of the Ozarks—kind of like the old homesteaders. At the crack of dawn the scouts would head out to hold the spot, while those left behind would whip up a pancake-and-scrapple breakfast and take it to them later. Whoever did that early-morning shift didn't have to do anything else the whole day."

—Ethel Young
Springfield, Missouri

and the facility's manager should write out a letter of agreement stating all mutual expectations: date and hours of rental; when access for set-up will be provided; any limitations on the facility—i.e., no use of patio, no use of kitchen, no banners—what special equipment will be made available; the maximum number of people permitted in the facility; and cleanup expectations—who disposes of trash, for example, or if the family is expected to sweep or mop the room after use.

SITES FOR THE WEEKEND CLASSIC

Reunion sites are chosen for many reasons: the host family lives nearby, or the site is within driving distance for most of the relatives. Often the site lies on or near "sacred ground" with significance for the family: the grandparents' hometown or a church founded by the ancestors. Or it's near tourist attractions that make the time, effort, and expense of attending the reunion worthwhile.

When a reunion site is inconveniently located, its compensations usually include a lovely setting, inexpensive rates, and a variety of activities. The trick with these kinds of places is to make sure increased transportation costs don't offset savings in lodgings.

By this point in the planning, the reunion committee should have canvassed family members to find out where they'd like the reunion to be held and how much they're willing to spend. Now is the time to figure out which competing interests—convenience, pleasant surroundings, or expense—will play the most decisive roles.

And the search begins. Check with a travel agent, even though the less commercial, more rustic spots may not have made it onto her list. Refer to guidebooks on family vacations (see Appendix, pages 249–250). At the library, check the *Readers Guide to Periodical Literature* for recent magazine articles about family resorts and vacations. Place notices in church newsletters, on school bulletin boards, and on electronic bulletin boards at the office asking for suggestions.

Once you've narrowed down your location, call on local tourist boards, chambers of commerce, and convention and visitors bureaus. They all exist to steer business to their area—and family reunions are big business. They can help you find hotels, motels, and conference centers that meet your needs. And find out from them about ethnic and historic tours, photographers, florists, caterers, and disc jockeys in the area. They'll also send you maps and brochures, possibly enough to supply all your family members. Use them.

Planning the reunion from afar? Peruse a copy of the Yellow Pages for the reunion region about listings for florists, photographers, golf courses,

FAMILY FRIENDLY SITES

A reunion site should be well-suited for families with young kids. Virtually all hotels let kids under 12 stay free—but check. And put all sites to the family-friendly test. Are there

❑ playgrounds or parks nearby?

❑ laundry facilities?

❑ a pool (indoor or outdoor)?

❑ connecting rooms? double-doubles (two double beds)?

❑ suites? kitchenettes?

❑ low rates for a cot or crib?

❑ refrigerators in the rooms?

❑ baby-sitters the hotel recommends?

❑ recreational facilities for kids (including indoor game rooms)?

❑ on-site restaurants that aren't too formal for young children?

and tennis clubs. Telephone books for any area in the United States are available from your phone company (800) 848-8000, and they'll save you the cost of long-distance information, now about a dollar a call.

Hotels and Resorts

A resort's appeal lies in the wide variety of activities held on the premises—although a family could organize many of the same activities

ON-SITE INSPECTION CHECKLIST

Once you've narrowed down your choices, try to visit the sites. Even if the resort literature shows a spacious lobby and elegant banquet hall, all may not be as pictured. Know what you're looking for.

❑ Inspect the bedrooms yourself. There's plain and clean, and there's drab and musty, and you can't tell the difference over the phone.

❑ Check out the service. You don't need bowing and scraping, but you do need to feel welcome. If the sales manager is helpful and enthusiastic, that's a good first clue.

❑ Does the hotel host many re-unions? A hesitant answer may mean that the hotel is more accustomed to dealing with adults in business clothes than families in matching T-shirts. A weary response may mean that the hotel is a reunion mill, with your family one among dozens.

❑ Test the staff's friendliness by asking a passing staff person for directions to the rest room, or the person at the registration desk for change of a dollar.

❑ Does the variety of room options accommodate a range of financial abilities: suites, adjoining rooms? Are nonsmoking rooms available? Are meals served family-style? If this is a family resort, are there set mealtimes?

❑ What about access for disabled guests? Chances are your reunion party will include one or two dis-abled or older people who need extra support.

❑ Does the hotel have a disco or nightclub? Make sure your rooms are nowhere near it. Cinderblock conducts bass lines straight from the disco to your pillow.

❑ What are the restaurants like? Are the banquet rooms big enough? Do they offer a view? What room would serve as hospitality suite?

❑ Does the staff arrange for off-site activities like fishing trips, trail rides, tee times at nearby golf courses?

---

itself and pay much less by staying at a motel or hotel. The one nonnego-tiable feature for any location is a swimming pool or beach nearby. (In the warm-weather months, water washes away a multitude of sins for families with kids.)

Sometimes a locale can offer too many activities. "We were so involved with the Disney activities we barely saw each other," says one woman whose family held a reunion in Orlando. "By the end of the day the kids were wiped out. They had a great vacation but not much in the way of a family reunion."

Family resorts are not glamor-ous, but they're reasonably priced, offer package rates that include all (or most) activities and meals, have family-oriented activities throughout the day and evening, and are usually located in rural settings.

If you'd like to hold a reunion in a suburban area, conference centers are an option. Designed with loads of meeting rooms, hospitality suites, and resortlike amenities, conference centers are well equipped to host reunions and may be reasonably priced in summer, when business traffic slows. Check with major hotel chains to find out where their conference centers are located.

Hotels in New York, Washington, D.C., and other big cities often offer excellent deals on summer weekends, when corporate business is zero and most tourists are at the beach.

Tip: Never make reservations via an 800 number; you can almost always get a better deal using the local reservation number.

Everything's Negotiable: How to Cut a Deal

Scoped out a few prime sites? Zero in on your best bet and negotiate a special reunion rate with the sales manager or group-sales person. The bigger the reunion, the better your deal should be, with more perks. By the way, if you're the kind of person who's always paid sticker price for a new car, maybe you should enlist the help of a master bargainer from the family.

ORGANIZER'S TIP SHEET

Designate a page in your notebook for each reunion site you call or visit. Note the address, phone number and contact person, the place's pros and cons, observations like "banquet manager has an attitude," quoted prices, and any questions you forgot to ask. Buy plenty of pocket folders in which to stash brochures and fact sheets from sites, too. And try to keep it legible: This notebook might be an invaluable resource for the next reunion organizer in the family.

Here are some tips.

Get a package deal. A typical reunion package includes breakfast vouchers, a discounted banquet, use of a common room, and a 15 percent discount off the standard room rate, as well as perks like prepared name tags or reunion signage. Find out what's included in the package, the minimum number of reservations needed to qualify, and how the costs differ from standard room rates. Other extras to request: a meeting room (or hospitality suite) without charge, one room thrown in free with every 20 or 30 rooms booked, a discount for those reserving early, late checkout on Sunday. Can't get at least two of these perks? Keep looking.

Know your opponent. The sales manager may claim that the hotel has an unalterable rate set by management, but almost everything is negotiable, so keep trying. Practice saying these four little words: "Can you do better?" But don't do any negotiating over the phone or in front of other customers—the salesperson won't want to be caught dead making concessions in public.

Arouse the sales manager's competitive instinct. Let it drop that you've visited comparable facilities and know what prices are reasonable. If you *do* think this is the ideal spot for your family, don't tip off the sales manager immediately. Be prepared to walk and return another day. Then, if you really like the place and it really is over your budget, ask the sales manager, "How can we make this work so we'll both be happy?"

Get detailed figures. Find out precisely how much everything costs: P.A. system, podium, audio/visual equipment set-up, dance floor, health club, coffee service in the hospitality suite, meeting rooms, children's rates for meals, parking, cribs and cots, fees for arrangements for off-site activities. Are charges per room or per person? Uncover any hidden costs—automatically applied gratuities, expected (presumably voluntary) gratuities, taxes, and parking (many cities have steep hotel taxes and parking charges)—and make sure to include them in the costs stated to the family in the explanatory letter. See if reservation forms can be sent directly to the reunion goers and returned to the hotel. It will save you a lot of paperwork.

Talk with the banquet manager. If you're holding a dinner at the hotel, ask about children's rates and if a gratuity is automatically applied to your bill. See if reunion goers can reserve and pay for the dinner directly. Don't commit to the banquet right away: You may be able to cut a better deal with a restaurant or have a meal catered in a common room nearby.

Ask about the deposit and cancellation policy. Use a credit card to make a deposit, so if there's a dispute about the contract or service, the credit-card company will withhold payment. Some facilities will apply your deposit to your group's bill, while others hold the deposit in case of damages until a week after the stay.

Get it in writing. Have the reunion site draw up a contract with everything you've agreed on, including the package room rates and minimum number of reserved rooms needed for them. You should also get in writing any discount for early reservations and when that discount ends, and the exact check-in and check-out times and dates. Make sure to spell out any other special features of your reunion package, such as meal-plan rates, coupons for breakfast, or discounted off-site activities, such as tennis or golf.

One benefit of early planning is that by locking in this year's agreed-on rates in writing, you get next year's rooms at this year's rates. Make a copy of your contract and take it with you to the reunion, in case any disagreements arise.

HOTELS, RESORTS, AND CONFERENCE CENTERS

Here's an eclectic mix of places where your family might converge for its reunion. Most of the resorts are moderate in price (unless otherwise noted), topping off at $100 per adult per day, including meals. What these places may lack in plush comfort, they make up for in their range of activities and splendid locations.

ASILOMAR CONFERENCE CENTER

800 Asilomar Boulevard
P.O. Box 537
Pacific Grove, California 93950
(408) 372-8016/Fax (408) 372-7227

This lovely nonprofit conference center on the Monterey Peninsula is run by the California State Park System. There's a mile-long beach just over the dunes, numerous walking trails, and a heated swimming pool. Evening barbecues and bonfires can be arranged, and golf, tennis, and fishing is available nearby. There are a number of architecturally pleasing lodges with capacities of up to 100 (most are around 40), and while rooms may not have TVs or phones, they do have private baths, and many have fireplaces. All buildings are nonsmoking. What's the catch? You have to plan wayyyyy in advance—two to three years in advance. Nearest airports: Mon-

terey, a 20-minute drive; San Jose, 1½ hours away.

ASPEN LODGE AT ESTES PARK

6120 Highway 7, Longs Peak Route
Estes Park, Colorado 80517
(970) 586-8133
(800) 332-6867 outside Colorado

This dude ranch on the edge of Rocky Mountain National Park has plenty to offer those with no interest in learning a figure-eight lasso twirl. Offering a choice of lodge rooms or cabins, Aspen Lodge features a kid-friendly array of Western resort activities: fishing, swimming in the heated pools, hiking, trail rides and hayrides, and outdoor barbecues and campfires. And that spectacular scenery, of course. Golf can be arranged nearby. Nearest major airport: Denver, 1½ hours away.

DRIFTWOOD SHORES RESORT AND CONFERENCE CENTER

88416 First Avenue
Florence, Oregon 97439-9112
(800) 422-5091/(541) 997-8263

Driftwood Shores, situated on a beautiful stretch of the Oregon coast, offers beauty (all the rooms have great views of the Pacific Ocean), golf (the Sandpines Golf Course was voted the Best Public Golf Course by *Golf Digest*), 10 miles of uninterrupted sandy beaches, and a variety of local attractions. Old Town Florence, a picturesque port and waterfront, is just minutes away. Other nearby activities include the Oregon Coast Aquarium and the Sea Lion Caves, where one can see Stellar sea lions and the largest sea cave in America, as well as catch a whale-watching trip. The resort has conference rooms that can hold up to 125 people, an indoor pool, and a spa. Nearest Airport: Eugene, 1 hour and 10 minutes.

FLYING L GUEST RANCH

P.O. Box 1959
Bandera, Texas 78003
(800) 292-5134

A real Texas time, with as much or as little ranching as you want and very little roughing it—accommodations are all newly upgraded two-room suites. The ranch offers an 18-hole golf course, outdoor pool, tennis, cookouts, and water sports on the Medina River, in addition to the expected rodeo activities, riding lessons, and trail rides of a typical dude ranch. Water parks are nearby, as is the Lone Star Brewery, which offers tours. Can accommodate as many as 150-member reunions and will handle all the mailings to family members directly. Discounts start at groups of 20 or more. Conference rooms available. Nearest airport: San Antonio, a 1-hour drive.

GRAND VIEW LODGE

134 Nokomis
Nisswa, Minnesota 56468
(218) 963-2234

You can stay either in the beautifully situated national historic site lodge or in the cabins scattered over this 900-acre resort on Gull Lake, about 2 hours north of Minneapolis/St. Paul. Even those accustomed to high-end lodgings will be happy with Grand View. A kids' program runs from morning till mid-afternoon, with activities ranging from arts and crafts in the Art Barn to hayrides. Facilities include a playground area and beach on the lake, indoor pool, tennis courts, and 9-hole golf course (an excellent 18-hole course, The Pines, is nearby). Activities include sailing, canoeing, waterskiing, and trips to the nearby Paul Bunyan Amusement Park. Nearest airports: Brainerd, a ½-hour drive; Minneapolis/St. Paul, 2 hours.

THE HERSHEY LODGE

The Hershey Highmeadow Campground
Hershey, Pennsylvania 17033
(800) HERSHEY

This big, well-managed, well-priced resort is the spot for the family that likes loads of activities to keep itself occupied. With its location accessible to family members in the Northeast, Midwest, and Mid-Atlantic states, it also offers a range of economic options for accommodations. Some can stay in the well-equipped campground while others can take it easy in the lodge, and all can meet for meals and activities.

The range of activities is exhaustive: 72 holes of golf, nearby Hersheypark, pools and tennis and spa facilities. And of course, the Chocolate World Official Visitor's Center. Nearest airport: Harrisburg International, 25 minutes.

HIGH HAMPTON INN AND COUNTRY CLUB

640 Hampton Road
Cashiers, North Carolina 28717
(704) 743-2411

©Lavidge & Associates, Inc.

This Blue Ridge Mountain resort is on the National Register of Historic Places and prides itself on its comfortable, rustic accommodations far from the madding crowd. No phones or TVs in rooms, no monuments to commercialism—but soaring mountains, gorgeous azalea gardens, a lake for boating and fishing (with fly-fishing lessons available and a children's beach), golf greens, donkey-cart rides, clay tennis courts, kids' club, and hiking trails—one to the peak of Chimney Top Mountain. Great-grandma and great-grandchild should be equally happy here. While the required coat and tie in the dining room for evening meals may put off some families, others will welcome the excuse to spruce themselves up. Nearest airport: Asheville, 1 hour.

Lake Quinault Lodge

P.O. 7
Quinault, Washington 98575-0007
(800) 562-6672/Fax (360) 288-2900

Slightly pricier and more remote than the other accommodations listed here, Lake Quinault Lodge's prices—and remoteness—are justified by its spectacular location: the heart of the Olympic National Forest, our only temperate mainland rain forest. There's canoeing, kayaking, and fishing on the lake, and hiking and mountain biking (or just plain walking) through the forest by day, and an indoor pool and sauna to return to at day's end. This is the spot for a nature-loving family. Nearest airport: SeaTac, 3 hours away.

Montecito Sequoia Lodge

Sequoia National Forest, California
(800) 227-9900 or
(415) 967-8612

By summer, this is a high-activity structured family camp in the Sequoia National Park, with all the activities you'd expect from a great camp: horseback riding, fishing, hiking, waterskiing, arts and crafts, and three meals a day served buffet-style in the main lodge. Family members can stay in cabins with a common bathhouse or in more luxurious accommodations in the lodge, with private bathrooms. In the other seasons, family groups can compose their own schedules, with cross-country skiing, snowshoeing, and sledding in winter, and canoeing, hiking, and paddleball in spring and fall. Nearest airports: Fresno or Visalia, both 1½ hours away.

Oglebay Resort/Wilson Lodge

Wheeling, West Virginia 26003
(304) 243-4060/(800) 972-1991

This year-round resort, with most of the grounds open to the public, has a wide array of activities: tennis, golf, indoor and outdoor pools, fishing, trails for walks and hikes, zoo and nature center, and many winter sports, including cross-country skiing, sledding, and ice skating. Accommodations range from small cottages to 20-bedroom "cottages" to rooms in the main lodge. Speak with the family reunion specialist to work out a package with meal plan and accommodations. Nearest airports: Pittsburgh International, 1 hour away; Wheeling, 15 minutes away.

POTAWATOMI INN RESORT & CONFERENCE CENTER

6 Lane 100 A Lake James
Angola, Indiana 46703
(219) 833-1077

L ocated within Pokagon State Park on Lake James, Potawatomi Inn is within driving distance of Chicago, Indianapolis, and Lansing, Michigan. There are two swimming beaches on the lake and an indoor pool, exercise room, whirlpool and sauna, crafts and games rooms, loads of meeting rooms, and stables for horseback riding. Excellently priced. Nearest airport: Fort Wayne, a 1-hour drive.

SLIDE ROCK LODGE

Star Route 3
Box 1141
Sedona, Arizona 86336
(520) 282-3531

W ith only 20 rooms (but accommodating up to 45 guests), this log-cabin lodge sits at the foot of the Red

Rock Buttes not far from stunning Sedona. No TVs or phones in the plain yet clean rooms (some with fireplaces), no restaurant (plenty in Sedona, though), but there are swimming holes, barbecue areas, and a magnificent setting unlike any other that is within easy driving distance of the Grand Canyon. Nearest airport: Flagstaff, less than a $\frac{1}{2}$-hour drive.

SUNRISE RESORT

Moodus, Connecticut 06469
(860) 873-8681

A family-run, camp-style resort in rural Connecticut, open from Memorial Day through Labor Day, with clusters of accommodations of differing costs dispersed over 200 acres of rolling hills and fields. Many planned activities, especially for kids, watersports on the Salmon River beachhead, and softball fields. Nearest airport: Hartford, a 1-hour drive.

The Camp Option

Unbeknownst to many, a number of sleep-away and day camps, church camps, Jewish camps, and YMCAs rent out their facilities to groups by the day, weekend, or week and are a reasonable (albeit not deluxe) alternative to resorts. While summer camps are usually booked with programs during the main summer months, many are available during weekends in June and September. Church camps are often available during the summer, since family togetherness and approaching God through fellowship with nature is part of their mission.

Camps are usually low cost, with all meals included, situated in bucolic settings, well-maintained and clean (if bare-bones), and tailor-made for group meetings and kids' and intergenerational activities. Facilitators and group leaders are often on hand to lead hikes, games, and other outdoor teamwork activities. Religious camps usually feature at least some lodgings better suited for older people than the traditionally spartan bunkhouse. Jewish camps almost always have Kosher kitchens, a great advantage for families with observant members.

The YMCA runs seven conference centers around the country in stunning rural settings ideal for family reunions. Among the many advantages of the Y conference centers are their unbeatable affordability and large, well-maintained lodges and private cottages with kitchens (alcohol may be consumed on these premises). Flexible meal plans let a family cook part of the time and take meals in the main dining halls at other times. There are crafts rooms and meeting rooms indoors, group leaders to help organize activities, and a wide range of outdoor activities that emphasize togetherness and teamwork, such as hiking, trail riding, and canoeing. Many are well suited for winter reunions, too, with cross-county and downhill skiing as well as other snow activities.

The drawbacks? Camps rarely have air-conditioning, usually do not permit alcohol on the grounds (especially true of church camps), limit or prohibit smoking, and may have dorm-style lodgings that are too "camplike" for your family's liking. Camps may also serve meals at hours out of sync with your family's eating habits; they may not always provide linen, pillows, and blankets; and they may be shared by other groups at the same time your family is there. Camp managers also may not be able to give you a firm date until fairly late in the game. And church camps and Jewish camps often feature religious symbols and a religious outlook that may make some family members uncomfortable.

For more information about Jewish, Christian, and nondenominational camps, see Appendix, pages 246–247; for a listing of YMCA conference centers, see pages 247–248.

CAMPSITE CHECKLIST

Before packing your knapsack and heading out with the whole family for camp, ask some questions.

❑ What are the dates of availability?

❑ Are facilities winterized? (A fall reunion at a camp could be glorious.)

❑ Is housekeeping provided? Linens? Meal service?

❑ What activities are available? Are staff members available for assistance with activities? What staff members are available at extra cost —lifeguards, rope-course guides?

❑ Are more comfortable rooms available for older family members or those with special needs?

❑ Does the family need to provide an insurance policy? (These are often available through a family member's existing umbrella policy.)

❑ Where is the nearest airport? What is the travel time to the nearest metropolitan center?

College Dorms and Prep Schools

Many colleges rent out dorm rooms, floors, or entire dorms in the summer at extremely affordable rates. Some families use colleges for all their reunion activities, but most use them just as clean, well-lit places to spend the night, with older folks and parents with small babies lodging at a good-quality motel nearby. Call the housing departments of colleges in the area in which you'd like to hold your reunion—many colleges don't advertise dorm availability because they don't want to jeopardize their nonprofit status or sour relations with town businesses, which would prefer to keep the lodging business for themselves. Or order the *Budget Lodging Guide* from B & J Publications, P.O. Box 5486, Fullerton, CA 92635, (800) 525-6633, for a comprehensive listing of college and university accommodations. Make your plans well in advance: colleges book early for summer programs and conferences.

More rarely, and almost never on a formal basis, prep schools are available. It usually helps if the family holding the reunion has some relationship with the school—and a contribution to the school substitutes for a standard fee. It can't hurt to give targeted schools a call. The *Vincent/Curtis Educational Register*, a directory of private boarding schools, can be ordered from Vincent/Curtis, (617) 536-0100.

State Resort Parks

Waterskiing, trapshooting, golf. Tennis, swimming, boating. Trail riding, miniature golf, water slides. These are some of the activities on offer at resorts run by state parks. Most resort parks have a recreation director, and in addition to the resort activities, they generally feature nature activities led by park rangers. Many offer a range of lodging options that run from the quite comfortable to the bracingly rustic, with rates sliding accordingly; almost all rates are well below those of commercial resorts. Each park varies in what it has to offer. Letchworth State Park, in Castile, New York, features whitewater rafting. Roman Nose Resort Park, in Watonga, Oklahoma, offers modernized teepees as an option for accommodations. Lake Barkley State Resort Park, in Cadiz, Kentucky, has racquetball and lighted tennis courts for nighttime family tournaments.

The most significant drawback of state resort parks is their inconvenient locations—by definition, they're *meant* to be in the middle of nowhere. But many families feel that state parks compensate for their difficult access with affordability, scenic beauty, and range of activities. (See Appendix, pages 248–249, for a list of some popular resort parks).

Houseboats

A small flotilla of houseboats makes a memorable reunion site—and when the bunks fill up at night with sweetly sleeping children, and the nightbirds are out and about, and the adults are sipping wine and talking quietly on the decks, the cramped shower stalls

THE HYBRID REUNION

If families are willing to work at it, a reunion held at a state or national park can be tailored to all the income and energy levels of the group. The family can patch together lodgings within the park, with some members camping out, others staying at an RV campground, some in rustic cabins, older relations in comfy digs at a lodge, and another contingent staying just outside the park in a conventional motel. The whole family can then convene during the day, lakeside or seaside, and at a campfire or at a catered dinner in the evening.

◆ The family gets the benefits of being in spectacular natural surroundings, removed from the commercialism of everyday life, so that even the in-laws come away with the feeling that this was a real "vacation" away from it all.

◆ Figuring out which parks are best suited for this kind of patchwork reunion can be time-consuming, and reservations must be made at least a year in advance. And while guests may reserve lodgings in cabins and lodges, many parks won't take reservations for campsites, which makes it a bit risky and stressful for the camping set.

"Our family is scattered across the West. At our reunions a third of us end up in tents, a third of us are in RVs, and a third of us are at a lodge. One year, the non-RV people rented houseboats on Lake Tahoe. It worked fantastically well. Most of our meals are potluck at the campsite. But on the first and last night we take over a room in a restaurant and make it our own. Last year we went to a ribs place the first night and on the last night, took over an entire pizzeria. We just had a blast. **"**

—Holly Hollinger Trumbull
Issaquah, Washington

seem worth it. Houseboats are far more common than most people realize—they can be found on Lake Tahoe, Lake Powell, the Erie Canal, Lake Cumberland in Kentucky, and the Lake of the Ozarks in Missouri, to name a few places.

While many of us would be happy simply staying in a "cottage on water," other families might actually want to travel together, trading off kids throughout the day, working the locks on canals. Houseboat rental companies differ, but almost all give lessons in how to steer and dock. Everyone but the smallest kids should attend; the lessons may come in handy when the master skipper is off fishing in the dinghy. (For a listing of some good houseboat companies and other resources, see Appendix, page 249.)

Condominiums and Beach, Lake, and Mountain Cabins

Some families rent groups of cottages at a beach, a large house, or condos for a week-long reunion. If the reunion is held in summer, houses should have swimming and parking rights at a lake or beach. Usually this kind of reunion lasts about a week and is limited to siblings, their spouses and children.

It helps if at least one family member knows the area and can steer the reunion leader to good neighborhoods and reputable rental agents. Ski resorts in summer offer bargains on condo rentals—although very few are downright cheap. Before deciding on where to rent, get brochures and other information from the chamber of commerce, tourist board, or convention and visitors bureau. When a family is all together in one house, there should be a few good rainy-day destinations lined up.

The advantages of a condo or house are the unbeatable privacy and togetherness that come from living and working together. And parents can put young kids to bed and still be able to hang out with other adults—which they can't do at a resort unless a baby-sitter is hired. If water, tennis courts, and a golf course are nearby, the family can enjoy a full range of activities, and high-quality condos rented in groups means that a high standard of living

A Camp Reunion

The Grange Family

What: *Extended weekend classic*

Who: *Three generations of Granges, originally from South Dakota*

Where: *Storm Mountain Center, South Dakota*

Number of Participants: *65*

Unofficial Family Motto: *"Families are like peanut brittle. It takes a lot of sugar to keep the nuts together"*

Family Traits: *Dancing eyes and laughing uproariously at own jokes*

Family Sport: *Chinwagging.*

A small sign, easily overshadowed by the much larger signs trumpeting Mt. Rushmore and Wall Drug, points the way to Storm Mountain Center, a few miles outside Rapid City. Wind down a dirt road into the heart of the Black Hills National Forest, and a few miles later appear a cluster of lodges and cabins, amid soaring rock spires and scrubby pines.

A quick glance at the license plates in the parking lot tells you that you're at either an annual sales convention or a family reunion: Oklahoma, Colorado, Washington, South Dakota, Texas, Nebraska. The range of bumper stickers, too, lets you know that nobody here has gathered in a show of political solidarity. One bumper sticker rails against Planned Parenthood, while another reads "Pro-Family, Pro-Children, Pro-Choice." The air-conditioning of a giant RV grinds away at the dry heat of the early evening, the family within having driven down from Vancouver, Washington. They don't need to spend money on rooms at the lodge.

Family members come from all over the country.

The Grange family is the group here at Storm Mountain—a self-contained world of Granges. At night the ventilation is minimal, the mattresses on the bunk beds feel thinner by the hour, and to catch a breeze, you need to keep the door open. But these discomforts are far outweighed by Storm Mountain's strong suits. The swimming hole is ringed with granite spires and fed by a stream suitable for tubing or trout fishing. The miles of hiking trails, a ropes course for a group challenge, a community room for the talent show, a rec room for downtime Foosball and Ping-Pong. And

Father and son snag some alone-time.

the air here smells fresh and clean, pure oxygen and scrub pine.

It's the second day of a four-day reunion. On a grassy patch just off the parking lot is a cluster of folding lawn chairs, a cooler filled with liquor, mixers, and beer, and a convivial bunch of Grange family members. They meet here every evening before dinner, just outside the Storm Mountain Center's official boundaries: Here they are allowed to drink. One disadvantage of holding a reunion at a church camp is that drinking gets relegated to a tailgate party. But to judge from the easy sociability of this group, it may not be such a disadvantage after all. The cocktail hour outside the loop has a "we happy few" feeling about it.

The dinner gong is struck. Six o'clock. Way too early for half the adults and just right for the other half. But everyone eats at the same time, breakfast, lunch, and dinner. "Let me have a try," says Ross Grange, II, hovering over the gong. *Bong!* It's the family's responsibility to set up for dinner, and everyone

Nearby Mt. Rushmore is a reunion day trip for the Grange clan.

pitches in without hesitation. They unfold chairs and put pitchers of water and lemonade on each table. After dinner, they'll bus their plates, fold up the chairs, and wipe down the tables. The food is plain but decent—spaghetti and sauce, Italian bread, salad, pudding for dessert—like school food on a good day.

The staff who fix the

Assuming the Grange identity in a reunion T-shirt.

meals are clean-cut young people who are so nice, it's almost scary; it's reassuring to know that they're listening to a typical teenage rock station in the kitchen. Apart from the T-shirts worn by the staff, "It's not a job—It's a mission," Storm Mountain is not overwhelmed by religious imagery.

But there's enough to trouble Robin Goldston, the only family member who's Jewish. Robin could do without the crosses down at the swimming hole and on the wall of the main lodge. But, apart from Robin, lots of Christian sects are represented within the family: Mormons, Catholics, Protestants, as well as more than a few in quest of something beyond organized religion. What you can say about the Granges, and those who've married in, is that they're open and unpretentious and laugh easily—recognizable to the rest of the world as a family from the American West.

A hot topic at the cocktail hour and at dinner is the family accomplishments on the ropes course earlier in the day. With scenery like this it was easy to get a group to accept the challenge. The mood was one of anxious anticipation when the family gathered in the morning. No one was sure what to expect. "Can we wear sunglasses? High heels? Lipstick?" asked one Grange cousin.

"Yes, no, and lipstick is always a good idea," said Chris Coleman.

At the course the family divided itself into three groups, evenly distributing the big and little people among them. One group approached a wooden wall about 10 feet high, with a raised platform behind it, so that those who have made it over can help pull up the next. From below, it seemed insurmountable. They looked up, then at each other, and started to make a plan. For a family whose

To get over the wall takes cooperation and trust.

preferred sport is chinwagging, the discussion of strategy is half the fun.

A few people made it over the wall, when, suddenly, Kitty was dangling from the hands of relatives, with a look of panic on her face. "Walk the wall, woman!" yelled her cousin Mary Pat. Somehow Kitty's sneakers found the wall and she clambered up and over.

Close family: 13 Granges on a 2-by-2-foot platform.

The most challenging station required everybody in the group to fit on a 2-by-2-foot platform and balance there for five seconds. There were a multitude of theories and attempts: little people on the outside, big people counterbalancing each other, and little children holding on while dangling one leg off the platform like figurines on an Italian fountain. But three seconds later they would all totter off.

At last, the four children were pressed to the core of the platform, the bigger people surrounded them, arms linked, and the medium-size people clung to the edge. They counted to five in about two seconds, then let out a cheer. "Let the children out! They need to breathe!"

"Talk about your close families," John Urquhart muttered.

Chris Coleman, a Grange granddaughter and Rapid City resident, is the reunion's host. Her sons had gone on youth-group retreats to this church camp, and when she volunteered three years ago to host this year's reunion, she had this place in mind. But

The Group Shot: Capturing the event on film.

there was a hitch: Storm Mountain Center's manager knew he could fit in the Granges sometime that summer, but he couldn't say exactly when until church groups around the state solidified their own plans.

It wasn't until December that Chris was able to tell the family that the reunion would be held the week of July 4th. By then, some workplaces had already given time off to those who had put in earlier requests for that plum vacation week, and as a result attendance was down 25 percent.

But 65 Granges go a long way. A fresh contingent bursts into the dining hall, having just returned from a family history tour to Mobridge, the once-thriving railroad town where the Granges had originally settled. They had seen the old

The youngest and oldest Granges span four generations.

house and old friends, and Will Grange had attended his 50th high school reunion. "There was a girl I was close to in high school, and then somehow we stopped being close. I never could understand why and I was too proud to ask her at the time.

"But we met again today and she explained it all. What it was about, that's our secret. But I've been troubled by it for 50 years, 50 years! And now, I feel light as a feather, as free as the wind, walking on air!" Will does a little jig that does seem light and airy.

Anyone can see that a great weight has been thrown off his shoulders. Raising the collective spirit of the room even higher, he sits down and joins his family to eat, smiling all the while.

A SIBLINGS' REUNION

"My nine siblings and I rented three houses in a row at a seaside community. The rental agent was a friend of mine, so I trusted her judgment and didn't have to travel to see the houses. We designated one house for families with teenagers, one for families with younger kids (they could play together, go to bed earlier, and wake up earlier), and a quiet house for our father and the older siblings with grown kids. The quiet house was a great success. It was where we'd all go, even the kids, to have one-on-ones with our father, who finds it difficult to talk when there's lots of background noise now that his hearing isn't what it was. Every night the teenagers roamed from house to house, dragging their air mattresses and sleeping bags behind them. Some mornings we'd peek into a bedroom and there'd be no cousins at all, while in the next room over there'd be five lying in a sleepy heap. That was what it was all about.

"The houses were all on a short road, and during the day everyone would walk back and forth. It was like the street had become our family's street, our little family village.

"Each night, two families would be in charge of every aspect of dinner—shopping, cooking, cleaning up—which was always cooked in the kitchen of one house, since that's where we kept all the staples and cooking supplies. Our last night we held a grand-finale dinner in a private room at a hotel. My father sat and looked out over everyone and murmured, 'I can't believe I'm responsible for all these great people being here.' We needed privacy then, because after that it got pretty teary."

—*Ellie von Wellsheim*

becomes affordable. Since condos are available at all the major resorts, the reunion can take on the aura of a deluxe vacation without the usual price tag.

But there are disadvantages. A house's quality may be difficult to determine from afar, and finding a trustworthy rental agent can be hard. (You might want to check your rental agent with the local Better Business Bureau.) And living together for a week may be *too* much "togetherness" for some families.

Because activities aren't on site, more organization is required of the family. A cash deposit may be needed early on, before everyone has committed to the reunion, and may not be returned until weeks after the reunion, pending assessment of possible damages. And since the family is responsible for cooking and cleaning, this may not be the vacation break some family members had in mind. See pages 114–115 for more information on how to divide up cooking chores at a sibling reunion.

OLD COUNTRY REUNIONS

To say that people return to a country where they've never been is an oxymoron. But for those whose parents came from the Old Country, going there for the first time often feels like returning; the sense of familiarity and connection are stronger than one could possibly have imagined. Placing one's ancestors in context, visualizing how their day-to-day lives must have been, and getting a sense of the culture that formed them (and hence you) can be illuminating. But does that mean the Old Country is a fine place for a reunion?

It can be—if the reunion includes meeting up with members of the family left behind, a once-in-a-lifetime gathering that may justify dipping into the retirement fund. But otherwise, while a personal exploration of the Old Country may be a wonderful vacation to be shared with a few others, unless the family has lots of financial resources well distributed across the family branches, such a trip probably doesn't make sense for a reunion. Apart from the expense, a trip to the ancestral home would

"My father came from a small fishing village in Italy, the kind you reach only by boat or by descending steep stone steps down a steep mountainside. When I visited for the first time, we went by boat. It was amazing. As soon as we stepped off the boat, there we were—in his world! All the men were talking like him. They looked like him— they had the same kind of nose, same eyes, same hand gestures. And I realized, 'This isn't just where he came from. This is where I come from.'"
—Sister Pauline Chirchirillo
New York, New York

probably be lost on younger children, who would either have to be left at home (hardly the goal of most reunions) or wind up kicking at cobblestones on quaint village lanes whose charm eludes them.

Perhaps the best idea is to hold an American reunion and then have one person try to organize an Old Country trip with some of the relatives—most likely it will be older people with the time and resources to travel. The American Society of Travel Agents (1101 King St., Alexandria, VA 22314) can help families find travel agents who specialize in ethnic travel. But the sponsoring family members should do most of the digging into the family history themselves. Experienced travel agents report that overseas travel agents and self-styled genealogists often take advantage of Americans in quest of their roots, performing shoddy yet expensive fact finding into a family's history. Like genealogy, this kind of history is best undertaken as a labor of love. The National Genealogical Society sells a wide selection of books on how to explore one's Old Country genealogical roots. (See Appendix, page 252.)

The search for the reunion site is tough—it rattles the nerves. But once the decision is made, there's a kind of liberation, a release, from the uncertainty whether the reunion will actually happen. The reunion site is the reunion's home, and once that place comes into focus, your thoughts can turn to the faces and voices that will soon be filling that place—all that family, coming home.

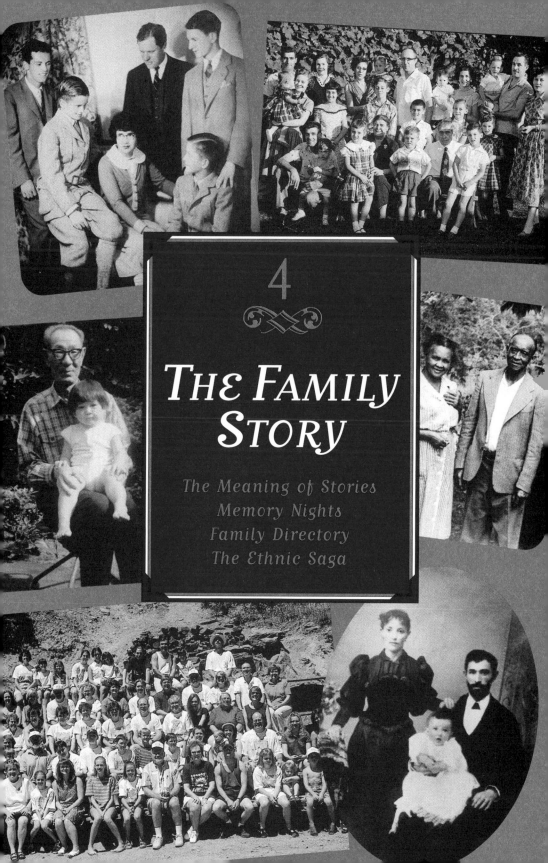

4

THE FAMILY STORY

The Meaning of Stories
Memory Nights
Family Directory
The Ethnic Saga

Our identity as a family is shaped by our stories. What do we choose to tell about ourselves, what do we embellish, what do we leave out? Family stories, writes Elizabeth Stone in *Black Sheep and Kissing Cousins,* "fasten the identity in place and keep it from floating off, slithering away, or losing its shape." These stories remind us of who we are. They instruct us on how we as family members are to act: We are this way, they announce, and not that way. These stories mark the distinctions that characterize your family as different and special, whether a sense of specialness is justified or not. Even families who haven't enjoyed great financial success or who have been dealt a bad hand in life tell tales of their unique and superior qualities: generosity, physical strength, the good looks of its women, or the wily ways it has out-maneuvered authority figures.

Harvesting stories may be a reunion's most important job. "Stories are an essential way for a family to create bonds," says folklorist Steve Zeitlin. "We use stories not only to re-create memories, but to create new memories." Stories become shared experience—they are what we have in common with cousins we see only once a year.

"Remember when Uncle Bill broke his leg at Uncle Ed's ranch?" Nobody who tells the story or hears the story of Uncle Bill's leg may have been there to see it break, but it's an experience shared by cousins nonetheless. Once a story is told, it becomes yours, part of you. Shared memory, shared history, shared stories: That's what defines family.

Every American family has its saga. We are who and where we are because of an epic struggle in the not-so-distant past. The family's genesis myth memorializes the arrival: how it's first forebear arrived on these shores.

The classic American migration story has three essential parts, says Steve Zeitlin. The first part explains why the family left its old home back East, down South, in Mother Africa, or in the Old Country. The second details how hard and rigorous the journey to the new home was. The third shows how confusing and difficult the struggle was to build a new life in a strange land.

These stories personalize the immigration experience in ways that make it special to your family. The flipside, exploring how your own family saga connects to the larger ethnic experience, is discussed in "The Immigrant Saga," pages 87–94.

How a family's name was changed in the process of coming to America is often a feature of these stories. The name change is the perfect metaphor for the sea change a family undergoes in coming to America, shedding or shifting its old identity, willingly or not. It's the first step of the ensuing struggle to become assimilated—losing part of one's old family identity in pursuit of cultural acceptability.

The courtship tale, detailing how the grandparents or great-grand-parents managed to find each other, is another genesis story told in families:

"In Russia, our family's name was Kozlovsky. When Harry Kozlovsky emigrated to America, they asked him his name when he got off the boat but he didn't understand a word of English. The man ahead of him had said, 'Gross' and had been moved along, so he said 'Gross' too, thinking that was what you said if you wanted to get into America. And that's how our family came to be Gross. Or one version of it, at least. I've heard other versions..."

—Gale Robinson
New York, New York

how a family came to be. These stories are often love-at-first-sight tales, implying that destiny played a hand in bringing the two people together. This sense of destiny imbues the couple and thus the family with significance. Parental disapproval or another obstacle the lovers had to overcome is a familiar component—proving how special your origins were.

Hardship tales and struggles of survival are the most directly useful of family stories, illustrating the trials a family has faced in the past, and how they were endured and overcome. Vacation disaster stories act as modern versions of hardship tales, Mary Pipher points out in *The Shelter of the Family*. They provide life lessons in the same way old-time stories did: "These stories are important because they say this family can not only survive adversity but can laugh

"Our family always felt itself special—the soil on our grandpa's farm was the best soil, our Uncle Ernest was the very best singer. Was he really all that great a singer? Probably not. At our reunions, the sense of specialness in the minds of the elders gets transmitted to the young people and acts as a filter against the worst elements. As a member of this family, there are certain things you can't do, and certain things you must do because it's expected of you. In our family, you're expected to be one of those people other people turn to in times of trouble—and you are."
—*William Raspberry*
Washington, D.C.

at it and keep on loving each other." Stories that tell how a family has outwitted authority or persevered through illness by pulling together teach children that the ability to prevail over disaster exists. It's almost a family responsibility to pass on the lesson that just because the odds are against you, the game is not necessarily lost.

The hero of the survival tales is often the family trickster—the one who traded an old horse for train tickets out of town before an unjust creditor caught up with him and his family, the one who scored the last train tickets out of Vienna before the Nazis marched in, the one who bottled witch hazel on the Dakota Plains

and called it the Superior Salve of the Sioux. He's the family antihero: roguish, wily, limber enough in wits, spirit, and body to slip through authority's nets.

But for every trickster, there is the illustrious ancestor—somewhere back in the mists of time we *were* Somebody—endowing the family with a much-needed sense of specialness. Tales of the illustrious ancestor are most common in families that feel a little out of sync with the culture around them; they are a way of families "making themselves feel more comfortable, of defending against slights and disparagement," writes Elizabeth Stone.

The other ancestor to which Americans often stake an unjustified claim is the Native American. Certainly many European and African American families have an American Indian forebear somewhere in the family tree. But many families use a fictitious Indian forebear to explain a strain of wildness—often an attractively rebellious kind of wildness. In Europe, the same myth is employed —but there, families attribute the wild strain to Gypsy blood.

In the end, family stories are explanatory myths, trying to make sense of why things are the way they are, as the lost fortune story does: The house the family sold turned out to be sitting on an oil reserve; a great-uncle was invited to buy stock in something called the telephone but was sure the new contraption would never work. These tales suggest that riches are acquired less by superior personal talents than by sheer luck, of being in the right place at the right time.

And then there are the family stories rarely told above a whisper—the private world of grief and loss relayed under one's breath to the newest members of the family as a kind of covenant—family history of the most personal sort. "You know, Bill left her, and then two months later, she lost the baby. . . ." Because the stories are told only under hushed conditions, rather than being dealt with directly, they are received almost without question, the explanation beyond faith, not to be challenged.

By exploring the themes running through your family's stories, you can isolate and celebrate what your family values—or challenge those articles of faith at the core of family stories that may be contrary to what you've learned in your own life lessons. By listening to relatives tell stories, you hear the components of your family's character—and your own.

HARVESTING THE FAMILY STORY

Reunions are great pools of stories. You dive into a sea of relatives and emerge dripping in family lore. Some reunions focus on nothing but talk and food, both flowing easily and naturally. But for many of us, the storytelling is not so effortlessly woven into the day-to-day. And when the family is scattered during a reunion, one group headed for a golf course, another drifting downstream in inner tubes, a structured venue may help get the storytelling on a roll.

Memory Night

Many reunions designate a memory night, or liars' night as some families call them, relishing the embellishments

---

DOWNSIDE OF FAMILY STORIES

Family definition stories—which convey not only what a family is like, but what it thinks it should be like—may have their downside, when they're used to ostracize or exclude those who don't measure up. What of those family members who find themselves squeezed out of the family definition—the bookish person who can't be the tough athlete, the dull-but-worthy one who can't play the cunning trickster? Must they always feel they've let themselves and their family down? For more on being outside looking in on the family tradition, see Chapter Nine, page 201.

"If my homework was done, I could sit with them and listen until ten o'clock struck.... I loved the sense of family warmth that radiated through those long kitchen nights of talk.... Usually I listened uncritically, for around that table, under the unshaded light bulb, I was receiving an education in the world and how to think about it. What I absorbed most deeply was not information but attitudes, ways of looking at the world that were to stay with me for many years."

—Russell Baker
GROWING UP

and narrative excess indulged in by the storytellers. Memory night is time, usually after dinner, when family members are invited to share a story.

If the reunion is very big, a time limit of 5 minutes may have to be set, a microphone is essential, and there should be comfortable seats for older family members. Memory night may be the best time to videotape a reunion. Those speaking are prepared to address the public. Their hair is done, their clothes are spruced up, their conversation is tailor-made for public consumption, and they're not in the middle of eating drippy coleslaw.

Question-and-Answer Night

Family members may spend a lifetime brooding about unanswered family questions. Where did Great-Uncle Martin go to college? And why did he go to college, but not his brother Jacob? Why did Grandmother Alice move to St. Louis after Grandpa died? The reunion goers should be given notice of this event ahead of time so that they can write down the questions that have been flitting in and out of their minds for years.

There may also be an in-laws' question night, when those who've married into the family train an inquiring spotlight on the family they have loved, yet never completely understood.

A master of ceremonies should lead the Q&A, introducing speakers by both first and last names. Less an emcee than a facilitator, he or she should repeat or rephrase questions, weave Oprah-like through the family with a microphone, assign questions to family members to answer, and listen with the ears of an outsider in order to ask for clarification or elaboration when speakers make references to obscure points of family history or refer to relatives by first name only.

Photos spur the telling of stories, and a slide show brings the whole group into the act, even the hyper-visual younger kids, as they laugh over Aunt Betty's bouffant hairdo and the much-prized Mediterranean-style TV and stereo console Pop brought home in 1963. For a slide show with a small group, one person should sort the slides, put them in chronological order, aim for equal

TEASING OUT THE STORY

Denver storyteller Cherie Karo Schwartz is an expert at harvesting stories from people who claim that they have no stories. She uses "story starters" to spark vivid reminiscences, and she asks prospective storytellers to think of the following:

- rooms of a house they grew up in
- family hero
- family wisecracker
- coldest or hottest time
- trick played on someone in the family
- how their family came to live in the town they grew up in
- very funny family story
- special object in the family

She then encourages storytellers to shape these memories into story form by giving them a title (even if not used, it lends focus and cohesion), setting (time and place), a great first line, a climax, and a "kicker" or great last line.

Novice storytellers also need to rehearse. Even great storytellers constantly rework and shape their material, with stories becoming richer and details more refined with each retelling.

You may want to photocopy these ideas for shaping stories and include them with registration materials so that family members will be primed for storytelling night.

---

representation of family members, and arrange for the projector and screen. For a larger group, ask each family to bring slides (set a limit: five slides per family, for instance) and to supply who-what-where-and-when exposition for each slide as it comes up.

Should kids be included at memory night? Some parents want their children to absorb the old stories, while other parents feel that being force-fed stories produces only alienation from the prospect of future reunion going. For the shaky storyteller, there's nothing so dismaying as a resistant or bored audience and lots of fidgeting.

A middle ground may be to designate a nearby room—stocked with a baby-sitter, perhaps a VCR with tapes of kids' movies, and a few toys. Young kids can be situated there from the start, while older kids can go there when they feel restless, then drift back to the main room when roars of laughter suggest that perhaps those old stories aren't so boring after all.

FAMILY FOLKWAYS

It's in the way your uncle slaps your back when he sees you and punches your brother's arm (because

A Family of Storytellers

The Crichton Clan

What: *Weekend classic*

Who: *The descendants of Scottish coal miners, William and Margaret Crichton*

Where: *Deep Creek Lake, Maryland*

Number Of Participants: *125*

Family Motto: *"Proud to be your cousin!"*

Family Traits: *Long faces, ruddy complexions, indifference to food, the gift of gab*

"Remember, you descend from dukes and earls," Andy Crichton's grandmother Margaret would tell him when he was a boy, back in the 1930s. The Crichtons haven't been dukes and earls in title since the 1600s, except in their collective memories. "Come on, Duke," Andy would say to his brother Bob. "Okay, Earl," Bob would answer. This family values telling their stories and passing their history down through each generation. Now they are gathered in Crichton Country to tell more stories—about themselves, as well as the past.

Crichton Country, that part of America where the coal veins run thickest and deepest—West Virginia, western Pennsylvania, Tennessee—was where William and Margaret Crichton settled when they emigrated from Scotland to America in the 1860s. They raised a family of coal miners, ten children in all, and went on to buy a mine, then more mines, and a trucking company.

When the American dream was achieved, the Crichton family business was dissolved, and with it much of the original family unity. Still, coal is the family's roots, and it has brought them all together again. A slab of anthracite, mounted on a wood stand, sits on the welcome desk in the reunion's hospitality suite. The banquet room is

A bagpiper and a young Crichton share a moment of ethnic pride.

full of people with longish faces, broad smiles, and thin, sandy-colored hair. They talk loudly and expressively, slap backs, and rarely kiss or hug.

Half the family is clutching Diet Cokes while the other half works on their gin and tonics.

"Did you notice how many Crichtons in the directory list themselves as volunteers in alcoholic rehab centers?" one cousin asks another between sips of cola.

"Alcoholism . . . the family disease," the second

cousin says, raising her soda. "Cheers."

Another common thread that runs through the family is a propensity for joining handbell choirs. Evidently, Crichtons love to get together and chime the hours away. "Do you think there's a relationship between the handbell choirs and giving up drinking?" the first cousin asks.

The second cousin thinks for a moment and says, "Well, I sure as hell would hate to be hungover for handbell practice Sunday morning."

"Are all these Crichtons?" 4-year-old Andrew Collier Emil asks his mother.

"They are all Crichtons," she assures him.

"Oh, cool." He pauses and asks, "What's a Crichton?"

That is the question that will be answered tonight, by sharing the family myths, stories, and legends. After dinner Jean Crichton, the reunion organizer, walks to the front of the banquet room to open the floor for the evening's storytelling. "We're here to share memories, to answer questions, to talk about what it means to be a Crichton."

Rob Crichton, of Seattle, Washington, is first to pipe up. "I heard a story from my father, that the Crichtons would act superior to the other coal miners. For example, there was one Crichton who would always take a watercress sandwich with the crusts cut off to work. The other miners would

razz him for it unmercifully."

Jack Crichton, a grandson of William and Margaret, answers, "It is true, in its way." He is a tall, robust man in plaid golf pants. He holds up his hand to quiet a roar, and says, with a gentle smile, "When I was first married, my wife, Barbara, made me watercress sandwiches one day, and one day only, because watercress was on sale that day. I took them down to work with me. But as to whether we Crichtons thought we were special—" He makes an understated yet eloquent gesture with his hand, as if to say, "Well . . . to deny it would be a lie."

"If there's one thing a

Crichtons let off steam in a conga line after an emotional Memories Night.

Crichton can't stand," says Andy Crichton, "it's snobbery and pretension. I remember when we moved 'up' in the world, in the 1940s into an exclusive neighborhood. Not long after moving in, my mother received a welcome call from the local women's club. 'Mrs. Crichton, we welcome you to the neighborhood and are happy to be able to tell you that in our town there are no Polacks, no Negroes, and no Jews,' to which my mother replied, 'Well, isn't that too goddamned bad!' and slammed down the phone.

"The picture of our devout mother using a curse word was hard to believe,

Cherishing the oldest Crichton, 91-year-old Margaret Kerr.

Mudd, who married into the family. "I'd like to know more about my father-in-law, Kyle, and the FBI."

Now, Kyle was the youngest of William and Margaret's ten children, and he came of age when the family had already attained a level of prosperity. He was sent to prep school, then on

frowns, leans across the table, and whispers loudly, "He wasn't really a Communist. More of a liberal, really. It's just that in those days a liberal seemed so much like a Communist."

But Sarah Crichton, who had written her college thesis on her grandfather's activities, shakes her head. "I'd always heard that during the McCarthy years, Kyle was called on to testify before the House Un-American Activities Committee, but the subpoena was rescinded at the last moment."

Those at the table of Kyle's descendants glance apprehensively at a nearby table, occupied by Kyle's

Half with Diet Cokes, the rest with beers, the Crichtons are masters of cocktail-hour conviviality.

but single-handedly fighting social injustice is something every Crichton feels deep in his bones. We honor 'the good fight.'"

Next to speak is Clayton

to college, while his older brothers were "down pit," working in the mines. He became a writer, a left-winger, possibly a Communist.

An older Crichton cousin

brother Harry's well-heeled descendants. Harry was a Republican businessman who may have pulled some strings to help Kyle avoid the HUAC hearings.

Rain forces the clan inside for its group portrait, shot with a wide-angle lens.

Kyle's story is an uncomfortable paradox, proving by its mixture of components that the family is not so united. There are the Republican country-club Crichtons, the Communist brother who fought the kind of private enterprise that created the privileges he enjoyed, and the older brothers who never benefited from a college education. Yet despite the mixture, there remains a mutual affection and respect.

Andy Crichton's son Kyle, named after his much-discussed grandfather, takes the stand. "We appreciate your efforts, Jean, in pulling this reunion together—even if I haven't seen architecture this brutal since the time I was in the Soviet Union. There's that same lack of—

what would you call it?"

"Grace and proportion!" someone supplies.

Sardonic, it would seem, is what the Crichtons are.

The oldest person at the reunion, a spry and quick 91-year-old, leaps to her feet when introduced. She is Margaret Kerr, the daughter of Margaret Crichton McAnulty, the oldest of William and Margaret's ten children. Their sarcasm abandoned for the moment, the Crichtons burst into resounding applause.

"I'd like to talk about my grandmother for a minute," she says. "Grandmother never kissed or hugged any of us. It would not really have occurred to her—or to us. And you never complained. In the summer, we stayed outside all day and

didn't came back in until dinnertime. But she never had a harsh word for any of us."

The room falls quiet as the family imagines how life was for Margaret Crichton, who came to America with nothing, raised a family of coal miners, made sure they stuck together, then moved everyone into a big house on the hill in Johnstown, Pennsylvania.

Cheers follow the end of Margaret Kerr's talk, and the surge of emotion is full and complex. They cheer for Margaret, for her grandmother, for the dukes and earls in the distant past, and the coal miners in the recent past. They cheer for the past already starting to slip away, but still so much a part of them.

in this family, a slap on the back equals a kiss, a punch on the arm is better than a hug). It's in the way the entire family roars and cheers when the last straggler arrives for the family portrait. It's in the way the family uses phrases—"He's talking through his hat!"—that nobody else seems to use anymore. Similar responses to life, ways of handling sentiment, means of applying pressure to others to stay in line are the family folkways that have shaped you, giving you more than just a family name in common with the cousins you've never met.

Family culture is conveyed and absorbed without thinking too much about it, atmospheric pressures as real and as invisible as the oxygen and humidity levels that surround us. And every family atmpshphere is different.

A reunion is where we can focus on what makes our family distinctive—and reinforce those qualities, if only by recognizing and appreciating them. Of course, what a family considers special or superior about itself may not strike outside observers as all that stellar—a much-vaunted family sense of humor may appear more like an everyday ability to tell and appreciate a joke. Yet a family's self-definition, however broad, still lays down what traits the family values in—and often demands from—its members.

As folklorist Amanda Dargan has pointed out, "A relative who is unlike his father's family will be explained as being more like his mother's or his grandmother's side of the family." Or the contradiction itself may be explained as a family trait.

Taking Stock: Family Questionnaire

Create your own database to find out what makes your family tick. How is your family special in its differences? Driving all reunions are the questions "Who are we?" "How did we get here?" "Where are we going?" and "When do we eat?"

To sound out what it really means to be a member of your family, a questionnaire (facing page) can be distributed with the registration form or when everyone checks in at the reunion. (All kids who can read and write should get their own questionnaires.) Completed questionnaires can be read later to the group at large. For unedited responses (the good kind), encourage anonymous entries. The family shouldn't be worried about the less-than-flattering answers that might emerge: A group meeting should always be flavored with a soupçon of self-mockery, if only to allow family members to prove to themselves and others what confident insiders they are.

Family Expressions

A family's culture lives vividly in the expressions, slang, and nicknames you see and hear among family and just about nowhere else. Ask family

Family Stock Questionnaire

One word that defines the essential quality of this family _____

Too tough? Okay, two or three words_____

One physical trait this family could do without_____

One physical trait you hope gets passed down through the generations_____

Family character flaw_____

Best family characteristic _____

You can count on a _____ to_____
          (your family name here)

What I love about this family is _____

What drives me a little/quite a bit/completely crazy (*circle one*) about this family is

_____

Family member (other than parent) who has taught me the most, and in what way

_____

All-time funniest family member_____

Expressions you hardly hear anywhere else but this family_____

_____

If there were a family sport, it would be_____

❖ ❖ ❖

If you're feeling less ambitious, scale the activity back and collect nominations for family characters. Before dinner, pass around sheets of paper and ask family members for nominations. The master of ceremonies can read the selections after dinner, category by category, and ask for anecdotes to back up the claims.

◆ most mischievous
◆ most psychic
◆ most reckless
◆ most sympathetic
◆ best hair

◆ fastest talker
◆ person you'd most likely call if it was 2:00 A.M. and you had a flat tire on a dark and lonely road
◆ any other category you can cook up

IN-LAW QUESTIONNAIRE

Just as an aerial view of your hometown can give you a different understanding of familiar landmarks, so the point of view of in-laws and significant others can help you see your family with new insight. At the very least, it's helpful to remember that in-laws, however well they fit in and are loved, are usually taking in the family with at least a bit of detachment. Let's just hope they find it all somewhat amusing. Pass around an in-law questionnaire to see what they're really thinking about this crazy bunch they married into.

What most surprised/confused/alarmed/excited me (circle as many as you like) about this family when I first married _____

Ways in which this family is most unlike my own family or any other family I know _____

Family member most like someone in my own family _____
_____

Idiosyncrasy of my spouse's that I now realize is a family trait _____

Chief way in which I am like this family _____

One thing that drives me nuts about this family (please limit it to one!)
_____

What I love most about this family is _____

members to write down expressions that capture the quintessence of family. (Place a 3-by-5-inch card at each table setting, and collect them after dinner to be read aloud.)

Reciting biblical and other proverbs is an integral component of child rearing in many families. Proverbs get internalized, become part of what you believe, help direct the way you act. What proverbs did you hear often as a child? Which stuck with you? Which never made sense to you as a child—but now do make sense? What proverb remains a baffling yet poetically wonderful phrase? Which do you repeat to your own children? Which family member was the quickest draw with a proverb? Include this information on the expressions cards as well.

FAMILY DIRECTORY

A family directory serves as a map for navigating the tricky social shoals of a family reunion and a field guide for in-laws who need help sorting out the flock of new relations. But the directory can also become a reunion's most treasured keepsake—saved, browsed through, used for reference and reinforcing family connections for years. The best-organized families often send out directories in advance of the reunion, so family members can bone up on the latest deaths and births, marriages, divorces, and family relocations. Lesser models of efficiency can distribute the directories at the reunion's start.

People who can't attend the reunion can and should be included in the directory, but respect the privacy of the alienated or estranged family member. When requesting directory information, include the option "If you do NOT want to be listed in the family directory, check here and return."

A no-frills, low-cost directory is simple to pull off. Reproduce the reunion mailing list. Use everyone's first and last name—no Mr. and Mrs. Husband's Name (otherwise known as the case of the disappearing wife)—and include all the kids' names. Create a dated cover sheet—Miller Family Directory, 1997—preferably on heavier stock. Duplicate the directory on a computer printer or photocopy it, staple, and, if possible, send it out with the other reunion materials.

A directory with more frills might be organized by family branch, with one page for each nuclear family. Collect information on birth dates,

ASSORTATIVE KINSHIP

There is, of course, the truism that as couples age together, they begin to look alike. But most anthropologists believe they always looked pretty much alike—youthful glow and flow of abundant hair just threw observers off the track, at first. Even when they believe they're "marrying out," humans tend to marry others physically and culturally like themselves. It's called assortative kinship, and it's why even nuclear families—mom, dad, kids—give the appearance that they've always been family, even though mom and dad may have met only a few years back. It's one of the reasons why a tribal feeling reigns at reunions: Strong family traits are coming to the fore, traits that are shared by in-laws and blood relations alike. They're assorted kin—they've put themselves into families where somehow they already belonged.

professions, hobbies, volunteer work, sports, and school activities through a questionnaire (see the sample form in the Appendix, page 251). Offer to collect responses through E-mail, if that's possible. Each family might also give a statement elaborating on recent accomplishments and hopes for the future. Set a space limit of 100 words to rein in the more enthusiastic family members and reduce the intimidation factor for the shy ones.

Include a family tree: Even a less-than-complete tree showing the main family branches is useful for getting a grip on where one fits in. (For more on family trees, see Chapter Five.) You might also run scanned-in or glued-on photos with the family info. (Even poor photocopies help attach names to faces.) Consider running a black-bordered list of family members who have died within the past year or so, and a list (on another page not adjacent to the death notices) of the family's newest members: spouses, babies, stepkids. To

> **"M**y father had died a year before the reunion. When I stepped into the meeting room, I nearly burst into tears. I could see my father in his cousins—the charming grin, the hooded eyes, the big hands holding a cocktail, the ruddy complexion, the back slapping. I felt such a longing to be with my father again, and then his cousin John beckoned me over and said, 'We miss your father terribly—we had such fine times together.' I almost lost it then—but it was such a relief to see those traits I'd loved in my father, and to be surrounded by people who knew and remembered him. He no longer seemed so terribly gone."
>
> —Catherine Collier
> Old Chatham, New York

bind the directory, three-hole punch the pages, fit them into a paper folder with inside pockets (for holding reunion schedules, brochures, and family trees), use tabbed dividers to separate the family branches, label the cover with printed or handprinted stick-on labels with the family name, date, and reunion logo, and run fasteners through the holes. To give the directory the feel of a real book, have it spiral-bound at a copy shop with a heavy stock cover printed with the family name and logo.

Since the directory is an important form of family adhesive, the publishing costs might be included in the reunion registration fee. If your family has been taxed to the max, ask those who'd like to receive a directory through the mail to pay for printing and mailing costs.

Family Demographics

When family information is gathered, the map of the family grows more textured, like raised maps in which the mountain ranges are clearly visible. One can see how a family tends toward certain professions and hobbies—lots of lawyers, scarcely a doctor, many home woodworkers, few soccer players.

Every family has a few statistics-minded members—the kind who can quote the footnotes of the *Consumer Reports* toaster oven survey. Organizing the statistics is a good job for them or for the computer guy (see page 31). If you've ever yearned to

"Sure, you can be assimilated, and you don't have to have ties with the culture you came from. But that puts such pressure on the nuclear family and their relatives to be everything to everybody. Caring about a family means you care about its past. The more you want to give life and your family a larger meaning, the more you appreciate and want to conjure up the past."
—Steve Zeitlin

see the family graphically summarized in a pie chart, here's your chance. Find out which careers, hobbies, and sports dominate in the family, the most common family size, the number of girl and boy children, how the family is geographically distributed, even the number of family members represented in astrological signs (the Chien family sorted its members by the Chinese zodiac).

THE IMMIGRANT SAGA

At the heart of every reunion is the desire to link with the past, to make sense of the movement of the family through time and space, and to place the family in the context of the larger American immigrant saga. How did we get here from there, so different from what we were, so far from where we were? A handful of families may have experienced envi-

able continuity over the past century, but for most families, the past hundred years have been a whirlwind of change. Between 1880 and 1925, 25 million immigrants came to America—and most of us descend directly from at least one set of great-grandparents who were part of this extraordinary wave, the largest migration ever known.

There were good reasons why our immigrant forebears wanted to break from the past, why they rushed to America and, with mixed feelings, watched their children assimilate as quickly as they could. For the first generation, the past was pain: deprivation, persecution, the unyielding simple fact of hunger. There was pain, too, in having to leave it all behind, in losing one's whole known world. For the second generation, the past meant funny accents, old-fashioned superstitions, and Old Country clothes, embarrassing to children who wanted nothing more and nothing less than to fit in. To the third generation, the past is no longer so painful or so embarrassing. "I see my great-grandparents and grandparents as heroes, really," says Shira Rosan, "as giants."

As journalist Ted Solataroff puts it so memorably, "The first generation tries to preserve. The second generation tries to forget. The third generation tries to remember." Since many of us are third-generation descendants, at least metaphorically, we feel a need to remember, to fit our family into the larger American

100 YEARS OF FREEDOM

THE FABER FAMILY

What: Weekend classic

Who: Descendants of Ephraim Jacob Faber, who left Russia for America in 1896. They traveled from England, Germany, California, Illinois, Colorado, and many other states

Where: New York City

Number of Participants: 125

Family Motto: "100 years of freedom"

The banquet room in the hotel in downtown Manhattan is swelling with Fabers. Eighty registered to come, but only half an hour into the welcoming cocktail party, the room is filled with at least 100 people.

"Why didn't you think I would come?" cousins ask Lewis Faber, who organized the event. "Family members think you don't have to RSVP like other people," Lewis explains later.

Lewis's wife, Helen Rubinstein, who is experienced in corporate training, says, "It's always preferable to have a room appropriate to the size of the crowd, or a little small, to create a sense of excitement." This room buzzes with human energy as people hover over copies of the family album Lewis has

Mingling over the family book.

prepared. "The album is the best icebreaker," Helen says.

Lewis Faber is deeply pleased. To the gathered Fabers he explains what this event is about. "One hundred years ago, our great-grandparents took the leap and came over to America from Russia. With noble intentions, with selfish intentions, who can say? But what might have happened to us if they'd stayed? Conscription in the czar's army for decades, pogroms, World War I, Stalin, the Holocaust. As a family, we now enjoy a kind of affluence and freedom our great-grandparents could not have

Lewis Faber conducts a short history lesson on opening night.

imagined. I wanted to pay homage to the risk our great-grandparents took that changed the lives of their descendants for the better. A leap into the unknown that made it possible for us even to exist."

Now Lewis works the room. "He's the soul of the reunion," his wife explains. Lewis is the big-picture guy; Helen makes it all happen. Lewis envisions his cousins schmoozing all weekend long; Helen realizes that to do so, they'll need a hospitality suite with snacks and sodas. Lewis envisions the family delving into its ethnic history; Helen hires a school bus to transport frailer family members on the excursions they've planned.

The next morning, the family heads out on the bus to the Ellis Island ferry. Lewis and Helen have found a tour guide to walk them through Ellis Island and relate the typical experience of an eastern European Jew-

Lewis and Helen and the ubiquitous family bus.

ish immigrant. Many have toured Ellis Island before, but they've never experienced it so personally.

The kids listen intently as

the guide describes how Ellis Island officials would boom out, "Are there any Hebrews here?" The Jewish immigrants, who had left Europe to avoid persecution, would shake with fear, thinking they were again being singled out for persecution. The guide explains that the well-meaning but thoughtless immigration officials were only trying to lead the immigrants to kosher meals.

After lunch, the family visits the Tenement Museum on Manhattan's Lower East Side for a glimpse of the living conditions probably experienced by their Faber forebears. The narrow stairwells and cramped apartments of the museum mean that the family visits in

The Fabers pay homage to their forebears on Ellis Island.

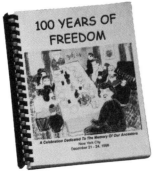

The Faber Family Book, with cover by Helen Rubinstein.

shifts, but the logistical snags are worth it. "We don't know many facts about our great-grandparents. Nobody stopped to take notes in those days. This way, we have a good idea of what life must have been for them," Lewis explains. The older members, who couldn't manage the Tenement Museum's stairs, were taken by bus to the Jewish Museum on upper Fifth Avenue.

That evening, family members head out to a nightclub in the thriving Russian neighborhood of Brighton Beach. The bus has become a bonding experience in its own right, and there's singing and talking all the way out to this oceanside enclave.

At the nightclub, long tables are already prepared with smoked fish appetizers and bottles of vodka. "I'd like to make a toast," says a Faber cousin from England. "To our ancestors . . . if they hadn't left Russia, we couldn't be here, in 'Russia!'" The family cheers.

The next day the Fabers prepare for a more formal celebration of their roots. The hotel's banquet room is decorated with easel-mounted posters of Faber relations and archival photos from the period when the great-grandparents lived. They are all captioned "100 Years of Freedom." A young Faber cousin, who is a lawyer by day and a budding stand-up comedian by night, acts as the emcee for a program of impromptu stories and memories.

Lewis Faber (left) receives a plaque from his cousins.

Lewis's cousins give him a plaque, commending him for the "mitzvah" of bringing together the descendants of Ephraim Jacob Faber.

"There's a Hebrew term, *gesher*, meaning a bridge, but more than a bridge," says Lewis. "It's a metaphor for what connects generation to generation. This is one of the best things I did in my entire life, bringing this family together. This *gesher* is something alive, this family is alive. All I ask is that everyone keeps connecting!"

Dancing at the Saturday night banquet in "Little Russia."

saga. How does our family's personal experience relate to that of the larger ethnic group and how does our family's genesis story fit into the framework of a historical movement?

Connecting to Ethnic Roots

It's hard to separate the characteristics that are true only of your family and those that can be credited to an ethnic culture—our ways of talking, of telling stories, the kind of jokes we find funny, the sort of food we eat, our predilection for plain geometric designs or swirling patterns. Still, it's fascinating to discover and celebrate in your family culture elements you have in common with your ethnic group. The vision of the melting pot has been supplanted by a view of the marvelous mosaic—nothing "melts" away; everything instead contributes to the rich complexity of American life. And since much of the impulse to hold a reunion is to honor those who have made your life possible, it's a good time to reflect on how those ancestors still affect our lives.

A big question, though, may be "Which culture to celebrate?" Few families are entirely Irish or Italian or Norwegian, as they may have been even 50 years ago. But even when ethnic components don't apply to the entire group, they remain an important way to link with your forebears and what touched them. Here are some ways to celebrate a family's ethnic heritage at a family reunion.

Celebrate your family's 100th anniversary in America. Hold the reunion in the town or city where your ancestors first put down roots.

Set up a display table commemorating the family's immigrant saga. Display copies of naturalization papers, passports, clothes from the time, family ledgers, diaries, and letters from the Old Country. If your family does not have a well-documented past, photocopy written descriptions of immigrant conditions that would have applied to your family. Display books of ethnic history as well—a librarian can help you find suitable ones.

Create an ethnic heritage trail. Visiting places with strong meaning for your ancestors can be a moving experience, placing your ancestors' lives in context. Get help from the family historian, a historical society, or a tour guide. Use car caravans or a chartered bus to visit ethnic neighborhoods and the industries your ancestors worked in—steel and textile mills, coal mines, working farms, breweries. Visit the neighborhoods your family's ethnic group aspired to move to. Or tour historical museums and sites with relevance for your family—for example, the Chinese Culture Center in San Francisco, California; the Czech Village, Museum and Immigrant Home in Cedar Rapids, Iowa; the Museum of African American History in Detroit, Michigan, to name a few. (For a list of ethnic guidebooks, see Appendix, pages 249–250.)

ELLIS ISLAND

Ellis Island has become *the* monument to the American immigration experience. After all, more than 100 million of all living Americans descend directly from at least one of the 12 million immigrants who passed through Ellis Island between 1892 and 1954.

The American Immigrant Wall of Honor has become the favorite focus of many New York and New Jersey reunions, as families contribute money to have their first immigrant ancestors' names inscribed on the wall and then gather there to pay homage to the forebears and explore the Immigration Museum. For more information on how to include your family name on the Wall of Honor, contact:

The American Immigrant Wall of Honor
The Statue of Liberty–Ellis Island Foundation, Inc.
52 Vanderbilt Avenue
New York, NY 10017-3898

Celebrate with ethnic food. Food is still the touchstone of ethnic identity. Hold a reunion lunch at an ethnic restaurant. Go to the old neighborhood (if it still survives) and bring back foods unique to your ethnic group. Give caterers an old family recipe to adapt for an evening meal. Or create an entire meal composed of ethnic favorites.

Establish a ritual of remembrance. The Raspberry family reports to the long-deceased family matriarch, bringing her up to date on what all her descendants have done since the previous reunion. What important, meaningful things would you want to report to your first forebears in this country?

Write and perform a skit illustrating the family's saga. When young people act out a skit of a historical incident unique to their family, which also happens to speak to a larger truth, the story becomes personal and internalized—it becomes *their* story.

Bring the Old Country home with music. Ethnic musicians are often gifted amateurs who charge less than professional rates. To find them, call ethnic restaurants and bars and speak with the manager. Tapes of ethnic music capture the mood, too; the large music chains boast huge world music sections. As for folk dancing, don't be so idealistic as to expect the male relatives to jump up and join the circle—unless, of course, they're Greek.

Reproduce photos of great-grandparents in poster-size prints. Or post a map of the world, tracing where the ancestors came from, marking their route to their first home in the United States, giving a graphic view of the family's movement through time and place.

Don't overdo the ethnic history. You don't want to neglect the present in quest of the past.

Ethnic Questionniare

Tracking the family's ethnic identity as it assimilates or as it maintains its ethnic character through the years can be an elusive challenge. And now that so many ethnic neighborhoods have dissolved, being with family may be the one time we can share a sense of ethnic identity. Set aside a time at the reunion to share stories about what it means not only to be a member of the family but to be a member of the larger ethnic group. Some questions that may be raised:

Does anyone in the family still remember the first ancestors to come to America?
_____

What Old Country habits did they continue? How did they dress?
_____

What sayings did they bring with them from the Old Country? What superstitions or beliefs? _____

What qualities were most highly valued in people?_____
_____

What were the hierarchies in the neighborhood—who were the powerful people, who were the most admired people? _____

How were the older people treated? _____

What was your ancestors' "comfort food"? What foods that come from that heritage do you all still enjoy? _____

Which features of American culture did your forebears immediately embrace? Which did they resolutely refuse to accept? _____

How did they deal with language barriers? Religious customs? The loss of those left behind? _____

What happened to family members who stayed in the Old Country?
_____

What prejudices did the family elders confront? What prejudices do members of the ethnic group still confront? _____

What was the stereotype of your ethnic group? In what ways did the stereotype ring true and in what ways did it seem ignorant and inaccurate?
_____

What ethnic characteristics do you and the family as a whole still possess? (If you do not, can you think of reasons why you don't?)_____

Which ethnic characteristics, rituals, sayings are you passing on to your own children?
_____

What ethnic jokes can you tell on yourselves that only the ethnic group itself is permitted to tell? _____

THE STORIES WE TELL OURSELVES

The immigrant drama is the tension between the impulse to assimilate and the American tendency to draw ethnic distinctions. Between a family's sense of itself as unique and its deep connection to a wider, older tradition than itself. We are all wrestling to discover at what point we are no longer hyphenated Americans—not Croatian-American or Italian-American but simply, complicatedly American—in our own eyes and the eyes of others.

How our families as wholes feel toward our ethnic origins often mirrors how individual members feel about their family. Like adolescents seeking individuation, many immigrant families turned uneasily away from their ethnic backgrounds, unwilling to let tradition dictate identity and sense of possibility. But now families can turn back again, the threat lessened, acknowledging that if we don't see ourselves through the prism of our ethnicity—at least part of the time—we are missing much of the story of ourselves.

The search for identity is the American story, and the questions and quests of identity for individuals, families, and ethnic groups continue to unfold. It's at a reunion that we can gather our stories, shape our identity, and collect a head of steam to make the big push out into the world again, a little bit more sure of our footing in the nation.

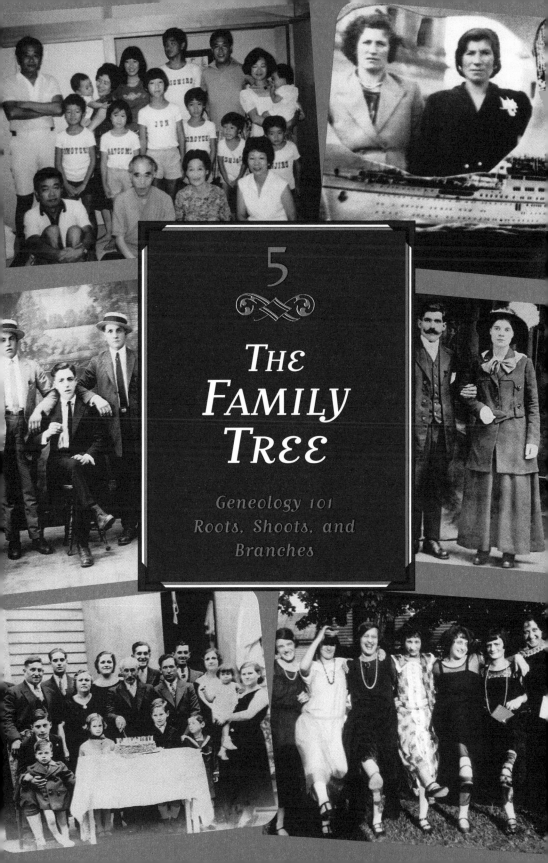

5

THE FAMILY TREE

Geneology 101
Roots, Shoots, and
Branches

Genealogy is tricky. First, you connect names to your name. Then you connect those names to the people who came before them. Then—well, that's when it gets *really* tricky. How many of our ancestors left home back East, down South, or in the Old Country to escape bad debts, family feuds, or love affairs gone wrong? We remember the laudable relations, the ones who came to pursue democratic ideals or religious freedom. But in genealogy, *all* the names emerge to be recalled. The more illustrious family members may be better documented—they've left a paper trail of deeds, newspaper clippings, and respectful obituaries. But in the end it's the darker characters' stories that usually receive most of the attention.

Every extended family holds within it the full scope of human experience, and genealogy can give us the whole picture, the picturesque, prodigal, or prosaic lives of our ancestors, captured through the schematics of genealogical charts.

Genealogy was once the exclusive province of those of the upper classes in search of proof (or something that looked like proof) to fortify their claims of rank, property, or status. In fact, one of the early English definitions of nobleman was "he knows his pedigree."

Keeping track of one's ancestors began as far back as 1,000 B.C. in China, where entire halls were designated to house family trees. Much later, Hindu royalty of the 16th century kept a *bhat* on hand to chant the ruler's pedigree, which always managed to move back in time to find its source in the sun, the moon, or a god. *Griots* of western Africa were—and in some places still are—similar sources of pedigree information, as well as being counselors and storytellers. In Iceland, the sagas and *eddas* of families going back more than a 1,000 years are still kept on file in national archives, much as oral histories are now preserved here: Family history equals the history of nations. In Christian tradition, the Gospel of Matthew links Jesus back to King David. The Bible itself contains some of the most genealogically complex tables ever written.

Where genealogy took note of the common folk, it was not to stake a claim but to serve the practical purpose of making clear who was or was not too closely linked to be marriageable. It wasn't until Alex Haley's *Roots* was published in 1977 that America's interest in genealogy went beyond that of bluebloods hoping to document their upper-crust lineage.

All genealogical associations will agree that *Roots* changed everything. For the first time it occurred to the "common folk," Black and white, that their past really mattered; that their families' lives were part of history. When our forebears moved, history moved with them.

The genealogical search is a labor of love; for the amateur genealogist, learning the name and hometown of a great-uncle may constitute the challenge of a lifetime. The activity of genealogy involves the sometimes tedious work of plowing through reams of paperwork, conducting long, often fruitless phone conversations—and the exhilaration of discovery, even if (or especially because) that discovery will have meaning only to a precious few.

"I undertook to reconstruct the history of my family, and I found a certain satisfaction in the genealogical research the project involved, in resuscitating and making posthumous contact with forgotten forebears. Some of their names sounded beautiful to me... Their names resonated in the depths of my being because they were prenatal fragments of myself, my people. Tracing one's ancestors may heighten one's own awareness of kinship, but it is ultimately a private matter, a communing with personal spirits."
—Alex Shoumatoff
The Mountain of Names

"Genealogy is an enormous jigsaw puzzle, and you're not sure all the pieces even exist," says family genealogist Margot Feiner Conte. "Assembling it goes piece by piece, and sometimes when you're on a roll, a whole clump of pieces. But if you have to force a piece to make it fit, it probably doesn't belong. Best of all is that 'bingo!' moment all genealogists eventually have, when the hours of poring over microfilm records pay off."

And then came the Internet, which changed everything. The Internet collapses distance and time: As genealogists link databases, seek out and find individuals in the vastness of cyberspace, the New World and the Old World shake hands and fuse. America Online's Genealogy forum is one of the most frequently visited sites on line. It offers help and "chats" on every conceivable area of genealogy, including family reunions, and is well set up for the novice, anticipating the most basic questions and inviting you to pose your own. If you want to start on the World Wide Web directly, head for the World Wide Genealogy Resource home page, www.genhomepage.com/world.html. From there you can link up to a wide array of ethnic and national genealogical Web sites and bulletin boards, from Slovenia to Jamaica to Norway.

A new wave of reunions has resulted from the desire to see in the flesh the names clustered on a computer-generated family tree. Genealogical reunions are adult-oriented events held at hotels, with the focus on gathering and sharing genealogical and historical information.

Because genealogy brings together people who have never met, such gatherings aren't considered "reunions." "We've never united before, so we can't really say we're holding a reunion," says Georgia Baldwin, who helped organize the first Baldwin Union in Connecticut. "When we hold our second one, then it'll be a reunion."

In the genealogical quest, personal issues often merge with those of the larger ethnic group: For many African American families genealogy makes whole—if only on paper—families ripped apart by slavery. There's something consoling in nam-

ing and remembering those who, having had no choice in their destinies, would otherwise have been forgotten long ago. Genealogy documents, and so celebrates, the triumph of longstanding family stability.

For Jewish families, genealogy often ties together cousins scattered across the world not only by the Holocaust but by anti-Semitic pogroms in Europe long before World War II. Completed family trees record and honor those who perished while pulling together those who made it through. And while the numbers of Holocaust victims are so overwhelming as to be impossible to absorb, those numbers come into heartbreakingly human scale on a family tree with name after name on branch after branch recorded with the words "Died 1943," "Died 1944," "Died 1945," surrounded by black borders, and with a complete absence of descendants.

One-World Genealogy

If one group keeps the most detailed genealogical records in America, it would have to be the Church of Jesus Christ of Latter-Day Saints, headquartered in Salt Lake City, Utah. The Church of Latter-Day Saints, otherwise known as the Mormons, emphasizes the fact that in the end we're all related, often much more closely than we know. For Mormons, genealogy has the moral imperative of a spiritual quest. In their belief, those alive today may choose to make covenants—special promises—with ancestors who have gone ahead to the spirit world, covenants that may one day unite the entire extended family.

But those ancestors must be accurately identified first, which is why the Church of Latter-Day Saints has taken on the mammoth task of collecting genealogical information about families all over the world. This tremendous resource for all genealogists amounts to more than 1 1/2 billion names—perhaps your name, my name, the names of our grandparents, and those of great-great-uncles we never knew existed—all stashed away in the Saints' "mountain of names." Branch offices, the LDS Family History Centers, can be found across the country and are open to all genealogists, amateur as well as experienced. (See Appendix, page 252, for more on the LDS Family History Centers.)

Although genealogy is a highly complex field, there are many resources available for the budding genealogist. A beginner's project aimed at bringing your family's lineage into focus may be easier than you think. Following are some tips that will get even the rankest beginner going.

FAMILY TREE 101

The project is to construct a family tree that explores one side of your family (presumably the one gathering for your reunion). It involves setting up a descendancy chart that works its way from your great-grandparents on one side and includes all their descendants and spouses down to the present generation. You might start—or even finish—with a nutshell family history (see Appendix, page 253).

The assumption of this project is that you're not using genealogy software (although software programs can be found in the sidebar, below.)

GENEALOGY SOFTWARE

The genealogy software most highly regarded by amateur and professional genealogists is Reunion 5 (Leister Productions) —although it is for Macintosh only. Genealogists cite its ease of use: You enter the data for each individual on a "card"; the program makes the connections for you and tells you how everyone is related, and even assembles family sheets. The database of names and addresses can also be used as a mailing list, and you can create stellar family trees with it as well.

Family Tree Maker II (Broderbund) has many similar features and is both Windows- and Macintosh-compatible. It also comes with CDs full of archival materials drawn from census and marriage records.

A SEARCH FOR FAMILY

THE KING FAMILY

What: *Homecoming*

Who: *A northern branch of a family meets for the first time its southern cousins*

Where: *Ancestral hometown of Columbia, Tennessee*

Number of Participants: *36*

G rowing up in Farmington, Connecticut, Katharine King had never known her father's family. She had only a vague, uncertain sense that family and cousins were out there, somewhere, but Katharine's father, John King, had died when she was 7—and her parents were divorced sometime before then.

John King had been an only child, whose father had also died at a young age, and so John, who had moved North from Tennessee, had very little contact with the paternal side of his family. Katharine had had none at all. And since the King family

was predominantly female, most of the surviving members of his family had different surnames, changed when the women had married.

All these factors conspired to sweep clean the trail that led to Tennessee. Katharine had no idea of how to begin to find her family. Now living in Los Angeles, Katharine was pur-

The nuclear King family.

John King, Katharine's only connection to southern roots.

suing a career as a concert producer. Despite a full and successful life, she felt an underlying sense that something was missing, something left unsettled and lost. Most of her friends viewed family

as powerful and unshakable, but Katharine was keenly aware of "how easily families could lose each other."

It was by accident that Katharine discovered her first clue, putting form and face on the lost branch of her family. While visiting her mother one holiday, Katharine found herself poking through the attic—and came upon a letter from a great-aunt to her father, mentioning the married names of cousins and where they had gone to live.

But what does one do with names and places? Do you call up strangers out of the blue and ask if they're related to you? That's exactly what Katharine did. The letter had mentioned that one branch of the family had moved to Louisville, and Katharine called directory assistance for a list of numbers belonging to that surname. She started calling.

"This is Katharine King. I'm the granddaughter of James Joseph King…" There were flat hang-ups. There was, "Gee, I wish I could be of help, but…" After eight or nine calls, finally one—like a key turning in a lock and the door opening: "Why, you must be Jimmy Joe's granddaughter!" cried her second cousin Maynard Howell.

While Katharine had always felt a longing for connection, she never imagined that her cousins in Tennessee might feel the same way. But the next remark from her newly dis-covered cousin confirmed it: "The question of what had happened to Jimmy Joe's line has been burning a hole in our hearts."

Katharine and Maynard planned a reunion to bring the branches of the family together again. Another second cousin, Marilyn Howell Holcomb, asked everyone to write an auto-biography, which she then photocopied for family dis-tribution. For Katharine,

this was "an invaluable head start on who all these people, my family, were."

Katharine had always known that her father's family came from the South, but the abstract knowledge was nothing like the force of true expe-rience. "It was a shock to my identity to realize I had this Southern her-itage," she recalls. "I had to rethink so much of his-tory. Now the Rebels in the Civil War, whom I'd always seen as the villains, were my great-great-grand-parents."

The reunion was held in the community room of the historic Zion Presbyter-

Katharine embraced by her newfound cousins at a family farm in Tennessee.

The ancestral home of Jimmy Joe King.

At the reunion lunch, Katharine paused to compare this reunion—down-home-style, home-cooked food, paper tablecloths, casual clothes—with her mother's family's catered evening affairs in Connecticut. Those parties had been more social events, with a kind of formality that was *part* of her heritage, but not *all* of it.

"The Tennessee reunion was about healing, about closing up the wounds," Katharine remembers, "for me as well as for the whole King family. I hadn't really realized it, but the question of Jimmy Joe's line had been burning a hole in my heart, too. I just hadn't known, until the hole was finally filled."

ian Church in Columbia, where Katharine's grandfather and cousins were buried. "There I was, surrounded by all these cousins I just called 'aunt' because they had been like sisters to my father, and before the reunion I hadn't dared hope that I'd feel this immediate sense of kinship. But I did. And somehow I felt connected to my father in a way I hadn't since he was alive. Especially when the 'aunts' told stories about my father and saw physical resemblances to my father and to themselves in me."

On Sunday the family attended church together. "Even those who aren't very religious in my family were moved by it, there was this heightened sense of something spiritual…

hard to explain," Katharine says. "And after the service, we walked through the cemetery where the King family is buried, and it was stirring to be among the visible markers of those people's lives. I was encouraged to learn that there were cases of longevity in the King family, when I thought there were none."

Katharine sees her southern roots in a new light.

In this project, the software is paper and the hardware is a looseleaf binder, an extremely efficient data-processing and recording system with a universal interface (as long as your handwriting is legible).

You'll need:

- Three-ring binder
- Dividers with pockets
- Hole-punch
- Plastic sleeves for protecting documents
- Family group sheets

You'll be working from family group sheets, which are used to record when and where each person was born, married, and died. You can buy these in bulk from the National Genealogical Society (see Appendix, page 252 and 254) and distribute them at the reunion as a way of conducting a massive genealogical sweep. The format can be photocopied or input into your computer.

When recording the vital statistics of each family member who falls within the catchment of this project, be sure to include the following auxiliary information:

- Town, county, and state or country of birth
- Full names of both participants in a marriage, including the maiden name of the bride
- Place of burial of each member

To organize your binder, place a blank family tree on the first page. You'll probably go through several drafts so don't be afraid to cross things out or mark up this first "sloppy copy."

> **"When** I look down at this family tree, I see the whole scope of human nature in this one family. We have divorced people, gay people, victims of murder, financially successful and less successful people. The whole of human experience is on view in this one family. That's thrilling."
>
> —Joan Rumely Sparrow
> Lake Forest, Illinois

Using tabbed dividers, create a section in the binder for each branch—a branch being composed of one of the great-grandparents' children and all their offspring. Proceed chronologically, with the oldest family members down to the youngest. For each branch section, include:

- Family group sheet for each nuclear family
- Blank sheet for each direct ancestor in the family, on which to note occupation, educational history, medical history, religious affiliations, and other information that might prove useful someday. (Collect as much information as you can the first time around and sort through it later.)
- Research page for citing sources

How to harvest this information?

- Fill in the family group sheets as best you can. Don't sweat the minor points—like the parents' names of unrelated spouses—at this time. The object of this project is to get the names of and basic facts about only the *direct* descendants of your great-grandparents. Any other information can be pursued later, if it is not reaped as an unexpected bonus when you're doing research on direct descendants.

• Identify any major gaps that need to be filled. Draw up a list of questions and place it at the front of each branch section, crossing out each query as you discover the answer. Ask for help from relatives by sending a gracious letter, along with a brief questionnaire regarding the sought-for information and a self-addressed stamped envelope. The burden rests with you to make the process as easy and painless as possible for your informants. Always make copies of the letters you send, and keep a log of correspondence.

If you know your ancestors' religion, you may be able to find their church or synagogue as well, and with that a mother lode of documents: baptismal certificates, wedding certificates, and funeral records.

• When you chat with family members, ask them if they recall any relative having done genealogical research on the family—a family genealogist may very well have trod much of this ground before.

• Is there a family source—a Bible or other family history compendium? A shoe box? Documents to look for include:

Birth certificates
Armed forces records
School transcripts and diplomas
Insurance papers
Marriage licenses
Passports
School yearbooks
Wills

Death certificates, while good sources for medical histories, are not reliable for other vital statistics, such as place of birth or names of parents. That information may have been given to the doctor filing the certificate by a person who had little accurate knowledge.

GENEALOGICAL ABBREVIATIONS

Here are the standard genealogical abbreviations, but you can make up your own abbreviations so long as you note the full meaning elsewhere on the page, i.e., Breaux Bridge, Louisiana = B.B., LA:

b.	=	born	bap.	=	baptized
m.	=	married	c.	=	circa
d.	=	died	NMI	=	no middle initial
bd.	=	buried	nd	=	no date given

Never use numbers to indicate months—otherwise readers may be confused between the day and the month. Genealogists write out the month

• Obviously, the planning stage of the reunion offers a great chance to collect information. Mention in one of the reunion letters what genealogical data you're looking for, and people may volunteer it.

• At the reunion itself, distribute family group sheets to be filled out by each family. Encourage the Boy Scouts in the family to join you—Boy Scouting offers a genealogy merit badge, and many of its requirements can be met at a reunion.

When recording genealogical data:

• Record names with the last names first, then first names, then middle names and nicknames in parentheses—nicknames are essential, since some people are known only by their nicknames.

• Note, in parentheses next to the name, whether a particular child is from a second marriage.

Experienced genealogists are as scrupulous as historians in citing their sources, preferring primary sources (documents created at the time of an event, such as a marriage certificate) to secondary ones (a wedding date recorded years later by the bride's cousin). Citing and sourcing may be a pain in the neck, but the point of proceeding this way is to create usable historical material. If your information is well sourced, the genealogists and family historians who follow won't have to duplicate your efforts.

Create a research page for each family group sheet. On your research pages:

GENEALOGY WORKSHOP

Schedule a workshop during the reunion itself, inviting all the family members who've been working on genealogy. Ask them to bring copies of their work for you to collate and add to. You'll need to know how many copies of your own research to make, so request preregistration, but make a few extra copies for last-minute drop-ins.

• Cite a source for each fact, whether it's an aunt in a phone conversation (give the date), a birth certificate found in a county courthouse, or your grandfather's old passport.

• Add photocopies of primary documents and note where the originals can be found.

What to do with secondary source material? On each of the pages you've set up for researching a direct ancestor, include hearsay information, but note that the information is unsourced by following it with a question mark and the name of the informant: "Gigi Martin's maiden name was Hamburg (?), according to Martha Strauss (aunt)."

Hit a wall in your research? Now we really begin: into the spiral of genealogical research, like Alice down the rabbit hole, where time gets twisted, strange characters are met, and you are much changed by journey's end. You'll need to go to county courthouses, learn your way

THE CRICHTON FAMILY TREE

Nancy

William IV

Edward

William Crichton III

Helen (Crichton) Summers

| WILLIAM CRICHTON 1884–1946 |

Valery

Judy

Willis

Philip

Andrew B. Crichton Jr.

Harlan

Richard

John

Robert Jr.

Clarendon "Shorty" Crichton

Alan Crichton

Andrew "Don"

Robert Crichton

Jean Crichton

| ANDREW B. CRICHTON 1882–1952 |

Ann

Sandra

William Jr.

Mary

Mary Edith (Crichton) Mardis

Sally

Charles

Margie Lou

Sue

Joe Jr.

Nicholas

Nancy

Jim Jr.

Fain

Tony

James Miller

William Miller

J. Howard "Bud" Miller

Todd

Joseph Miller

Harry Miller

Sarah

Margaret (Miller) Burchard

Peter

| SARAH (CRICHTON) MILLER 1879–1938 |

Bruce

Hal

Sarah

Jane

Elizabeth (McAnulty) Zook

Margaret

Martha (McAnulty) Zook

| MARGARET (CRICHTON) McANULTY 1877–1976 |

Emily

Margaret (McAnulty) Kerr

| ROBERT CRICHTON 1875–1917 |

This artistic family tree shows four generations. The founding parents are at the base, and each of their offspring is on a major branch, with the name boxed. The first-born Crichton is at the left of the base of the tree, and the names move clockwise around the tree according to birth order. The names of the founding parents' grandchildren are underlined, and the names of their great-grandkids, at the ends of the branches, are not.

| William Crichton 1850–1927 |

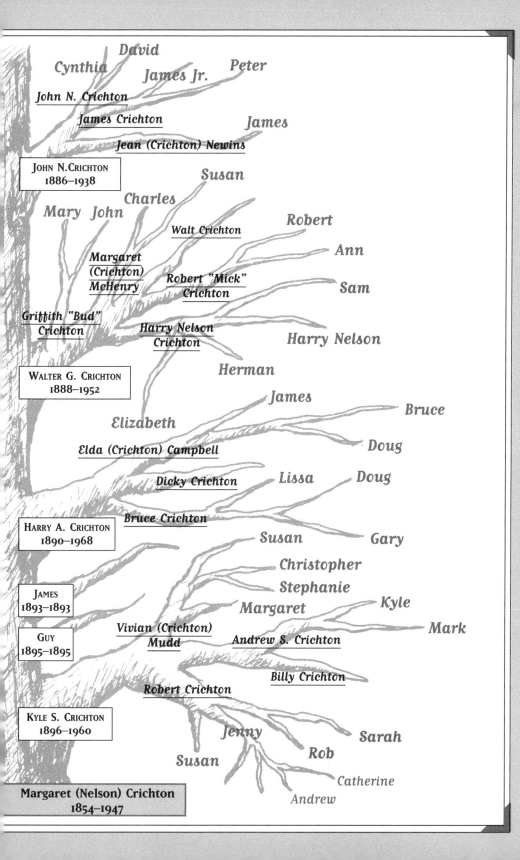

David
Cynthia
James Jr.
Peter
John N. Crichton
James Crichton
James
Jean (Crichton) Newins

JOHN N. CRICHTON
1886–1938

Susan
Charles
Mary   John
Robert
Walt Crichton
Ann
Margaret
(Crichton)
McHenry
Robert "Mick"
Crichton
Sam
Griffith "Bud"
Crichton
Harry Nelson
Crichton
Harry Nelson

WALTER G. CRICHTON
1888–1952

Herman
James
Bruce
Elizabeth
Elda (Crichton) Campbell
Doug
Dicky Crichton
Lissa
Doug
Bruce Crichton

HARRY A. CRICHTON
1890–1968

Susan
Gary
Christopher
Stephanie

JAMES
1893–1893

Margaret
Kyle
Mark

GUY
1895–1895

Vivian (Crichton)
Mudd
Andrew S. Crichton
Billy Crichton
Robert Crichton

KYLE S. CRICHTON
1896–1960

Jenny
Sarah
Rob
Susan
Catherine
Andrew

Margaret (Nelson) Crichton
1854–1947

around the National Archives in Washington, D.C. (which contains census records and immigrant ship passenger lists, among a zillion other things), and master the use of microfilm at the Family History Centers run by the Mormons. (See Appendix, pages 252 and 254, for starting points.)

Model Family Trees

An *artistic* family tree, like the one on pages 106–107, may not be genealogically perfect—genealogists prefer only the direct descendants to be listed—but it gives a good sense of who the family players are and where you and your immediate family fit in. And that's really the point of the excercise.

If you've finished the family tree before the reunion, send it out with the other reunion materials. It will excite family members; help orient them in the context of the family, making them realize how many relatively close cousins they have; locate the family in history; give your project the weight and gravitas of a substantial enterprise; and, most important, provide the answer to the question that always emerges at reunions: "Exactly how is it that we're related again?" And in case you're wondering how you get to be a first cousin once removed, or if you can legally do more than just flirt with that cute cousin, consult the Cousins Chart in the Appendix, pages 257–258.

AMONG THE ANCESTORS

For many families, a reunion isn't complete without paying a visit to those who've gone ahead—to that place which in the old days was rightly called the boneyard. When Joan Sparrow conducted her family

MEDICAL FAMILY TREE

Our ancestors live within us, often through their secret influence in forming our medical legacy: our genetic propensity to various forms of heart disease, diabetes, and cancer. Why know any of this gloomy stuff? Not only can we adjust our lifestyle habits to improve our odds, we can monitor our health more vigilantly by knowing which warning signs to look for, which diagnostic tests to have performed earlier or more often than other people, and whether we should see a specialist in the diseases for which we are genetically at risk.

While family reunions may not be the place and time to investigate the family's medical history, you may be able to put the newly restored family links to work creating a medical family tree after the fact. (For how to construct a medical family tree, see the Appendix, pages 255–256.)

Kids' Family Tree

❖❖❖

Kids ought to have their own family tree, one that puts them at the center of the family universe and includes *both* parents and their families: To kids, it's counterintuitive to focus on only one side of their pedigree to the exclusion of a mother or father. Photocopy this tree so that your family's kids can use it at the reunion, filling in the boxes with the pictures or names of their relatives, or an imaginative combination of both.

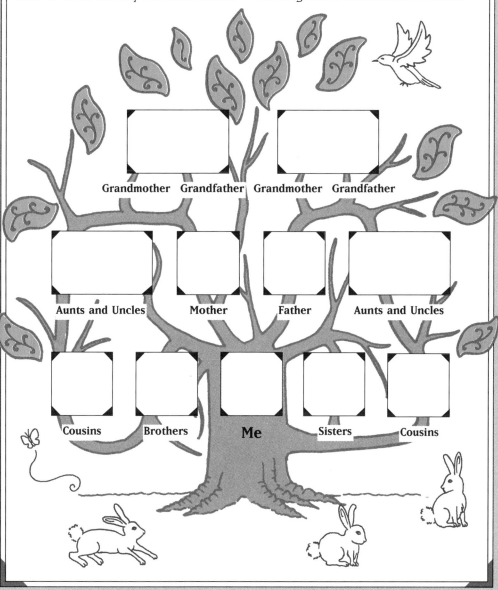

Grandmother   Grandfather   Grandmother   Grandfather

Aunts and Uncles   Mother   Father   Aunts and Uncles

Cousins   Brothers   Me   Sisters   Cousins

tour of "Rumely Abodes: Past, Present and Forever," the "forever" abodes weren't located in downtown La Porte, Indiana. They were the grassy family plots where all those Rumelys lay underfoot.

"It's a strange, powerful feeling to be among all those Rumelys," says Joan Sparrow. "It was one of the reunion's high points, at a reunion with a lot of high points. There's nothing like a trip to the cemetery to put things in perspective."

Winifred Coleman, of the Raspberry family, concurs. "There are very few original names in our family, and most of us, if not all, are named for one of the ancestors," she says. "We always visit the cemetery where the ancestors are buried, and find the people we were named for. We have a special, private, quiet time with them." The kids always make gravestone rubbings.

Unless the cemetery is extremely well maintained, wear long pants and shoes and socks to guard against poison ivy, which thrives at cemeteries. Doing grave rubbings? Wear long sleeves. Clearing the graves? Add work gloves. And don't forget your hat. It will keep the spirits from entering your head—or so they say.

Graves as Primary Documents

Where are those forebears buried? Family Bibles and church records will often tell you. Death certificates don't usually mention burial sites,

> "**My** family tree does not branch. It never has. As with many Black families in the rural South, the distinction between nuclear and extended faded long ago. Today, as it has been for centuries, cousins are siblings, aunts are mothers, uncles are fathers.... What sustained us was a reliance upon each other."
> —John Simpkins
> **The New Republic**

but New Englanders of the 19th century were often buried in church cemeteries; Southerners were typically buried in family graveyards, many overgrown and lost now. County courthouses often have county maps from the year your ancestor died, which may show cemeteries (although not private plots). Know the exact address of your ancestor? Usually folks were buried no more than 5 miles from home. Your ancestor's address may be found on records from probate court, deeds, or a grantee index, where purchasers and sellers of land were listed—which can be found at the county courthouse. Know that your ancestor was buried at a large, "active" cemetery? The cemetery office should have a "plat" showing precisely where.

Visiting graves can provide the missing pieces of genealogical puzzles. While death certificates weren't commonplace until around 1900,

GRAVESTONE RUBBINGS

Gravestone rubbings are excellent keepsakes; making them can also provide a fun, creepy adventure for the younger reunion goers.

To rub a gravestone, you'll need:

◆ Large sheets of tracing, architect's, or shelf paper, or newsprint

◆ Sticks of graphite or charcoal, or black crayon

◆ Masking or freezer tape

◆ Scissors

◆ Fixative or hairspray

Clean gravestone as described below.

◆ Cut paper down to size of stone. Tape tautly to gravestone. Start rubbing at upper left corner of stone, using diagonal strokes. Don't rub up and down; that's too much wear and tear on the paper.

◆ Detach rubbing and lay it flat. Fix rubbing with fixative, or spray lightly with hairspray from about 8 inches distance.

◆ If the tape left any sticky residue on the gravestone, gently rub off with soap and water.

---

headstones served the same function. Many old gravestone inscriptions give the dates of the deceased's birth and death; the names of first wives and husbands as well as those that followed; the names of the deceased's parents and children; occupation; and even the year of the deceased's arrival in America. Treat the headstone as you would any other source document, and transcribe it with complete accuracy.

For a trip to an old graveyard, you'll need:
- Rags
- Water
- Dishwashing liquid
- Whisk broom
- White chalk
- Clipboard or notebook, paper, and pen
- Graph paper
- Garden spade (to dig out weeds around the base of the tombstone)

To clean and read an old gravestone:

• Remove dust and dirt gently with whisk broom.

• Rinse with water and wash with dishwashing liquid and rags (scrub brushes can abrade the stone). Dry with rags. Moss, which can protect against the elements, is not always bad for gravestones, so don't be overzealous in rubbing it off.

• Has wording been eroded by time and the elements? Fill in the letters with white chalk, which should bring letters into high relief and improve readability. Don't use shaving cream, as is sometimes suggested; its sticky residue can attract dirt and bugs.

• Copy the gravestone exactly as it reads, line for line, as though copying a poem. Transcribe all symbols and designs, too.

• Don't rely on photographs to transcribe the headstone, but if you do photograph, use black-and-white film and spread aluminum foil at the stone's base to reflect light onto the surface. Photograph from 4 feet away.

• Because families were usually buried in clusters, look around for other relatives.

• Make a map of the graveyard on the graph paper, marking roughly where all your ancestors lie. The map is now a primary document of its own. Include it in your genealogy binder.

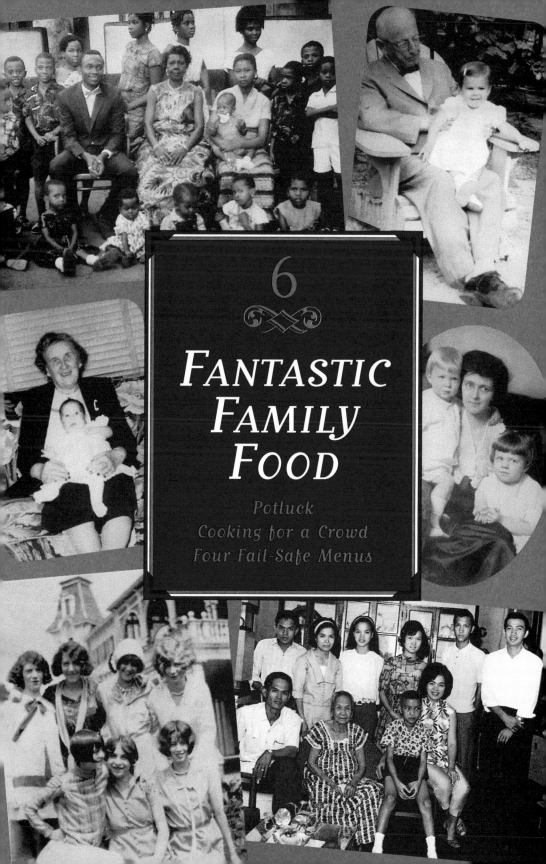

6

FANTASTIC FAMILY FOOD

Potluck
Cooking for a Crowd
Four Fail-Safe Menus

The role food plays at a reunion is an important one, ranking a close second to the actual act of bringing people together. What's great about reunion food is that you can make it unique to your own clan, showcasing generations of family recipes and blending together ethnic flavors and all-time family favorites, for example, Sofia's famous pirogies next to Aunt Maggie's chocolate chip cookies. But food has plenty of tricky variables. You have to decide what to feed the family, organize the menus, decide who will bring what, prepare the food, set up, and serve, while contending with the issues of cost, equipment, and storage. Following are four ways of feeding the family: cooperative cooking, catering, potluck, or do-it-yourself, along with sample menus and recipes to make everyone's work easier. Whichever option you choose, the more strategy and advance planning, the better. And if you go the do-it-yourself route, think about having one evening meal out in a restaurant where *everyone* gets to relax.

COOPERATIVE COOKING

This option works best at a week-long camp reunion, with meal planning and preparation divided among the families or "dinner teams." Leave breakfast and lunch up to the individual families—for these meals, stock the pantry and refrigerator with cold cereal, bagels, cold cuts, premade salads, and fresh fruits. Let dinner be the shared meal. Assign each family a night to cook. If the dinner schedule is distributed before the reunion, the families can browse through their favorite cookbooks or gather their family recipes to share with the group. To avoid duplications in dinner menus, make up a calendar and rotate it among the families. Each family writes down its menu and then passes it on to the next group.

Another option is to draw up simple dinner menus and assign each family a night to cook. Or mix it up a little by assigning members of different nuclear families to "dinner teams." One family decided to let the kids make the opening night dinner, a job they took very seriously. To get ready, the cousins all wrote notes to each other prior to the event. The result? Chicken fingers, French fries, potato chips, chocolate eclairs, and eight thrilled, bonded cousins with some great memories.

Whatever the system, the rules should be articulated and agreed on well before the reunion itself. Decide if each family or "dinner team" will shop, cook, and clean up on their day to cook, or if those three chores will be divided among three different families or teams each day. Draw up a list of what each family considers "pantry basics" and use that as the primary shopping list. Avoid money issues by either establishing a "shopping kitty" at the beginning of the reunion—each family contributes a designated amount for supplies—or have one person front the grocery money and save all food receipts (if you lose one, just jot down the sum on a scrap of paper). At the reunion's end, a calculator-assisted reckoning can divide the costs equally among the families. If

"We never called it soul food. We only called it southern cooking. It was a big part of why we traveled all that way for the reunion. We always assumed it was not all that healthy for you, the black-eyed peas, the fish fry we always held on the Friday, the cracklin' pork, the cornbread made with lard. But we didn't think of the health aspects all that much; it was just too good. None of us eats pork now, except my uncle. But still, we think about it... We miss that good old food."
—Jenice Zniew
Baltimore, Maryland

there is a large discrepancy in the sizes of families, costs can be divided on a per-person rather than per-family basis. Either way, make sure this is all decided before the start of the reunion. Don't try and even out the costs according to who eats what unless you want a family war.

CATERED EVENTS

Having some or all of the reunion meals catered can be a huge stress reducer for the reunion organizers. You can hire a caterer to drop off food or to provide just the entrée or to coordinate the entire event—including organizing rentals, deliveries, and set-ups. Most caterers will include family recipes in menus.

Start the search for a caterer about six to eight months before the event. The best way to find one is to ask around—check with friends or the staff at your favorite restaurants to see who they recommend. Ask for references from prospective caterers—and call those people. What previous customers have to say may help you make important decisions. Also, check with the county health department (which inspects kitchens for cleanliness and food safety) to make sure your caterer is licensed.

Talk with your caterer about what foods you want and how much money you are planning to spend. If you find catering too costly, many restaurants will prepare large amounts of food for take-out. Consider a great ribs, barbecue, or chili restaurant in your neighborhood and build the rest of your meal around that entrée.

Most caterers will require a deposit at the time the date is secured as well as an estimated guest count. (They'll need a final guest count about a week before the event.) Include 10 percent more guests than your total to factor in last-minute drop-ins and unforeseen guests. When doing business with a caterer, tell the caterer you want a signed contract stating the date, time, and place of the reunion, the menu, the list of rental items and the cost of each item, the date when rentals will be delivered (make sure it is no later than the day before), the number of staff and cost of labor, the time the

"**A**t our first reunion years ago, Mother had insisted on cooking and cooking and cooking to produce food that's very... ordinary. I decided to preempt Mother for our next reunion. We found these caterers of southern food from the hills of Kentucky—for a little over six dollars per person, this couple would come out of the hills with an oil tank on wheels, set the fire up early in the morning, and make the most incredible pulled barbecue and fried chicken and biscuits and coleslaw. They sort of became part of the family by being there, friendly and enthusiastically heaping food on people's plates. Mother, of course, was furious at first. But when she saw how easy it all was, and how much fun she could have, she got over it.**"**

—Mimi La Camera
Cambridge, Mass.

caterer and staff will arrive, the time everything will be set up and ready to go, itemized costs along with the total, and how any leftovers will be handled (caterers usually do not leave leftovers with clients).

POTLUCK

Potlucks are a fantastic way to blend family tradition and ethnic flavors—if a little order is imposed to keep the contributions balanced. To take the luck out of potluck, the reunion organizer should act as (or designate someone else as) the food coordinator. The reunion invitation should instruct each family to bring two dishes to serve 8 or one to serve 16 and to contact the potluck coordinator about what dish they are contributing. (The coordinator will probably have to phone many of the families.) Each family should expect their dish to be served in the same container it was brought in, and should bring appropriate serving utensils, marked with the family's name; the dish shouldn't need refrigeration, reheating, or any further preparation. Out-of-towners can contribute bread, desserts, or beverages. It works best if the host family (or reunion committee) provides the entrée and general supplies such as napkins, paper plates, and charcoal.

To coordinate the potluck, divide a large sheet of paper into six squares, one for each food category (see chart on page 118). When a family decides what it will bring, note it in the square: name, dish, how many servings. When a category has enough servings to feed the expected number of attendees, close out the category. As the reunion date nears, the coordinator should drop cards or make brief phone calls to remind families what they've agreed to bring.

Potluck Categories

This list doesn't include meat or poultry. Unless the menu calls for something simple like hot dogs or burgers, the host family (or food committee) should provide the entrée and have the guests bring appropriate side dishes and desserts.

Appetizer: raw vegetable platters, pickles, olives, tortilla chips and dip (or salsa), pita triangles and hummus and bean dips, cheese and crackers

Vegetable salad: coleslaw, tossed salad (dressing separate), cucumber or tomato slices, green beans, carrot sticks, marinated cucumbers, marinated beets

Starchy salad: rice, potato, pasta, three-bean, grains

Fruit: melon, assorted fresh whole fruits (peaches, plums, apples, etc.), fruit salad

Bread: loaves, rolls, bread sticks, biscuits, cornbread

Dessert: sturdy desserts that don't need refrigeration—fruit pies, cobblers, pound cakes, quick breads (banana, zucchini, etc.), cookies, brownies

DO-IT-YOURSELF

While providing and preparing all the food for a reunion is undoubtedly labor-intensive, this option usually works best for smaller reunions, ones at which most of the guests are from out of town, or when the reunion organizer welcomes the challenge and satisfaction of creating

POTLUCK COORDINATOR'S CHART

Appetizer	Vegetable Salad	Starchy Salad
Dish: Family: Servings:	Dish: Family: Servings:	Dish: Family: Servings:
Dish: Family: Servings:	Dish: Family: Servings:	Dish: Family: Servings:
Dish: Family: Servings:	Dish: Family: Servings:	Dish: Family: Servings:
Fruit	Bread	Dessert
Dish: Family: Servings:	Dish: Family: Servings:	Dish: Family: Servings:
Dish: Family: Servings:	Dish: Family: Servings:	Dish: Family: Servings:
Dish: Family: Servings:	Dish: Family: Servings:	Dish: Family: Servings:

and preparing an entire menu. (See the Hubbard family's Cousins Day profile on pages 120–122.)

If you choose to go this route, check out the four menu ideas in this chapter. Each recipe serves 25 and can be easily doubled or tripled, if need be. Even if Thanksgiving is the largest dinner you've ever cooked, don't worry too much about cooking for a crowd. If you can boil water and chop vegetables, you can prepare our recipes. You won't need special equipment, either, although you may need more equipment than you have at hand now. Just remember to make your menu as unfussy as possible, and leave nothing to the last minute. Make a game plan of what needs to be done when, especially on the day of the reunion, right down to details as minor as "dress and toss the salad," and consider asking relatives who live nearby to come early (or the day before) to lend a hand with easy-to-explain tasks.

Getting Ready to Cook for a Crowd

Because you'll need all the surface room you can get, remove nonessentials from kitchen counters and store them in a box in the basement until the kitchen is no longer command central. Clear out the refrigerator, and determine its limits—most fridges can't accommodate meals for more than 50—and borrow extra coolers for overnight storage of packaged meats and other items that can withstand a deluge of melted ice.

"*We always thought Aunt Helen was the most incredible cook, because at every reunion, she would put her own food on a plate, take a forkful, shut her eyes and murmur, 'Mmmmmm... fabulous!' and everyone would follow her lead and take a forkful of what she was having and murmur, 'Fabulous!' and believe it was fabulous. But in truth Aunt Helen was just about the worst cook this family has. But what a technique!*"

—Sarah Martin
Brooklyn, New York

Consider asking neighbors if they'll refrigerate some items for you, but be sure to make a note to yourself to retrieve those items before the reunion begins.

Cooking for a crowd always takes longer than you imagine—so give yourself more time than you think you'll need. When you start to think, "I ought to be through by now," you've probably only reached the halfway point. Make things easy on yourself. Before preparing a recipe, round up and dust off all the equipment you'll need, from start to finish: mixers, bowls, storage containers, knives, cutting boards. Find the appropriate serving spoons and dishes, even if you won't be serving the dish for a few days, so there'll be no last-minute searches. Draw the garbage can right up to where you're

A ONE-WOMAN SHOW

THE HUBBARD FAMILY

What: Backyard reunion/ Cousins Day

Who: The Hubbard family siblings and cousins from nearby states, all brought together by Eleanor Hubbard

Where: Backyard of a Connecticut home

Number of Participants: 50

Family Trait: Easy sociability

Seventy-six-year-old Eleanor Hubbard rises at 6:00 A.M. on Cousins Day for her usual half-hour swim. Heading down the sloping lawn to the lake in her swimsuit, towel over her arm, tapping along in flip-flops, she surveys the scene. The branches of two-hundred-year-old oak and maple trees spread out over the lawn, shading the slate patio where lunch and dinner will be served. "If the weather turns bad, we go into the house," Mrs. Hubbard says. "But it won't turn bad."

The day before, she directed her husband, Ed, as he arranged the lawn furniture. After 45 years of marriage, Mrs. Hubbard knows when and how to ask her husband for help. She gave him a list of his Cousins Day responsibilities four days before, not so far in advance that he'd put the list away and forget about it, nor so close that he would feel pressured and rushed. He must clean and prepare the grills, check on the charcoal supplies, stock the bar, dust off the lawn furniture, and find and insert the extra leaves for the table that can seat 30.

Mrs. Hubbard prepares the entire Cousins Day menu herself. "Fifty people is not all that much," she says. "It's only the sound of 50 that's frightening. Rather like your 50th birthday. Sounds terrifying. Isn't really. Why don't I hire some help? Nobody cares as much as I care. That's why I prefer to do it all myself." (As for serving and cleanup, however, Mrs. Hubbard enlists the help of anybody who crosses her path.) "They call me the General," she says. "You have to have someone in charge, or it all falls apart."

By 10 A.M. the backyard is all set for the 50 family members about to descend.

After her swim, Mrs. Hubbard changes into her work clothes and consults the master list, written on two sheets of yellow legal-pad paper. "I challenge any computer to match this for efficiency," she says, holding up a pencil and the paper. One page bears the guest list. On the next sheet are the ingredients of each recipe.

LUNCH MENU

Homemade baked beans
◆
Hot dogs on the grill
◆
Cottage cheese with chopped herbs
◆
Sliced peeled tomatoes with fresh basil
◆
Homemade coleslaw
◆
Dill and cucumber salad
◆
Stuffed eggs
◆
Mexican dip: layers of guacamole, sour cream, shredded cheddar, hot salsa, green scallions, and chopped seeded tomatoes

Dessert and lasagna for dinner are in the freezer.

Mrs. Hubbard has started the water boiling for iced tea, which she will make

with mint from her garden. "For lunch you can drink this or water," she says. "No matter how much stuff you put out, some kid will always ask for something else. The trick for this kind of party is to establish a rule, or else you would just go out of your head. My

A guacamole dip made from scratch tempts nibblers.

rule is: If I don't have it showing, forget it, kiddo."

Mrs. Hubbard begins rolling the forks in good-stock paper napkins. "When you know you'll be doing this sort of event year after year, you can start investing in it. I bought this complete set of flatware at a church bazaar years ago for $15.00, and it's paid off royally. It would have cost much more to keep buying plastic utensils all these years."

Mrs. Hubbard also bought good-quality plastic

plates, supposedly disposable, but which she washes and puts away for the next year. On the kitchen floor are boxes of wine glasses, purchased on sale at an outlet shop. She starts to fill the salt and pepper shakers, which she has bought at yard sales over the years.

"Now I've got a set for every five people."

Eleanor Hubbard has been preparing for this event for a week. Last weekend she made and stored in the freezer 75 ice cream sandwiches. She takes chocolate wafers and a little scoop of vanilla ice cream, puts them into a gadget she bought years ago, twists it and voilà—a perfect little ice cream sandwich. A few days ago, Mrs. Hubbard made and froze the spinach lasagna that will be served for dinner. Yesterday, she cooked two pounds of bacon (one pound for the baked beans, the other pound to serve on the hot dogs), cleaned and chopped chives, watercress, dill, and parsley, and also chopped the cabbage for the coleslaw. Today she mixes it with mayonnaise and yogurt.

At 8:00 A.M., Mrs. Hubbard makes the guacamole and assembles the Mexican dip. Taking out a two-dollar cheese grater, she says, "My daughter uses her food processor to shred cheese. Is it really easier than this?" In a few minutes, she's got two cups of shredded cheddar on a sheet of waxed paper. Mrs. Hubbard uses commercially prepared salsa and chops up some scallions to decorate the top.

She stirs the baked beans. "Old family recipe," she says, then winks. "Fannie Farmer, in other words." She slices two ripe honeydews, cuts off the rinds, and arranges the slices on a platter. "The perfect Cousins Day food: finger food, and no rinds to dispose of."

Dinner is actually easier than lunch. The tables are set with the good silver, china, and wine glasses. All she needs to do is heat the lasagna, whip up

For starters: Mrs Hubbard's famous peach dacquiri.

savory muffins with fresh sage, thyme, and rosemary from her garden, and tell the kids to shuck the corn.

"Now for dessert—the pièce de résistance." It is a truly American dish, with the recipe sent north by a Georgia cousin. It has a base of smashed Oreo cookies and layers of ice cream, chocolate sauce, and nondairy whipped topping with shredded chocolate on top. "There's only one word for it," says Mrs. Hubbard. "Divine."

Before dinner, Mrs. Hubbard serves her famous peach daiquiris. She has ripened 30 peaches for a week so that the skins slip

off easily. She slices them in the morning and lets them rest in orange juice. In the evening she tosses them into the blender with loads of ice and a splash of peach juice blend for the kids' drink. The grown-up version contains an ample dose of rum. "Good grief, it's a messy thing," says Mrs. Hubbard. "It spills, it's sticky, it's altogether god-awful and wonderful."

At 10:55 A.M. it's nearly time for the family to arrive. Mrs. Hubbard has yet to change into the flowered shift she calls her muu-muu. She glances out the kitchen window. There are voices and car doors slamming, and a beaming young woman in a pretty pink gingham shift proudly bears a dish wrapped in aluminum foil toward the house. "Who's that? My niece Melissa. Oh, what's she got? A wrapped dish of something? Oh, I wish they wouldn't do that, when I've got it so nicely planned, down to the last teaspoon."

Then she is out the door. "Oh, dear, Melissa!" she exclaims. "You shouldn't have!" And Cousins Day begins.

ROMANTIC ILLUSIONS

We understand the seductive allure of the clambake, the pit barbecue, hand-cranked ice cream. But flirt with these culinary charmers at your own risk—in the end, they're heartbreakers.

◆ CLAMBAKE: Ah, the romance! Starting at eight in the morning for dinner by seven, you'll be standing in line for a fire permit, digging ditches, searching for rocks to shore up the sides, collecting driftwood, heaping seaweed. It's dinner as endurance test, as epic saga—as sheer exhaustion.

◆ PIT BARBECUE: This involves digging a pit 8 feet deep and 6 feet long out of packed earth. There's a reason kettle grills were invented.

◆ PIG ROAST: Unless the family is 100 percent southern folk, the sight of a pig on a spit will send half the 12-and-under set sobbing for their dog-eared copies of *Charlotte's Web*. It's an acknowledged fact: Kids prefer their meat without a face.

◆ HAND-CRANKED ICE CREAM: The adults love this, because the kids do all the painful cranking. And the result of the sore wrists and sweat is as often as not barely chilled whipped goo with lumps of not-quite-ripe peaches. It all made sense when there wasn't an ice cream parlor down the street—but now, it makes no sense at all.

---

cooking and wear your most comfortable walking shoes—when cooking for a crowd, extra steps add up. If you'll be in the kitchen when the family arrives, brighten up your act by investing in clean oven mitts and a dark-colored apron to hide stains.

When calculating number of servings, factor in one extra serving for every six people if the food is to be served buffet style; when folks serve themselves, they tend to take larger portions than they need. And if you intend to reheat a dish, reduce cooking time by 10 minutes, allow the dish to cool, and refrigerate. When the dish is reheated, it can finish cooking and won't be overdone.

All the recipes in this chapter can be prepared completely or substantially in advance—so you'll be able to take off your apron, enjoy the company and praises of family, and sit down and eat with them.

EQUIPMENT

Once the menu is set, the food committee should figure out what equipment is needed. Picture the entire day and write down what you will need for each dish. The best way not to spend a fortune on equipment is to pull together everyone's equipment or borrow from friends or neighbors. If that is not feasible, you can always rent equipment—from glasses to large tents—at local rental or party supply companies (for information on renting tents and tables, see Appendix, page 259; for equipment and supplies checklists, see pages 260–261). Also, check out discount or party supply stores for heavy-duty plastic or aluminum serving platters and utensils.

SERVING

The most efficient way to serve everyone is buffet style. Do you have enough tables for serving the food and for seating people (see Appendix, page 259, for information on numbers of tables you'll need)? If it is a hot day, is there a shady place for people to stay cool?

The best way to set up the buffet station is to have people take their plates, move through the buffet, then pick up silverware and beverages at the end of the line. Wrapping each set of silverware in a napkin makes it easy for guests to grab a set, and it prevents napkins from blowing away.

Follow the old standbys for food safety—especially important with older and younger guests attending. Don't return cooked meat, chicken, or fish to a plate or platter that held raw food, and discard any marinade that's been used with raw meat. Keep any dishes with mayonnaise, and all meat, chicken, and fish to be grilled in a cooler packed with ice. Make sure knives used to cut fruit and breads are completely clean. Don't keep any cooked meats outside for longer than 1 hour if you plan to save

"I am Irish, I'm married to an Italian, and I cook Italian. So I was a little worried about what all my Irish relatives would say about all this Italian food. Where's the corned beef? Where's the cabbage? How can we eat this? So for the first reunion I made a few Irish staples—had to have potatoes—and prayed. But I knew I was in like Flynn when I looked across the yard and saw my great-uncle from Ireland making his way to a picnic table, grinning ear to ear, holding on to a plate—a plate heaped with mashed potatoes and then, right in the middle of the potatoes, a great big Italian sausage."
—Winifred Infante
New Windsor, New York

them for leftovers. Most people take about 45 minutes to eat at a leisurely pace. If your family still wants to munch after that, keep the leftovers accessible in the cooler or fridge. Or leave the meat out an hour longer—and then give it the heave-ho.

TRASH

Make sure you have several trash cans in various locations around the reunion area and keep a good supply of liners nearby. If you are recycling bottles and cans, place recycling bins next to the trash cans where people will find and use them. If you are not using disposable plates and cups, set up several stations where people can scrape and stack dishes so that they don't pile up with uneaten food.

Beverages

Ice is no minor detail. When you're holding your reunion outdoors during summer, the whole event depends on it. Since ice is relatively inexpensive, be generous, and buy too much rather than too little. Use these guidelines when purchasing ice:

• For drinks: 1 pound per person. If the reunion is all day, 2 pounds per person.

• For chilling drinks in coolers and tubs: 1 pound per person. If the reunion is all day, 2 pounds per person.

If possible, buy the ice in quantity at an ice company. Check their hours; many companies close by noon on Saturdays. Beverage supply companies are also good sources for bulk orders of ice. Take coolers with you when picking up the ice.

SOFT DRINKS

Many beverage-supply companies allow you to return cans of soda that you don't use, so find one that does. Err on the side of buying too much and save your receipts to return the extras later. Use these guidelines when estimating for soft drinks:

• Two 10-ounce glasses of soda or 2 cans per person.

• One 2-liter bottle of soda = 6 generous servings.

• For 25 people, you'll need at least eight 2-liter bottles. For an all-day summer reunion, double that amount.

Purchase an assortment of caffeinated, decaffeinated, and diet soft drinks in a variety of flavors. Include a few jugs of spring water and seltzer water, too.

ICED TEA

Iced tea is the cheapest and possibly the most refreshing beverage to offer. Use well-scrubbed gallon-size mayonnaise containers that a local deli may be happy to hand over to you. To serve 25 at an all-day summer reunion, you'll want to make 5 gallons of iced tea. Use 10–14 tea bags per gallon jar; to avoid boiling large quantities of water, boil half the amount called for, then top off with cold water after the tea has brewed for 30 minutes. Serve with lemon and sugar and chopped fresh mint leaves (if you have mint) on the side. Offer 2 large lemons, sliced, per gallon of tea.

BEER

It's not easy to get a fix on how much beer you'll need. Go down the guest list and make an educated guess as to who drinks beer and how much. Beer by the keg makes sense for a crowd. The beer supply companies rent the tap and tub to chill the keg. Each tub needs about five 7-pound bags of ice (have extra ice on hand to replace melted ice). Half a keg yields 200 10-ounce glasses of beer. A quarter keg yields 100 glasses. Remember that as a host, you're

"I *grew up in the 1960s, in the suburbs, and when it comes to ethnic foods, I'm at a total loss. Soul food to me is macaroni and Velveeta, frozen peas, iceberg-lettuce salad with Russian dressing (mayonnaise and ketchup blended together), fish sticks, frozen apple pie, and for dessert, Jell-O with bananas or maybe some canned fruit cocktail. We kids all fought over the cherries—had to have those 100 percent artificial cherries. That's American cooking—that's my soul food, and I love it.* **"**

—Stacey Mayer
Kingston, Rhode Island

liable—legally and morally—for guests who are drinking. Organize rides home for reunion goers who may have overindulged.

COFFEE

Coffee is serious reunion business. When people hit the road after a long day under the sun, many need to crank up with a "go cup" of solid caffeine.

• Rent two 55-cup coffee urns from a local rental company: one for regular, one for decaf. (Mark which is which with a masking tape label.)

• Use 4 cups of ground coffee (about 1 pound) for each urn. Canned coffee comes in 13-ounce containers: One container will produce 55 cups of perked coffee.

• Big coffee urns draw a lot of electricity, so don't plug both urns into the same outlet or you might blow a fuse.

• Count on 2 ounces of half-and-half or milk for each person: about 3 quarts for 25 people. Set out cartons or good-sized pitchers of milk on ice.

• You'll need 2 pounds of sugar and a box of sugar substitute.

• Buy coffee stirrers: They're less wasteful than plastic spoons.

• Put a small wastebasket below or near the coffee table for napkins, stirrers, and sugar substitute packets.

• Heat water for tea in the kitchen, and let people fix their own.

FOUR MENUS: COOKING FOR COUSINS

Here are four complete dinner menus with recipes to suit a wide range of tastes. All these recipes create 25 servings and, unless otherwise noted, can be doubled or even tripled. There are no culinary tricks required and no expensive ingredients. All the dishes can be prepared substantially or completely a day in advance, so the cooks-in-charge can spend reunion day with the family, not the stove.

Since these recipes are basic blueprints, feel free to improvise on the ingredients wherever you want to. For those holding their first reunion, these recipes can help create fond memories to be savored in the years to come.

With the exception of hobos and cowboys, Americans didn't really cook over open fires outdoors until after World War II. Charcoal wasn't even invented until the 1920s, when Henry Ford wanted to recycle excess wood from his factories into something productive and called on Thomas Edison to design briquette factories. But when Americans tamed the wilds and called it Suburbia, we found the ideal way to get men to help out with dinner, return to nature, and commune with the spirits of Henry Ford, Thomas Edison, cowboys, cars, and hobos all at the same time, while creating the most evocative American aroma: beef blackening over an open fire.

Ode to Suburbia Barbecue

❖❖❖

Marinated grilled
flank steak
❖
Rosemary chicken
❖
Fresh corn salad
❖
Fresh tomato platters
❖
Dijon potato salad
❖
Lemon pound cake with
fresh berries

Feeding 25 people? Serve just the grilled flank steak or just the rosemary chicken. If you're having 50 people, serve both the steak and the chicken. The chicken is delicious cold and can be made a day ahead.

Marinated Grilled Flank Steak

Zip-lock plastic bags are a high point of technological convenience, a hundred times more useful than the microwave. Marinate the meat in these bags, stacking them and turning them every now and then. On the day of the reunion, you have no oily bowls to pile up in the sink. Squeeze out any extra air before sealing. (You can draw the air out with a straw slipped into an unzipped corner, but be careful not to get a mouthful of marinade.)

Marinade:
4 cloves garlic, crushed
4 onions, diced
6 tablespoons peeled and
    minced fresh ginger
1 tablespoon Tabasco sauce or
    1 jalapeño pepper, seeded and
    minced (wear plastic gloves)
1¼ cups soy sauce
1¼ cups honey
1½ cups sesame, peanut, or
    canola oil

12 pounds flank steak

SHORTCUT: Substitute three bottles of commercial Italian dressing for the homemade marinade.

1. Combine all marinade ingredients in a bowl, blender, or food processor. Marinate beef in three 2-gallon zip-lock bags, turning occasionally, at least 8 hours or up to 24 hours.

2. Remove meat from marinade, shake off excess marinade, and pat meat dry with paper towels. You want to sear natural juices inside the meat; if the meat is wet, it will steam, not brown, and searing will not occur.

GRILLING TIPS

Equipment

If you are grilling the entrée, you'll need three standard-size kettle or propane grills to feed 25 guests. Propane grills are the most fuss-free, as no warm-up is needed. Since each kind operates a little differently, read the instructions. Or you can rent a 2-by-5-foot grill. You will also need grilling utensils: two pairs of long-handled tongs (one for turning food and another for spreading or moving coals), a spray bottle filled with water for flare-ups, a long-handled basting brush (if you are saucing meats), clean platters to hold the cooked meats (never use the same plates that carried the raw meats), and a table near the grill to hold the platters of raw and cooked meat as well as the grilling equipment. If there's any chance of rain, set up the grill under a carport or covered porch—but never in an enclosed area.

To prepare the grilling rack

If using a home-style grill, scrub the rack clean with dishwashing soap, hot water, and a scrub brush. Dry the rack and, using an old dish towel, coat it lightly with vegetable oil (do not use olive oil) to prevent food from sticking.

If using a rental grill, heat the rack, then use a long-handled wire brush (steel wool tends to flake off) to remove any burnt-on pieces of debris—the rack is easier to scrape clean when it's hot.

To start the charcoal

For a kettle grill, use a metal chimney filled with newspapers and charcoal. The less starter fluid you use, the better for your food and the environment.

In a 2-by-5-foot grill, start the coals an hour before cooking. Lay two 20-pound bags of charcoal flat in the grill bed, slice the bags lengthwise, and leave the bags in place—they will help start the charcoal. Follow the manufacturer's directions on the starter fluid container, and carefully light the charcoal, making sure your sleeves are rolled up and long hair is tied back. Keep a smaller bag of charcoal in reserve to add if coals get low.

3. Grill meat for 4 minutes on each side for medium-rare doneness. (See Grilling Tips on opposite page.)

4. Let meat rest for 5 minutes so juices can redistribute themselves. Slice meat into ¼-inch strips across the grain.

Yield: 25 servings

Rosemary Chicken

If rosemary chicken is being served as the main course, allow 1 pound of bone-in chicken per person. The average whole fryer chicken (3 pounds) will serve three people. If chicken is being served with other meats, a whole chicken will feed four people. The chicken can be cut up and the marinade prepared a day ahead of time, but don't marinate the chicken any longer than 2 hours: The acidic lemon juice will break down the chicken's texture.

8 whole chickens, cut into eighths

Marinade:
Juice of 6 whole lemons (approximately 1 cup)
3¼ cup Dijon mustard
3 cups olive oil
12 garlic cloves, crushed
6 tablespoons chopped fresh rosemary or 2 tablespoons dried
Salt and pepper to taste

1. Rinse chicken pieces under cold running water. Drain and pat dry with paper towels. Pierce each chicken piece several times with a fork or the tip of a sharp knife.

2. Prepare marinade by combining lemon juice, mustard, olive oil, garlic, rosemary, and salt and pepper in a medium-size glass bowl or jar. Put chicken in eight 1-gallon (or four 2-gallon) zip-lock bags. Distribute the marinade evenly over chicken in bags. Refrigerate for 2 hours.

3. Preheat oven to 350°F. Remove chicken from the marinade and shake off any excess oil. Bake in three large roasting pans for 45 minutes to 1 hour, until chicken reaches an internal temperature of 160°F, meat close to the bone is white, not pink, and juices run clear.

Yield: 24 servings

Fresh Corn Salad

Corn on the cob is one of the great American classics—few things are better than just-picked corn boiled for five minutes and spread with a light coat of butter. But sometimes the huge vats of boiling water required to bring 50 ears to the table is too much to take on a steamy day. Our way to bring this summer treasure to the table is in fresh corn salad. Prepared for the most part a day in advance, add only the cucumbers, tomatoes, and vinaigrette the day of serving. Use fresh corn if corn is in season, otherwise frozen. But don't use canned corn—it's way too mushy.

18 ears of fresh corn or 5 1-pound
    bags of frozen
4 scallions, cleaned and finely
    sliced
3 large red peppers, cut into
    1/2-inch dice
3 large green peppers, cut into
    1/2-inch dice
3 cucumbers, peeled, seeded, and
    chopped
1 pint cherry tomatoes sliced
    in half (optional)
1 1/2 cups extra-virgin olive oil
1/2 cup balsamic vinegar
Salt and pepper to taste
1/2 cup chopped fresh dill
    (about 1 bunch)

1. If using fresh corn, husk it, remove as much silk as possible, and rinse corn under cold running water.

2. Clean kitchen sink thoroughly, put a plug in the drain, and place a cutting board in the sink. Slice corn in sink: hold each cob upright and slice downward with a sharp serrated knife.

3. For fresh corn: Bring a 10-quart pot or two 5-quart pots of water to boil. Don't salt water—that can toughen corn. Boil corn for 4 minutes. Skim any pieces of silk or husks from water. Drain corn and run under cold water to stop cooking process.

For frozen corn: Allow to thaw, then cook in boiling water for 2 minutes. Drain and run under cold water.

4. Prepare the remaining vegetables and add to the cooled corn (except for cucumbers and optional tomatoes, if you are cooking corn a day in advance). Mix together the olive oil, balsamic vinegar, salt, pepper, and dill and toss all the vegetables with the vinaigrette at least 1 hour but no more than 2 hours before serving.

Yield: 25 servings

Dijon Potato Salad

Mayonnaise can overwhelm the potatoes in potato salad—as though it, not the spuds, were the star of the show. But this potato salad avoids that problem by elbowing the mayo out of the act completely. Prepare the potatoes and vinaigrette the day before, but don't dress the salad until an hour or two before serving. This amount fits perfectly in a 10-quart bowl. To save even more time, prepare the vinaigrette up to three days in advance. Then just toss the vinaigrette with the cooked potatoes and chill before serving.

12 pounds small potatoes, either
    red bliss or white

Vinaigrette:
2 cups olive oil
4 tablespoons white wine vinegar
4 tablespoons fresh (or frozen)
    lemon juice
4 teaspoons Dijon mustard
6 cloves garlic, crushed
1/2 cup chopped Italian flat-leaf
    parsley
2 shallots or 2 scallions minced
Salt and pepper to taste

1. Scrub potatoes, skin on, under cold water. Cut into halves or quarters.

2. Put potatoes into a large pot and fill with cold water. Agitate for 1 minute with your hand to take off excess starch, drain, and fill with cold water to cover potatoes.

3. Bring to a gentle boil and cook potatoes until tender—cooking time will vary with freshness of potatoes. Potatoes should be intact, not flaking apart. Test after 10 minutes by removing a piece of potato, cooling it slightly, and eating it.

4. Drain potatoes gently, but don't rinse with cold water, which might remove skins. Cool potatoes by spreading them out on cookie sheets. Transfer potatoes to a large bowl, cover, and refrigerate.

5. About 2 hours before serving, toss potatoes gently with vinaigrette. Refrigerate. About 30 minutes before serving, remove salad from refrigerator and allow it to come to room temperature.

Yield: 25 servings

Fresh Tomato Platter

If your reunion coincides with tomato season, slice up 10 of the summer's best large Beefsteak tomatoes, and arrange them nicely on a large serving platter. Sprinkle ½ cup chopped basil and ½ cup extra-virgin olive oil on top. Season with salt and freshly ground black pepper, decorate with 1 pint of red cherry tomatoes and 1 pint of yellow cherry tomatoes, sliced in half, and serve.

Yield: 25 servings

Glazed Lemon Pound Cake with Berries

We love traditional shortcake with a bed of buttermilk biscuits soaked in berry juices. But biscuits taste best served straight out of the oven. So we've substituted this pound cake, which can be baked three days ahead and refrigerated, wrapped tightly in plastic wrap after the glaze has dried. Put out both forks and spoons with the dessert plates, and let everyone assemble his or her own.

Pound cake:
5¹⁄₂ cups cake flour
1 teaspoon salt
1 teaspoon baking soda
3 lemons
2 cups (1 pound) unsalted butter
6 cups sugar
10 large eggs
2 teaspoons pure vanilla extract
2 cups plain yogurt

Glaze:
2 cups sugar
1 cup fresh (about 6 lemons) or
*   frozen lemon juice*
5 quarts fresh strawberries
1 cup sugar (or to taste)
2 quarts fresh blueberries
2 pints fresh raspberries

1. Preheat oven to 350°F. Grease two 10-inch springform tube pans or bundt pans and dust with flour.

2. Prepare pound cake: Sift together flour, salt, and baking soda and set aside. Zest two lemons; then squeeze enough juice from the 3 lemons to make ½ cup. Set aside zest and juice.

3. Using an electric mixer, cream butter and sugar together in a large bowl on medium-high speed. Add eggs, one at a time, and blend thoroughly after each addition. Add vanilla, lemon juice, and zest. Add flour mixture and yogurt alternately, using half of the ingredients each time. Mix well after each addition. Fill both pans evenly.

4. Bake cakes 1¼ hours or until a cake tester inserted into the center of the cakes comes out clean. Cool cakes for 15 minutes, then gently unmold them onto racks.

5. Prepare glaze: Combine sugar and lemon juice in a medium-size heavy-bottomed saucepan. Simmer over medium-low heat until somewhat thickened and syrupy, about 5 minutes. Remove from heat. Spoon glaze onto cakes while both glaze and cakes are still warm.

6. Prepare berries: Gently wash strawberries in a colander under cool running water. Drain, then spread them out on paper towels to dry.

Remove hulls and place strawberries in a large bowl. Add sugar and gently crush berries with a potato masher or the back of a wooden spoon, just enough to release juices—do not purée.

7. Wash and drain blueberries, and pick them over for stems. Add blueberries to strawberries, and gently stir to mix. Refrigerate up to 4 hours, if you are not using them right away. Gently wash raspberries right before serving, then spread them out on a cookie sheet lined with paper towels to dry. Pick through to discard any unsuitable raspberries.

8. Sprinkle raspberries on top of strawberries and blueberries. Slice pound cake in advance and arrange on a pretty platter or plates, and keep it wrapped tightly until serving. Serve with a cake knife, with berries alongside in a big bright bowl. Top with whipped cream or ice cream, if desired.

SERVING TIP: If using whipped cream, plan on 2 quarts of heavy, or whipping, cream for 25 people. If using ice cream, plan on at least ½ cup per person—or 2 gallons for 25 people. Prescoop ice cream into two medium-size bowls, cover with plastic wrap, and return to freezer until ready to serve.

Yield: 25 servings

Italian-American Feast

❖❖❖

Antipasto platter

❖

Spinach lasagna

❖

Grilled Italian sausages

❖

Rustic vegetable salad

❖

Italian bread

❖

Homecoming apple cake

Lasagna has moved out of the ethnic sphere and into mainstream American cuisine. The antipasto platter is this meal's most authentic touch, and it's an easy way to provide a cocktail-hour atmosphere without passing hors d'oeuvres.

Antipasto Platter

Antipasto should suit your family's tastes—so from the ingredients list below, choose four or five items that most appeal to you. Scatter teaspoons and forks on the platter, as serving implements, and place small dishes and forks and cocktail napkins nearby. (Don't use toothpicks, which tend to get used again and again by different people.)

3 loaves French or Italian bread
2 pounds assorted cheeses: plain mozzarella, marinated mozzarella, sliced parmesan, asiago, fontina
2 pounds assorted olives
2 pounds roasted red peppers or stuffed cherry peppers
2 pounds dried sausages, sliced soppressata, salami, pepperoni
6 pounds mushrooms, cleaned
6 6-ounce jars marinated artichoke hearts
1 pound Italian bread sticks

1. Slice bread and serve plain, or spread it with olive oil and herbs and toast it. Fresh bread may be sliced up to 8 hours before use and stored in 2-gallon zip-lock bags until serving. Put in a towel-lined basket and cover until right before serving.

2. Use a board or platter about 16 inches wide for antipasto. Assemble antipasto ingredients as attractively as possible, creating an abundant, colorful appearance, with a small bowl full of olives, mushrooms, or bread sticks at the center. Cover and refrigerate for a maximum of 4 hours before serving (you don't want the flavors melding together).

Yield: 25 servings

Four-Cheese Spinach Lasagna

The tomato sauce can be made two days in advance. The lasagna may be assembled one day before baking. If you prepare the filling separately, it shouldn't be refrigerated for longer than one day. Remove the finished lasagna from the refrigerator for 1 hour before baking to bring it to room temperature. You'll need three 9-by-13-inch glass baking dishes for this recipe. To control the portion size, cut the servings yourself.

SHORTCUT: *Use fresh lasagna noodles or "oven-ready" ones that don't need to be boiled beforehand. Use commercially prepared tomato sauce. You'll need 6 cups for the baked lasagna, plus 10 cups to heat up and serve on the side.*

Tomato sauce:
- ¹⁄₃ cup olive oil
- 1 large Spanish onion, diced
- 6 carrots, peeled and cut into
  - ¹⁄₂-inch dice
- 6 cloves garlic, minced
- 4 35-ounce cans plum tomatoes
- 1 6-ounce can tomato paste
- 2 teaspoons salt
- 2 teaspoons sugar
- 2 teaspoons dried basil
  - (or 2 tablespoons fresh)
- 1 teaspoon black pepper

Four-cheese filling:
- 4 10-ounce boxes frozen
  - chopped spinach, thawed
- 4 pounds whole-milk ricotta
- 2 pounds mozzarella, whole milk or
  - part skim, grated
- 1 cup grated Parmesan cheese
- 1 pound cheddar, Havarti, or
  - Monterey Jack cheese, grated
- 4 large eggs
- 2 tablespoons olive oil
- 1 large Spanish onion, diced

- 2 teaspoons ground nutmeg
- 2 teaspoons salt
- 1 teaspoon black pepper

- 3 1-pound boxes lasagna
  - noodles, or 6 8-ounce boxes
  - "oven-ready" lasagna noodles
- 1¹⁄₂ cups grated Parmesan cheese
- 3 teaspoons olive oil

1. Prepare tomato sauce: In a large soup pot, heat oil over medium heat. Add onions, carrots, and garlic and cook, stirring occasionally, until onions are translucent, about 5 to 8 minutes; do not brown. Add remaining ingredients. Lower heat to a slow simmer and cook, stirring often to prevent sticking, for 1½ hours. Remove pot from stove and cool slightly. Process sauce in batches in a food processor or force through a food mill until smooth, and transfer to another bowl. Cover or refrigerate until ready to use.

2. Prepare filling: Defrost spinach and squeeze out excess water by pressing spinach against a sieve or colander over the sink. In a large mixing bowl, mix cheeses together. Add eggs and mix well. In a heavy pan, heat olive oil over moderate heat and cook onions until translucent, about 2 to 3 minutes. Add spinach, lower heat, and cook for 4 minutes. Do not brown onions. Allow spinach and onion mixture to cool, about 15 minutes, and add it to cheese mixture. Add nutmeg, salt, and pepper. Blend well, then cover and refrigerate until ready to use.

3. To finish: Cook lasagna noodles according to package directions.

4. Preheat oven to 375°F. Grease three 9-by-13-inch baking dishes with olive oil, then spread 1 cup of tomato sauce over bottom of each pan. Divide cheese mixture evenly into three separate bowls, one for each pan.

5. Place five lasagna noodles across length of each pan. They should overlap. Use half of cheese mixture in each bowl; distribute evenly across noodles in each pan. Cover each cheese layer with five more noodles. Spread remaining cheese over noodles, and cover with remaining noodles. Tuck under any side pieces. You should have two layers of cheese and three layers of noodles. Pour 1 cup of tomato sauce over each pan of lasagna. Sprinkle ½ cup Parmesan cheese over each pan. Cover each pan with aluminum foil and bake 1 hour.

6. To serve: Let lasagnas rest 15 minutes before cutting each into eight pieces. Heat up reserved tomato sauce and serve alongside lasagna in a bowl with a small ladle.

Yield: 24 servings

Grilled Italian Sausages

Some families would suffer a collective nervous collapse if the men were deprived of their opportunity to grill. The men fulfill their role as hunters by providing meat chunks for the tribe. And they've learned to effectively avoid family small talk by poking with studied concern at white-hot coals. So fire up the grill and throw on the sausages. Avoid any impulse to puncture the sausage casing when parboiling the sausage; the fat in the meat dissolves during parboiling and gently seeps through the casing, which retains enough fat to prevent the sausage from drying out. Parboil no longer than 1 hour before grilling (and don't refrigerate after parboiling, or the fat will harden again).

50 Italian sausages, mix of hot and sweet

1. Fill two large pots with water and bring to a boil. Add sausages. Allow water to return to a full boil, and cook 15 minutes. Turn off heat. Sausages can remain in the warm water (no longer than 1 hour) until grilling.

2. Prepare grills according to Grilling Tips, page 128. Grill sausages over medium-hot grill for 15 minutes, turning frequently. Again, be careful not to puncture casings.

Yield: 25 servings

Rustic Vegetable Salad

All the ingredients, except for the tomatoes and the optional cucumbers, can be assembled a day in advance. The vinaigrette may be made three days in advance. But don't dress the salad until an hour before serving, when you will also add the tomatoes and cukes.

Salad:

3 large bunches of broccoli,
about 1¹⁄₂ pounds each,
cut into florets
3 large bunches of cauliflower,
about 2¹⁄₂ pounds each,
cut into florets
3 large red bell peppers, seeded
and cut into ¹⁄₂-inch dice
3 large green bell peppers, seeded
and cut into ¹⁄₂-inch dice
6 carrots, peeled and sliced into
circles
1 red onion, thinly sliced
3 ribs celery, diced
10 fresh basil leaves, coarsely
chopped
12 good-quality black olives,
halved and pitted

Optional additions:

2 tablespoons capers, drained
¹⁄₂ pound ricotta salata (firm,
sliceable ricotta) or feta cheese,
crumbled
1 large fennel bulb, about 1 pound,
trimmed and thinly sliced
1 pound green beans, blanched
1 pint cherry tomatoes, halved
3 medium cucumbers, peeled, cut
lengthwise, deseeded and sliced

Vinaigrette:

1 cup olive oil
¹⁄₄ cup white wine vinegar
2 tablespoons fresh lemon juice
Salt and pepper, to taste

Optional:

2 tablespoons chopped chives,
2 tablespoons chopped parsley,
1 teaspoon fresh thyme
1 teaspoon fresh oregano

SHORTCUT: *Instead of making vinaigrette, use a 12-ounce bottle of good-quality commercial oil-and-vinegar dressing.*

1. Prepare salad: Bring two large pots of salted water to a boil. Add broccoli to one pot and cauliflower to the other, and cook about 2 minutes until fork tender but still crunchy. Drain in a collander and rinse under cold water to stop cooking. Combine the broccoli, cauliflower, bell peppers, carrots, onion, celery, basil, and olives, and any optional additions except the tomatoes and cucumbers; stir gently to combine.

2. Prepare vinaigrette: Combine all the vinaigrette ingredients in a small bowl. Mix well.

3. One hour before serving, remove vegetables from refrigerator and add optional tomatoes and cucumbers. Dress vegetables with vinaigrette; add optional chopped fresh herbs, if desired. Let salad remain at room temperature before serving.

Yield: 25 servings

Homecoming Apple Cake

To stay true to the Italian theme, head for the best Italian bakery around for some sfogliatelli and cannoli. But if you want to go homemade and you are no pastry chef, try this all-American cake. It really is the best apple cake ever. When selecting apples for this cake, look for Northern spy, Empire, Cortland, and Ida red. (Granny Smith are too dry.) Bake up to two days in advance, wrap well, and refrigerate. You'll need two tube pans.

> 6 cups cake flour
> 2 teaspoons salt
> 2 teaspoons baking soda
> 2 teaspoons cinnamon
> ¹⁄₂ teaspoon nutmeg
> 3 cups vegetable oil
> 1 cup granulated sugar
> 1 cup light brown sugar
> 6 large eggs
> 2 teaspoons pure vanilla extract
> 6 apples, about 3 pounds, peeled, cored and cut into ¹⁄₂-inch dice
> 1 cup walnuts, chopped
> 1 cup golden raisins (other raisins may be substituted)
>
> Confectioners' sugar or Cinnamon Whipped Cream (recipe follows) or 2 gallons vanilla ice cream

1. Preheat the oven to 350°F. Grease and flour two tube pans.

2. Sift together flour, salt, baking soda, cinnamon, and nutmeg. Set aside.

3. In a large bowl, beat together oil and both sugars with an electric mixer on medium speed until creamy. Add eggs, one at a time, beating well after each addition. Add vanilla, and beat until incorporated.

4. Stir in flour mixture. It will be very dense. Mix in diced apples, walnuts, and raisins, stirring until well distributed.

5. Divide batter evenly into pans. Bake for 1 hour or until a cake tester comes out clean.

6. Cool cakes completely before unmolding them from pans. To serve, dust cakes with confectioners' sugar sifted through a sieve and cut each cake into 12 slices.

Yield: 24 servings

Cinnamon Whipped Cream

> 2 quarts heavy, or whipping, cream
> 3 tablespoons sugar
> 2 teaspoons cinnamon

1. In a large bowl, beat the cream with an electric mixer on high speed until thickened.

2. Sprinkle in the sugar and cinnamon. Whip until the cream has

reached the desired consistency (soft or firm peaks). Refrigerate until serving, a maximum of 2 hours.

Old-Fashioned Country Ham Dinner

❖❖❖

Glazed country ham

❖

Festive coleslaw

❖

Summer confetti rice salad

❖

Rustic cornbread (see page 142)

❖

Sarah's famous cookies

We remember summer Sunday lunch at our grandmother's farm. It always consisted of a huge glazed ham, which seemed to take our uncle hours to carve, and cornbread that Grandmother would whip up effortlessly. She moved silently around the kitchen in the hours before church, in curlers and robe, magically making these golden cornbreads appear on top of the stove. Wonderful days, yes, but we wouldn't have objected if we'd had some of the salads and garnishes featured here to top off those long afternoon feasts.

SHORTCUT: Precooked, presliced, high-quality glazed hams are available through mail order—and can be ordered for next-day delivery, if need be. One excellent source is The Honey Baked Ham Company; call 800-343-HAMS.

Spice-Glazed Country Ham

A ham is the perfect main dish for a potluck. It's got dignity, substance, and an air of importance that announces, "This is a quality meal."

Two 7- to 8-pound fully cooked smoked boneless rindless hams

1 teaspoon nutmeg

2 teaspoons ground cardamom

2 teaspoons ground ginger

2 teaspoons cinnamon

4 teaspoons dry English-style mustard

$^1\!/_2$ cup molasses

$^1\!/_2$ cup light brown sugar

1 cup Dijon mustard

6 tablespoons whole cloves

1. Rinse hams with cold water and pat dry. Let them sit at room temperature for 45 minutes.

2. Preheat oven to 350°F. Place hams in a heavy roasting pan lined with aluminum foil and bake for one hour or until a meat thermometer (inserted into the thickest part) registers 140°F. Do not cover with foil.

3. Make the glaze. While hams are baking, in a small bowl, mix together nutmeg, cardamom, ginger, cinnamon, dry mustard, molasses, brown sugar, and Dijon mustard.

4. Remove hams from oven and let them sit until cool enough to handle, about 20 minutes. Score top and sides of hams in a diamond pattern, cutting through fat and meat about ½ inch. Insert whole cloves into diamonds. Generously spread glaze mixture deep into slits and over entire top and sides, using hands or a brush.

5. Return hams to oven and bake an additional hour, until they reach an internal temperature of 140° to 155°F. Hams will be dark brown and crusty. (Don't baste with fat from bottom of the pan.) Remove from oven.

6. Let hams rest 10 to 15 minutes before slicing them.

7. Serve slices on platters, accompanied by bowls (or jars) of good-quality prepared honey mustard.

Yield: 25 servings

Festive Coleslaw

To avoid the it-all-tastes-like-mayo blues, this coleslaw does not contain mayonnaise, and its colors look great. Make the dressing up to four days ahead of time, chop the slaw a day ahead of time, and dress it at the last minute.

Dressing:
1 cup vegetable oil
2 tablespoons sugar
⅓ cup cider vinegar

1 tablespoon whole-grain mustard
1 tablespoon celery seeds
1 tablespoon prepared white horseradish
1 teaspoon salt
¼ teaspoon white or black pepper

Slaw:
2 heads green cabbage, about 3 pounds each
1 head red cabbage, about 3 pounds
1 red onion, sliced thin
6 carrots, peeled and shredded
3 large red bell peppers, seeded and cut into thin strips
3 large green bell peppers, seeded and cut into thin strips
½ cup chopped fresh dill
¼ cup chopped parsley

1. Prepare dressing: Combine all dressing ingredients in a blender and mix well, about 30 seconds. Refrigerate, covered, at least 1 hour or up to four days.

2. Prepare slaw: Cut cabbages into quarters. Remove cores and shred quarters as fine as possible across the width. Toss all vegetables and dill and parsley together in a large bowl. Cover and refrigerate until ready to use, up to 24 hours.

3. Add dressing to vegetables 5 minutes before serving. Toss well.

Yield: 25 servings

Summer Confetti Rice Salad

You can make this salad a day ahead. Combine all the ingredients except the peas and cover and chill overnight. Add the peas just before serving.

Salad:

3 cups fresh green peas, cooked for 2 minutes, or 3 8-ounce packages of frozen peas, defrosted

9 cups cooked white or brown rice

3 cups peeled and diced carrots

3 19-ounce cans black-eyed peas or chick peas, rinsed and drained

3 stalks celery, diced

2 medium red onions, diced

2 medium red bell peppers, diced

3/4 cup chopped parsley

Dressing:

2 cups olive oil

3/4 cup fresh or frozen lemon juice

6 tablespoons water

1 tablespoon whole-grain mustard

3/4 teaspoon Tabasco sauce or

'1/4 teaspoon cayenne pepper

Salt and pepper to taste

1. Prepare salad: In a large bowl, combine salad ingredients. Mix gently.

2. Prepare dressing: Combine all dressing ingredients in a blender and mix well, about 30 seconds. Toss dressing with vegetable mixture. Cover well and refrigerate at least 4 hours. Add the peas before serving.

Yield: 25 servings

Sarah's Famous Cookies

Baking giant batches of cookies can be a great tradition. Invite some cousins over and spend an evening picking at the cookie dough. This recipe makes about eight dozen 2-inch cookies—more than three cookies per person if you're baking for 25. If you're baking for more than 25 people, don't double the recipe; just start over with another batch or two and make a marathon out of it. Store the cookies in airtight containers and serve on doily-covered plates.

7 cups all-purpose flour

2 teaspoons salt

2 teaspoons baking soda

2 teaspoons cream of tartar

2 cups toasted rice cereal

2 cups rolled oats (not instant)

2 cups flaked coconut, sweetened

1 cup chopped walnuts

2 cups granulated sugar

2 cups light brown sugar

2 cups (1 pound) unsalted butter

2 large eggs

2 teaspoons pure vanilla extract

2 cups corn oil

1. Preheat oven to 350°F. In a large bowl, sift together flour, salt, baking soda, and cream of tartar. Set aside.

2. In a medium-size bowl, combine toasted rice cereal, rolled oats, coconut, and walnuts. Set aside.

3. In a large mixing bowl, cream both sugars and butter with an electric mixer on medium-high speed, about 1 minute. Add eggs and vanilla, mixing well. Slowly add oil, and mix well to blend. Gradually add flour mixture and mix just until incorporated. Add cereal mixture and mix to blend.

4. Drop dough by rounded teaspoons about 2 inches apart onto an ungreased cookie sheet. Bake 10 to 12 minutes until lightly browned. Do not overbake. Remove cookies to a wire rack to cool. Allow each cookie sheet to cool before using it for a new batch.

Yield: 8 dozen cookies: 25 servings

Chili for a Crowd

❖❖❖

Texas-style chili
❖
*Green garden salad
with herbed ranch dressing*
❖
Rustic cornbread
❖
*Make-your-own sundaes
(see box, page 144)*

We know it's a point of honor for a Texas family to claim that they alone make the most authentic Texas chili. And though we've never put this chili to the test in the Lone Star State, you can count

on us boasting that this is the best, while casually glancing over our shoulders for any stray Texans.

Like most chili, this one tastes best made a day or two ahead, so the flavors can marry. This chili is medium-hot, but if your family likes it milder, reduce the amount of jalapeño peppers by half. If some like it hotter, have them indulge freely in hot sauce on the side.

Make assembling the chili even easier by having the butcher cut your meat for you. And remember to wear plastic gloves, or use a small food processor, when chopping all those jalapeño peppers, to prevent skin irritation.

Texas-Style Chili

*10 pounds trimmed beef
 shoulder, cut into 2-inch cubes*
*4 tablespoons olive oil, or more,
 if needed*
*6 12-ounce bottles of lager beer
 (look for a Texas microbrew)*
*4 35-ounce cans plum tomatoes,
 not packed in purée*
4 tablespoons salt
2 tablespoons black pepper
*20 fresh jalapeño peppers,
 seeded and finely chopped*
4 large onions, diced
*2 large heads garlic, cloves peeled
 and minced*
4 tablespoons ground cumin
2¹⁄₂ cups chili powder
*2 16-ounce cans kidney beans,
 rinsed and drained*

1. Pat meat dry with paper towels and allow it to reach room temperature, about 10 minutes. Heat 2 tablespoons olive oil in a large heavy-bottomed stockpot or Dutch oven. When the oil is very hot, brown meat, in batches, on all sides, stirring only once or twice. Do not overcrowd. Place browned meat in a large bowl between batches. Add more oil to the stockpot between batches, if needed. Don't worry if bits of meat stick to the pan; they're good for adding flavor. After last batch of meat has browned, return previous batches to stockpot, along with beer, tomatoes, salt and pepper. Stir, and turn off heat.

2. In a heavy saucepan, heat remaining 2 tablespoons of olive oil over medium heat. Add jalapeño peppers, onions and garlic, and cook, stirring, until onions and garlic are translucent, about 4 minutes. Add cumin and chili powder and cook, stirring to prevent burning, for 3 minutes.

3. Add pepper, garlic, and onion mixture to meat mixture. Reduce heat to low and simmer, partially covered, for about 3 hours, stirring often. Cook until meat is tender but not shredded. If chili becomes too dry, add more beer or water.

4. Ten minutes before serving, add kidney beans and heat through.

5. Serve chili with the following condiments.

2 pounds sour cream

3 pounds cheddar (cowboy, Monterey, Tillamook) cheese, grated

2 bunches cleaned and chopped scallions (green onions) or 3 medium red onions, chopped

2 bottles hot sauce

5 14½-ounce bags tortilla chips, served in baskets

Yield: 25 servings

Rustic Cornbread

This recipe makes a sturdier-than-usual cornbread. Serve it right in the pan, presliced, or in a big basket draped with a cloth napkin. If made a day in advance, wrap well in plastic and refrigerate. Before serving, reheat the bread in a 350°F oven for 10 minutes, if you like.

4 cups all-purpose flour

4 cups yellow cornmeal

2½ cups sugar

4 teaspoons baking powder

4 teaspoons baking soda

1 teaspoon salt

8 large eggs

5 cups sour cream

1 cup (2 sticks) melted butter

Optional additions:

1 cup grated cheddar or Monterey Jack cheese

1 tablespoon fresh dill or 1 teaspoon dried

1 cup frozen or fresh cooked corn

1. Preheat oven to 350°F. Grease four 9-by-5-inch loaf pans or two 9-by-13-inch pans. In a medium-size mixing bowl, combine flour, cornmeal, sugar, baking powder, baking soda, and salt.

2. In a large mixing bowl, beat together eggs, sour cream, and melted butter. Add cheese, dill, and corn, if desired.

3. Add flour mixture to egg mixture and stir just to incorporate. Do not overmix.

4. Pour batter evenly into prepared pans. Bake until tester inserted into center comes out clean, about 50 minutes.

Yield: 25 servings

Green Garden Salad

The hot bite of the chili cries out for a fresh green salad—preferably one with a ranch dressing to act as a mellow counterpart. Keep bottled, commercially prepared dressing capped on a bed of ice if the weather is hot. To serve 25, you'll need 8 heads of lettuce (romaine, red leaf, and Boston, in any combination), 4 cucumbers, 2 green bell peppers, 2 red bell peppers, 4 tomatoes cut into wedges or 1 pint of cherry tomatoes, halved, 1 red onion, sliced in thin half-circles, and 3 carrots, peeled and grated. With the exception of the tomatoes (which shouldn't be refrigerated), you can prepare all the salad ingredients a day before serving and store them separately in plastic bags in the vegetable crisper.

KID-FRIENDLY MENU

Kids today may seem sophisticated, but when it comes to food, they're picky, picky, picky. So no matter what you're planning for the main meal, keep on hand hot dogs, hot dog rolls, and ample ketchup for the kids—count on two hot dogs per child.

Cook the hot dogs to order—enlist a niece or nephew to take orders on a clipboard. Boil the hot dogs if the grill is occupied. Make sure the kids are sitting down and chewing while eating, rather than walking around gabbing, laughing, and jostling. Slicing the dogs in half lengthwise before putting them in the buns also reduces the risk of choking. Avoid other foods kids could choke on, especially round foods, such as grapes, raisins, olives, hard candies, nuts, carrots sliced into rounds, and pumpkin and sunflower seeds.

Keep a well-stocked fruit bowl on hand before, during, and after meals. Kids often grab and devour apples before realizing they've eaten something healthy. Sure, reunions are a holiday time, and health shouldn't be the overriding concern. But kids get grumpy when they eat nothing

Make-Your-Own Sundaes

❖❖❖

When adults see the variety of goodies that go on ice cream these days, they line up to make their own almost as quickly as the kids. To manage this many sundaes, scoop the ice cream in advance, so nobody leaves the reunion with tendonitis. We suggest sticking with vanilla to avoid jostling in line for favorite flavors.

ICE CREAM CUPS

25 10-ounce paper cups with lids (available from restaurant supply companies or local deli)

3¹⁄₂ gallons ice cream

1. Slightly soften the ice cream by allowing it to sit at room temperature for 10 minutes. Fill the paper cups three-quarters full (about 7 ounces). Use a regular kitchen tablespoon to pack in ice cream; an ice cream scoop will produce too many air pockets.

2. Cover the cups with the lids and stack them in the freezer. This can be done up to three days before serving.

TOPPINGS

We think it's best to choose five varieties of toppings plus fudge and caramel sauces, and whipped cream. Serve the toppings in many different dishes so they are accessible to several people at once. Count on 1¹⁄₂ ounces of topping per person. Here are some favorite toppings:

chocolate chips
M & M mini baking bits
mini Hershey's kisses
Nestlé Crunch baking pieces
butterscotch morsels
peanut butter chips
mini marshmallows
granola
fresh fruit, cut up or chopped berries
canned or fresh pineapple chunks
shredded coconut
chopped walnuts
chocolate-covered toffee bars, crushed

but junk food all day, and a piece of fresh fruit can set them right again.

Silly Desserts

Like reunions, silly desserts are an American tradition. Want to win the hearts and minds of your future reunion goers and givers? Make their desserts gooey, excessive, and silly.

WORMS IN THE DIRT

Prepare packaged chocolate pudding, fill paper or plastic cups two-thirds full, top with crushed chocolate-wafer crumbs, and place gummy worms in the chocolate mixture so they look like they're wiggling out. Serve with spoons. For a nonrefrigerated version, frost regular cupcakes with chocolate frosting, top with cookie crumbs, and feature a gummy worm wiggling its way out of the frosting. Older kids can be put to work making these for the younger kids. A 3.4-ounce box of instant pudding will make enough for four 4-ounce servings.

FISH IN THE SEA

A more benign version for the preschool set are gummy fish suspended in a clear plastic cup of blue raspberry Jell-O.

FROST-YOUR-OWN-CUPCAKE STATION

Set up a table in a shady corner of the lawn, preferably near a hose. Bake cupcakes from a mix (one box makes 24 cupcakes), buy cans of frostings

"We were more easily excited in those days....I recall my uncle always brought iced watermelon to the family picnic, a giant watermelon or two set in ice in a big washtub that he'd keep on the back of his truck until he thought we had finally earned it. When he'd cut into it, we'd be so hot and sweaty, it was beyond refreshing."
—Louise Martin
Lawrence, Kansas

(one can frosts 24 cupcakes), assorted sprinkles, gumdrops, and other small candies, and watch the kids enter sugar heaven. When everyone is finished, hose down bowls, tables, surrounding grass, and sticky kids.

HOMEMADE ICE CREAM SANDWICHES

This is how Mrs. Hubbard (page 121) makes hers. You'll need chocolate chip cookies or chocolate wafers (buy more than needed, since they do break). Allow ice cream to soften at room temperature for about 15 minutes, then put a spoonful on a cookie's flat side. Top with another cookie. Press them slowly and gently together. Put the sandwiches on a cookie sheet and place the sheet in the freezer for about 30 minutes. Then wrap each sandwich in plastic wrap. You can fix these about five days before serving. A half gallon of ice cream will make about 35 small sandwiches.

Special Reunion Cakes

❖❖❖

A big sheet cake pan (11 by 15 inches) lets you make big, silly cakes for a crowd with little effort and expense. Two boxes of yellow cake mix will fill the pan and feed 24.

Family Tree Cake features a family tree with the names of the families attending the reunion on the outstretched branches. Bake two sheet cakes, and refrigerate, well wrapped, at least two days: the harder the cake, the easier it is to frost. Place the cakes lengthwise side by side on sturdy cardboard or foamcore, and brush off crumbs. Sketch out a design of a large family tree on paper the same size as the cake. Start with four cans of white frosting. Create a background—blue sky, green grass—of frosting blended with food coloring, leaving space for the trunk of the tree. Refrigerate to harden, then blend food coloring with frosting for

Family tree cake.

the elements of the tree you "paint" on the background—bark, branches, leaves. Allow the frosting to harden again, then write in the family names on the tree's branches, first with a toothpick, then tracing over with white piped icing. Serves 50.

Family Reunion Cake features the name of every kid or every attendee at the reunion. Bake and refrigerate sheet cakes (as for the Family Tree Cake). Frost the cake, then trace the names into the frosting with a toothpick. Each name should represent one slice. Expect all the kids to

cluster around this cake, looking for their slice.

Flag Cake is fast becoming an American classic in the tradition of the Lipton's Onion Soup California dip. Frost a yellow or white single-package cake with vanilla icing or about 20 ounces of nondairy whipped cream (real whipped cream won't hold up for summertime display purposes). Use 2 cups of blueberries for the star field and 3 pints of halved strawberries for the stripes. Serves 12. Rather than doubling the recipe to feed 25, simply make two cakes.

Or frost a cake with the flag design of your country of origin. Lucky you if your flag is as manageable as the Irish or Italian flags. Frost the cake with the predominant field color or colors. Allow the frosted cake to harden under refrigeration, then mix colors into white frosting and add stars, stripes, and other flag symbols.

*"**O**ur reunion meals were always served in a barn that had been swept clean, with tree stumps as seats. The food committee was made up of my aunts—always the same aunts. Food was very bread-and-meat centered in those days. The aunts would pass around these giant cold-meat sandwiches on thick, home-baked bread, which we'd wash down with homemade lemonade. It never occurred to us that you could actually buy lemonade. "*

—Lindy Taggart
Walton, New York

THE GOOD-HUMORED FAMILY

Arrange with the operator of an ice cream truck to swing by the reunion site after dinner. He may be happy to do so if you guarantee a certain minimum of ice cream sales. Prepaying for that minimum will make his visit even more festive.

Sandwich for the Road

The family has had a big midday dinner, it's sundown, and people are ready to hit the road—but they also want to linger a bit longer. And perhaps they're a little hungry— although they don't want anything heavy or junk-foodish. Let family members build a sandwich to fit their needs at a sandwich buffet. The trickiest part is figuring out in advance how many people will actually partake. At almost every family reunion, a few guests plan to make an early break for it, only to change their minds, while others unexpectedly cut out early. We think it's always best to err on the side of having too many sandwich fixings instead of too few; if there are leftovers, they make great lunches for the week. Serve with a basket or two of chips and a freshly stocked bowl of fruit.

*3 ounces meat per person
(roast beef, ham, salami,
turkey, cold meat loaf)*
*2 ounces cheese per person
(sliced cheddar, Swiss, Jarlsberg,
provolone, American for the kids)*
*Leftover cooked food from the
major meal (sliced flank steak,
chicken, ham)*
10 sliced tomatoes
4 sliced onions
*6 heads lettuce (red leaf, green
leaf, Boston, iceberg)*
*6 cucumbers, peeled and
sliced*
6 avocados, peeled and sliced
*6 bunches watercress, large stems
removed*
*2 10-ounce bottles pitted olives,
drained, in a bowl*

1 dozen hard-boiled eggs, peeled
    and sliced, in bowls
2 12-ounce jars roasted peppers,
    cut in strips

Yield: 25 sandwiches

Condiments:
Butter (1 stick for every 8 people)
1 32-ounce jar mayonnaise (keep on
    a bed of ice, if it's warm out)
2 16-ounce containers of mustard
    (two different kinds)
Vinaigrette in a jar, bottle, or cruet
    (homemade or commercially
    prepared)
Sweet and sour pickles

Bread: Plan on 1½ bread servings per person. Check nutrition labels for number of servings in each loaf. Feature a variety of choices: pita bread, whole-grain bread, Italian bread, sandwich rolls.

Family Hero

There's something fitting about creating a family hero at a reunion. And devouring it. Order a super-long roll from a pizzeria or Italian deli and put the entire family to work (scrub those hands first) assembling a 6-foot-long family hero.

4 pounds cold cuts: salami,
    turkey, ham
3 pounds sliced cheese:
    provolone, cheddar, Swiss,
    Jarlsberg, American
5 cups shredded lettuce
3 sliced onions
1 10-ounce bottle pitted olives,
    drained
Salt and pepper to taste
1½ cups vinaigrette or oil
    and vinegar

1. Layer all ingredients on sliced roll. Sprinkle with vinaigrette or oil and vinegar and salt and pepper.

2. Close and tie with butcher's twine at 4-inch intervals. To serve, keep a serrated bread knife nearby (but out of reach of children) and let people slice off the amount they want to eat.

Yield: 20 servings

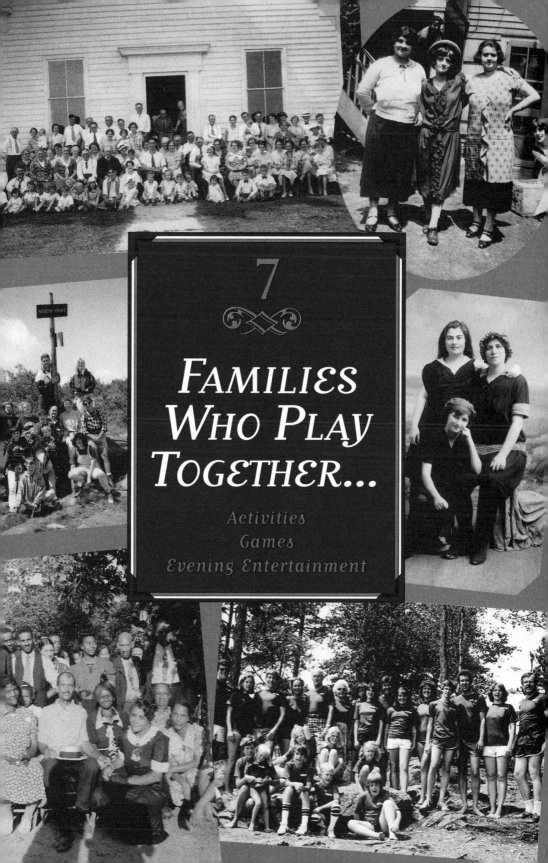

7

FAMILIES WHO PLAY TOGETHER...

Activities
Games
Evening Entertainment

A reunion can't be left to its own devices. Simply throwing related people together doesn't always result in a good time. Planning fun events to bring everyone together in a shared experience is vital. At the very least, activities create a bank of shared memories for the future. The most successful reunions alternate kids' games with intergenerational activities that have a component of doing rather than just schmoozing, with kids and grown-ups meeting on common ground for kite flying, a softball game, a scavenger hunt, or a talent show. The emphasis should be on fun, with games that are nonstrenuous and noncompetitive so that most of the older or less fit family members will be able to join in.

Planned events for kids help break up cliques of cousins who already know each other, and break ground for spontaneous play to flourish later in the day. An hour-long kids' activity in the morning is enough to give the day focus and supply a sense of togetherness, as long as other kid-friendly resources—arts and crafts, sports equipment, or swimming—are also available. Holding these events in the morning works best, because kids are fresh and least in need of naps.

At some point during the day, a reunion's structure should offer a period of do-nothing leisure for all its hardworking, hard-traveling members. There's a deliciousness to those quiet hours after a meal, when family members head off on their own for a few hours while others linger behind for quiet chats, a snooze while pretending to read the Lincoln biography, or a game of Scrabble with a favorite aunt. Downtimes can easily be a reunion's highlight.

A weekend reunion might feature an afternoon of "splinter activities" or "off-campus" trips that most likely won't interest the entire group: visits to a historical museum or a fishing trip, nine holes of golf or a genealogy workshop, stupid-fun activities for older kids, such as Gokarts or miniature golf. When the family reconvenes for dinner, the evening will be all the more fun and fulfilling for that period of separation, rest, and pursuit of individual interests. The reunion will soar on the gust of the family collectively getting its second wind.

GAMES FOR ALL AGES

Most of us grew up with competitive sports, which taught us to win and lose, use teamwork to eliminate the enemy, and apply other skills useful in the real world. But cooperation is useful, too—perhaps even more so in the world of family. In cooperative games nobody keeps score, nobody is eliminated or loses, everyone plays an essential role, and only teamwork guarantees success. Most of the following games can be played by all but the youngest or most frail.

What these games do need is a strong leader to make sure the participants are behaving safely and to stop the play if family members are horsing around. Because all generations are involved, kids will probably approach these games with an appropriate balance of seriousness and playfulness.

THE PULSE GAME
Imagine sending one invisible surging pulse of energy through the entire group. Everyone gathers in a circle and holds hands. The leader starts a hand squeeze, which the next person passes on. Now try sending the pulse in two directions. The leader sends two pulses at the same time. Try it with your eyes shut. Play with it: Speed it up, slow it down.

EYES-SHUT OBSTACLE COURSE
An obstacle course is set up: it could be tires flat on the ground, or a 2-by-4-inch "bridge" over a river, or a ravine made of two rows of chairs. One player keeps his eyes shut while he's led, without rushing, through the course by another player who is not allowed to speak, and guides the first player through gentle physical touch. The players then switch roles. This games relies on and builds up nonverbal communication and trust.

FAMILY TRUST
Each person takes a turn falling backward into the arms of the family from a height of anywhere from 6 inches to 2 feet. The person falling must let go and trust that the others will catch him. Even though it may feel as though he can't possibly be caught, the experience will change his mind. The group forms two fairly close lines, with just enough room to extend arms. Everyone should extend their arms, alternating arms with the person opposite. Arms should be straight, palms up, and nobody should hold hands or wrists. The leader should check the arms, making sure there are no gaps and insur-

Older and younger folks get to know one another through gentle competition, sharing, or just schmoozing and laughing over a game of hearts.

◆ Kite flying

◆ Tug-of-war

◆ Nature walk

◆ Ping-Pong or Horseshoes

◆ Clam digging

◆ Board games

◆ Card games

The basic kit might include:

• **Inexpensive badminton set,** with plenty of extra racquets and birdies.

• **Volleyball,** to be played over the badminton net or in a circle.

• **Old tennis balls** for monkey-in-the-middle, running bases, and playing catch.

• **Red rubber balls** for kickball, dodgeball, bouncing games.

• **Beach ball,** innocuous enough for tossing around indoors.

• **Frisbee** and its second-generation cousin, the WHOOSH.

• **Jump rope.** A few girls actually remember how to jump rope, and enjoy it. Get the mothers and aunts involved to show them a few turns

ing that the smaller people are interspersed with the bigger people. Family members should also be instructed not to horse around.

Having taken off his shoes, the jumper stands backward on something stable—a sturdy box or low footstool —and falls into the arms of family— and to his relief and joy, he's caught.

Unstructured Activities and Games

Tossing a ball around is an easy way to come together with other kids or with grown-ups, and it is the perfect response to the kid who says, "I'm bored." The reunion organizers might assign someone to bring a basic kit of sports gear—bought or borrowed for the occasion.

Scavenger and Treasure Hunts

Teamwork doesn't have to take an exclusively athletic form. When teams of cousins are thrown together in a quest, especially cousins of all generations and a grandparent or two, the result is supercharged, super-accelerated family bonding. What other family event has the air of triumph and the agony of defeat—both of which are quite meaningless—all in one hour's drive around town?

TREASURE HUNT

For the very ambitious family, a treasure hunt is pure excitement. The Seikis are just such a family. At their reunion, the organizers cooked up a "car rally," dividing the family into three teams, each of which included at least one representative from the five family branches. The teams were given local maps and sent off in minivans and Jeeps to chase clues through town—clues that had been taped to the underside of park benches and left in a dryer in the Laundromat, among other places.

Even the local pizzeria got into the act. The pizza man was cued to spill the beans when asked for "the secret recipe." The treasure hunt organizers trailed the pack with a cell phone at hand, ready to supply backup clues if the pizza man decided to take a badly timed coffee break or someone at the Laundromat accidentally removed the clue from the dryer. The "treasure"—novelty-store trinkets gift-wrapped in boxes, one for each team—was ultimately found under a tree at a cemetery.

PHOTO TREASURE HUNT

This variation on the treasure hunt is best played in locations where there is family history to be found. At the start of the hunt, each family team is given a camera and a list of places they must find, go to, and photograph themselves in as proof that they were there. Some clues might focus on family lore. For example, "The team must take a photo shot/ Where Alice and Ben tied the knot." And the team must rush to the church where great-grandparents were married. At the end of the hunt, take film to a one-hour photo developing shop for an instant memorialization of the morning's events.

LIVING CLUES TREASURE HUNT

A treasure hunt for kids, this one needs the cooperation of the grown-ups. Each adult participating directs the treasure hunters to the next adult through clues: "This member of the Martin family has been in the navy and runs a construction business." When the last adult is found, the child wins a prize from a stash only that adult knows about. This treasure hunt, like the family scavenger hunt on page 158, encourages kids to get to know something about the older folks.

TREASURE HUNT CLUES

◆ **The clues should rhyme. Why this is, no one knows—perhaps because forcing clues to rhyme makes them sound nonsensically cryptic and intriguing.**

◆ **Six stops before the treasure is found is about right.**

◆ **Use indelible ink on clues, and use masking tape to affix clues.**

◆ **Weekend mornings, when fewer people are out and about, are good times for holding a treasure hunt in a public area.**

◆ **Don't put clues into appealing-looking packages that strangers might be inclined to take.**

◆ **Involve a live civilian to add to the fun and excitement.**

THE OYSTERMAN TRIATHLON

THE KENNEY AND AUSTIN FAMILIES

What: Backyard barbecue mini reunion

Who: Two extended families joined by marriage

Where: Summer home, Cape Cod, Massachusetts

Number of Participants: 22

Family Traits: Supercharged energy levels, fierce competitiveness, verbal sparring

Official Family Motto: "No matter what, bursting with pride."

Unofficial Family Motto: "Winning is more fun."

Casey studies the triathlon route and plots her strategy.

Sibling rivalry is as old as the hills, and when some families get together, they want to engage in a Darwinian struggle of the fittest. Meet the Kenney-Austin family.

"We thrive on friendly competition," says Nancy Kenney Hays. When her sister Jane Kenney and Dr. Gregory Austin married, the Kenney and Austin families were joined not only by marriage but by a love of high-octane competition. Now the two families hold a mini reunion every year called the Oysterman Triathlon, named after the famous Cape Cod mollusk. The logo, designed by Donald Kenney, is an oyster jogging, swimming, and riding a bicycle.

Nancy Kenney Hays insists it's a "tryathlon." But for every family member who only wants to "try,"

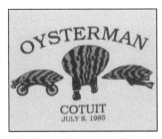

The famous Oysterman logo.

there's one who really wants to win. The triathlon consists of a 100-meter swim (flotation but not propulsion devices are permitted; if flippers are used, they must be worn for the remainder of the triathlon), a 3-mile bike ride, and a 2.3-mile run. The grandparent Austins work as a senior masters team: Betty Austin does the swimming and biking, while Al Austin does the running. Donald and Gerry Kenney provide technical support. As timekeeper and results recorder, they stand at the ready with stopwatch and clipboard.

On a beautiful summer evening before the triathlon, the family meets at Jane and Greg Austin's house in Cotuit to carbo-load—otherwise known as eating spaghetti. The family debates various race strategies and whether Greg Austin should remain in the youth category. At the age of 14, he is a shade taller than his aunt Nancy and has long sported bigger feet. The consensus is that this will be his last year in the junior class.

Showing off T-shirts at a post-triathlon minor league baseball game.

In the morning, nobody feels much like eating the breakfast spread. Adrenaline soars, and prerace jitters make it hard to manage more than half an English muffin. Dr. Greg Austin reminds the group, "It's only supposed to be fun."

The youngest contestant, 4-year-old Sam, arrives on his two-wheeler with training wheels, wearing helmet and goggles. He will avail himself of a flotation device for the swim, but he will not use flippers, according to the triathlon rules.

On the front lawn a map of the course, drawn on oak tag, is propped up against a hedge. George Reinhart, an Austin son-in-law, studies it. The bike course is proportionally shorter than in other triathlons. "The course favors running," he points out. "But you can really train for the running part if you want," says Dr. Greg Austin. "If you have a good racing bike, you would gain a huge advantage if the biking leg

Triathletes await the starting whistle before plunging into the cold water of Cotuit Bay for the 100-meter swim.

Nancy Kenney Hays is the first woman across the finish line.

line. Suzanne Austin, who gave birth a few months ago and is excused from the race this year only, stands by with a camera to record photo finishes.

Here comes the first winner, Dr. Greg, and then the rest, including Nancy Kenney Hays, the new Oysterwoman Champion.

Everybody collapses triumphantly on the lawn, exchanging notes on backchop, cross-currents, and psych-outs.

"I knew how demoralized you'd be if I blew you away at the start of the bike race," says winner Greg to his brother Ken, who grunts in acknowledgment.

Now the kids line up for their race. Adults patrol the course, watching for kids

were longer." He is thinking of his chief rival, brother Ken, who has a state-of-the-art bike, and bike shoes. Most of the bikes in the race are the classic Cape Cod three-speed models, with the occasional 10-speed-with-baby-seat-attachment variation.

The triathletes draw numbers from a cup. Each person's number is drawn on his arm with a purple lipstick bought just for this purpose.

At the water's edge competitors watch as the current moves in to their advantage (the race begins with a favorable tide). Donald Kenney, standing down the beach, waves a T-shirt in the air and they're off, heading for the big orange Tide container, marked "Oysterman Buoy," bobbing

at the end of the beach.

Dr. Greg Austin is first out of the water, pulling on socks and sneakers and heading for the house, followed by brother Ken. The bike leg begins while Ken searches for his bike shoes. Sabotage is suspected.

As the first runners come into sight, two young cousins unroll a crepe paper finish

Oysterkids heed a lecture in race protocol before triathlon start.

and cars. The kids walk down to the beach, looking warily at the water, and then they're off. Sam paddles in his life jacket, Greg Jr. slices along in a steady breaststroke, jumps out first, and charges up the hill to the house, glancing back

The *Rocky* soundtrack plays as the kids stumble breathlessly across the finish line. "I saw smoke and someone said it was Sam!" says his Aunt Joey.

"I ran with my hand behind my back," Sam says. "That's how I go so fast."

"He's out next year," someone cuts in.

Every kid gets a medal, standing up to take a bow.

"Now on to the women's division. We'll start with last place, which goes to me, Jane Austin." Applause. "I don't mind," Jane says.

At the evening awards, Oysterwoman winner struggles to don her medal.

at his sister Jen's progress. Eight-year-old Audrey McGrath emerges from the water yelling, "I've been bit by a jellyfish!" "I was bit by a jellyfish twice, and once by a crab!" yells Sam. Shedding goggles and life jacket, he runs barefoot up the hill to the house. As he mounts his bicycle, his father asks, "Where are your shoes, Sam?" A moment's thought. "I must have left them at the beach."

The family, sporting reunion T-shirts, meets again in the evening for an awards dinner of marinated, grilled chicken at Jane and Greg Austin's. George brings oysters and with them the Oysterman Final, a 10-question quiz filled with oyster trivia and brainteasers.

Jane Austin starts the awards ceremony, "Greg, we're not sure how long you'll be in the youth category—"

"Someone has to be last."

"But why does it always have to be the same person?" asks her husband.

George rings a bell to announce that Betty and Jane are the big winners of the Oysterman Final. Their prize? They get to draw up next year's quiz.

With that, everyone digs in and starts eating and most people hear, albeit faintly, Ken Austin mutter, "Wait until next year."

Family Scavenger Hunt

❖❖❖

This kind of hunt will appeal chiefly to kids, and as such it's a roundabout educational tool if the scavenger hunt is tailor-made to include obscure and less obscure family lore. Fill in your family name in the first blank, make multiple copies, and distribute them to the players.

DIRECTIONS: Find as many new members of your family as you can. If you find one who fits a question, have him or her sign the space. You may have the same person sign your form only TWICE!!! The player(s) with the most signatures will win a prize. HAPPY MEETING!!!

Find a _____ who has your birthday. _____
          FAMILY NAME

Find a _____ who has your profession. _____

Find a _____ who has a hobby you have. _____

Find a _____ you have never met before. _____

Find a _____ who has a pet you have. _____

Find a _____ who has the same number of children in their family as you.

_____

Find a _____ who was born in the same town as you. _____

Find a _____ who has the same birth order in their immediate family as you.

_____

Find a _____ who is the same age as you. _____

Find a _____ who has at least five grandchildren. _____

Find a _____ who has the most children. _____

Find a _____ who has been most recently married. _____

Find a _____ who has an unusual job. _____

Find a _____ who traveled the farthest to be here. _____

Find a _____ who came the shortest distance. _____

Find a _____ who has just graduated from high school. _____

Find a _____ who has just graduated from college. _____

Find a _____ who has just had a birthday. _____

KIDS' STRUCTURED ACTIVITIES

When we were kids, we played all summer long, taking breaks for meals, the occasional bath, and (reluctantly) bed. But kids are used to structure now. Concerned about their safety, parents keep them on a short leash, under supervision, and physical play takes place within the confines of the soccer league or gymnastics class. In cities, kids don't just stroll over to their friends' houses—they make play dates weeks in advance. And plenty of kids would rather stay home and monkey around in cyberspace than head outside and scale the monkeybars.

So while some kids at your reunion will be content simply to hang out with their cousins, others won't—and others would, if only they *knew* their cousins. Planned activities bring shy and outgoing kids together, create a shared experience, and let them know the reunion is as much about them as it is about the grown-ups gabbing away in the lawn chairs.

One adult for every eight kids should be on hand to explain and clarify the rules of the games and keep behavior in line. When forming teams, dispense with the pain of being picked last. Do away with captains altogether. Form teams by lining up kids from tallest to smallest. The first team takes the tallest and the smallest, the second team takes the next tallest and smallest, and so on. Teams are uneven in number? Who cares? If the number of boy and girl cousins is fairly equal, they may want to form into boy and girl teams.

Outdoor Games

BIRTHDAY LINEUP

Ask everyone to line up according to his or her birthday. The catch is, they're not allowed to speak. Sounds impossible? They can do it. You'll see. (Older kids can help the younger ones.) When everyone is lined up, go down the line, asking them to call out their birthdays, and test their accuracy.

OBSTACLE RACE

Get the kids themselves (or the older teenagers) to help plan the course. Here are some obstacles you could have.

- Water obstacle: Adult holds a hose so it sprays continually at one level; kids can either run through the water, duck under it, or jump over it
- Balancing act: Narrow plank or two the kids must walk along
- Slalom course: Cones or chairs around which the racers must weave
- Tire run: Running through tires laid out flat
- Crawl space: Tie an old sheet or tarp to four sturdy chairs and have the racers wriggle beneath them—warn big kids not to touch the sheet

Put the obstacles far enough apart so kids can do some real running between them. Don't include running up and down stairs as part of the race—there's nothing like a sprained ankle or a concussion to really put a damper on things.

Incorporate whatever is on the premises. If there's a pool and all the kids are swimmers, include the pool in the race. Have each kid paddle across the pool on a raft, for instance. If there's a basketball hoop, have each kid try to make a basket before proceeding on to the next obstacle, or dribble through a slalom course.

The adult in charge of the race might walk through the course to demonstrate how each of the obstacles should be handled—watching Uncle Ed wiggle through the crawl

---

STAY LOOSE

The Rumely reunion had planned a junior olympics, but those plans were jettisoned when the kids discovered a nearby lake and one another, and spent most of each day holding swimming races on their own and building a dam, fused together in happy busyness. What happened to the couple who planned the olympics? They sat back on the grass, watched, and sighed happily. While things hadn't gone as planned, things had gone exactly as everyone had hoped. So remember, don't fall in love with your activities.

---

space will be an unexpected source of entertainment. Either compile a team score or just keep track of individual times.

RELAY RACE

The more ridiculous the better! You just need two teams and a lot of enthusiasm.

- Relay course with ridiculous outfits and ridiculous stations: Kids put on flippers and goggles or snorkel masks. Run to station where they find a Ping-Pong ball hidden in shaving cream. Run with the Ping-Pong ball to sit and pop a balloon (don't use balloons near the face). Get sprayed with a hose for the length of time it takes to recite the Pledge of Allegiance or a funny sentence. Run back, still clutching the Ping-Pong ball.
- Dizzy relay: All the players take off their sneakers and sandals and throw them in a heap. About 25 feet away, the first players start—by putting their foreheads on the bottom of two baseball bat handles and circling around five times, the foreheads touching all the time. Dizzily the racers stand up and stagger to the heap of shoes, where they try to find their own pair and put them on as fast as they can to run back. The next players start the process again once the first have returned to home.
- Foot-to-foot baton pass: Mark out a track. Have a baton relay race. Each runner walks putting one foot ahead of the other—but with feet touching the entire time.

KIDS' SPORTSMANSHIP RULES

With PE classes reduced in time and number, some kids learn everything they know about sportsmanship from the NBA, the NFL, and Nike ads. A reunion is about role models, displays of good citizenship, and genuine teamwork. If a family member with sports credibility—a former high school football player, say—explains these rules, it changes the whole tenor of play.

◆ EVERYBODY PLAYS.
With the exception of grown-up games of basketball or golf, everyone should get to play in any game they want to. There are times and places where games are played in deadly earnest, but a reunion is not that time or that place.

◆ BIG KIDS LOOK AFTER LITTLE KIDS. Some kids only play sports in league situations, and have no experience with players younger and smaller than themselves. Tell your reunion kids that winning isn't everything. If there's a choice between getting to a ball and knocking over a little kid or missing the ball and missing the kid in the process, you miss the ball.

◆ NO TRASH-TALKING HERE. We don't go out to kick loser butt, we don't tell our opponents they stink in a slew of banal invectives, and we don't trash-talk ourselves—we don't curse ourselves out when we make a mistake.

Water Games

If adults are game, these classics work best with a mixture of kids and grown-ups—kids love to see the adults in their life get soaked. Because all these games involve water, it's best if everyone is in bathing suits and sandals (except for the super-competitive types, who will want the advantage of running shoes).

WATER BALLOON TOSS
Two lines of kid and adult pairs are formed, about 3 feet apart. The kid tosses the full balloon to the adult; the adult passes it back. Then everyone takes one step back, and the tosses continue, with partners eliminated when they drop or break their balloons. If all goes well, there are many unused water balloons left over with which to conduct a water balloon war.

WATER WAR
Bathing suits required. This should be the last activity, because it will degenerate into chaos. Since water balloons can hit pretty hard, it's not a good game for kids under 6. Two teams are formed. Each team is given an

equal number of water balloons. War cannot be declared until all the water balloons are prepared. There should be a 10-foot-wide zone between the teams. Guess what? They hurl water balloons at one another.

Prizes

Order lots of shiny prizes and medals from a novelty shop. For tin sheriff's badges, pirate's eyepatches by the dozen, smiley-face stickers, inexpensive beanbag animals, paper top hats, plastic leis, and other gimcracks that

THE CLASSICS

Remember when you played these games? They're probably your fondest memories of running with the pack and playing with oodles of cousins. Well, kids still love them.

◆ Wheelbarrow race

◆ Egg-in-the-spoon race (this also works with M&Ms)

◆ Three-legged race

◆ Back-to-back race (arms folded in front, kids run in pairs without separating)

◆ Telephone

◆ Dodgeball

◆ Simon says

◆ Giant step

◆ Statues

◆ Red rover

children love, contact:

Oriental Trading Company
P.O. Box 3407
Omaha, NB 68103-0407
Web site: www.oriental.com
Phone: (800) 228-2269

If a little extra expense is not too onerous, order engraved trophies and medals from sports supply companies with the family name and date of the reunion, one for each kid. And if you know for certain which kids are coming, have their names engraved on a medal and conduct a serious awards ceremony.

But distribute prizes only when all the games are over. Otherwise, kids get too caught up in the prizes to concentrate on playing. Invent lots of prize categories (ask teenagers to help), and make sure nobody is left out. If you have only one child of a certain age, for example, you can award him a medal for the "Best 7-year-old Boy" category. Reunions don't have to be schools of hard knocks. Leave that to real life.

Indoor and Rainy-Day Games

Every reunion needs to have a rainy-day contingency plan in place. As with any insurance policy, if you don't have one the catastrophe is certain to occur. A rainy-day activity should last longer than an hour, since the kids won't be able to play freely outside before and after the scheduled event.

DANCES

Dancing is the best indoor way for kids to blow off steam. For most kids, dancing involves hopping up and down, flailing arms, and occasionally wildly shaking their heads. After doing this for about an hour, they're ready to settle down to quieter play.

Rainy-day planners should have a tape deck and cassettes that studiously stay away from babyish music. No kid over the age of 3 will stay in the same room as a Barney tape, no kid over 4 will dance in public to Raffi, and no kid over 5 will be happy with music that exists primarily to instill values. Sharing is important, but as a musical motif it lacks a little something in the get-down department. Most kids like rap, rock and roll, and disco. Choose songs that sound tough and cool, are rhythmic and not sexually explicit—a sometimes elusive combination, to be sure. Those of us who lived through the 1970s never dreamed that the most-requested song from our youth would be "YMCA." But there you have it.

Here's a list of tunes kids love. You'll be a hero if you can find them all and record them on one tape.

"Hot, Hot, Hot"
"Rockin' Robin"
"Loco-Motion"
"La Bamba"
"Do You Love Me?"
"Bad"
"Friday I'm in Love"
"Electric Slide"
"ABC"
"Walking on Sunshine"
"Surfing U.S.A."
"YMCA"
"Macarena"
"16"—The Beatles
"Achy Breaky Heart"
"Hands Up"
Any kind of twist
Anything from *Saturday Night Fever*
The Limbo Song

In *freeze dancing,* everyone dances, then freezes in place when the music is cut off. Kids think it's cool to hold the strange position that their dancing trapped them in. The adult leaders can make a big show out of checking to see if the kids are moving or not, before letting the music rip. (If there has to be a real competition, kids who are caught moving three times can be told to sit out a dance. Or have kids dance with partners—freezing at the same time as a partner is more of a challenge.)

Assemble a *soul-train dance,* where the kids form an aisle and each kid takes a turn dancing through the crowd. The ultimate in photo ops.

The how-low-can-you-go song for the *limbo* is still alive and kicking. Line up the kids, shortest ones first. Don't be scrupulous in eliminating kids—keep them in as long as possible, and start eliminating only toward the end of the song. The only equipment you'll need is the time-honored broomstick, of course.

DANCE CONTEST

Get some teenagers to walk around with clipboards and judge a contest. Everyone wins, with a wide assortment of categories (let your teenage judges help invent them): "funkiest," "most energetic," "most graceful," "most different-drummer," "most horizontal," "most offbeat."

Don't forget a conga line. Gloria Estefan to the rescue! Or our new classic, the Macarena. And the Twist still works out those ants in the pants.

HAHA GAME

For some pure silliness, have all the kids lie down, with one kid's head on another's stomach, until they're all connected: head, stomach, head. Choose one kid to start. He says, "Ha." The second kid says, "Haha." The third kid says, "Hahaha." And so on. By the fifth kid, everyone has begun to laugh hysterically, feeling their laughs move the other kid's head, and another kid's head tickling their stomachs. By the end, everyone is giddy and happy.

CRACK-UP

An adult or teenage leader draws the kids around, instructs them not to smile, then tries to make them laugh. Those who crack leave the group and then try to crack up the remaining grim ones. The winner, if he can be called that, is the one left who refuses to grin. Eyes must remain open!

LINKED-ARMS RACE

Partners sit back to back, arms linked. They must stand up and run to the other end of the room and back.

COWS AND DUCKS*

Tell the group to shut their eyes and imagine they're either cows or ducks—their choice. Then ask them to move around the room (with their eyes still closed) making their animal sounds, until all the ducks are flocked together and all the cows are herded together. Keep the two groups separate, so that on opening their eyes everyone sees who are ducks and who are cows. If there are lots of kids, add more animals to choose from.

BEAUTY SHOP

What happens when you join older and younger girls together with cheap fingernail polish, a book of easy hairstyles, and a bunch of ribbons, barrettes, and elastics? For the younger kids the awesome chance to be done over by an older cousin they idolize; for the older girls a chance to play beautician, using the younger girls as models. Skip the makeup, unless you want packs of 8-year-olds running around like extras out of *Sunset Boulevard,* and park the fingernail polish on a porch or other well-ventilated spot.

Applying temporary tattoos is sure to appeal to both boys and girls—but none on the face. Those second-day tattoos do not show up well on family photos.

*Adapted from *New Games for the Whole Family,* by Dale N. LeFevre (Perigee).

MAGIC SHOW

Even if it doesn't rain, a magic show is a great idea, especially if you have six or eight kids to contend with. Buy a magic kit. Each child gets one trick to learn and perform. Show them how the trick is done and get them to practice for a few hours (or days). Paper top hats and canes (from a novelty shop) go a long way toward producing a magical effect. Have kids set a time for the show, draw up posters for it, make tickets (and see if they can sell them).

Crafts Cabin

For a weekend-long reunion, designate one room as the crafts "cabin" —a place for kids to hang out, do crafts, or have a little downtime. High-quality materials aren't important. Truth is, for kids, *quantity* is the real issue. The adult volunteer doesn't have to be in teacher mode: Kids like to show other kids how to braid lanyards or make friendship bracelets. And don't let sexist preconceptions mislead you: Boys like crafts, and most need and like quiet time, too—at least for a while.

Kids work well sitting cross-legged on the floor, so don't worry about having enough chairs. Give them paper plates to use as combination table mats and bowls for materials. Save up enough plastic containers to put crayons and markers in so that one bunch of materials is easily accessible to every four kids. At night, stow everything away in a good-sized plastic container. And, of course, keep a wastebasket visible and accessible and have everyone pick up after her- or himself.

As for assembling these supplies: Families with young kids too busy to help with other reunion events may

HIRED ENTERTAINMENT

Sometimes families have had enough doing and are in the mood for having things done for them. When this mood strikes, it's time to call in the professionals who supply fun for a living. Family members may be willing to spend a bit more for entertainment if other expenses are low. A few ideas:

◆ Carnival ride
◆ Ball pit: kids flail about amid hundreds of brightly colored plastic balls
◆ Hot-air-balloon ride (tethered to the ground)
◆ Horse or pony rides
◆ Hayride or wagon ride
◆ Fire engine
◆ Professional storyteller
◆ Fortune teller
◆ Portrait painter or caricaturist
◆ Magician
◆ Clown
◆ Handwriting analyst
◆ Other ideas appear in the Appendix, page 262.

A DOZEN COUSINS

I t's a summer morning, and a slight mist surrounds a big house on the Hudson River. Inside the house, four grown siblings, their spouses, and their dozen children are waking up. For two weeks every July, the Davidson brothers and sisters gather here, with their mother, for two weeks at Camp Highpoint. It's a way for the family to be together for an extended period of time and for young cousins to get to know each other deeply and well. The camp's structure allows the adults some time for their own interests as well. To be free to enjoy their vacation, the siblings hire a housekeeper to shop and help clean up.

Kids help grandma with the family tree cake. Left, Ben has his namesake cake and eats it too.

8:00 Breakfast The first adults downstairs set up a self-serve breakfast on the long kitchen table: boxes of cereal, pitchers of juice and

After a long dusty trail ride, a phalanx of girls splits for the pool.

milk, bowls of fruit, toast and jam, allowing all but the smallest toddlers to fix their own breakfasts. And they don't dawdle; at 8:30, the kitchen is pronounced "closed" and the cousins need little shooing to be swept out into the backyard.

9:00—11:30 Morning Outing

Each morning, the parents take turns leading one activity. Today the kids pile into cars to head to a nearby stable for riding lessons. Other days will find them visiting a llama farm, picking strawberries at a "you pick 'em" farm, and visiting caverns open to the public. The off-duty adults wave cheerfully at the cars of children as they are borne off down the driveway, then dance a jig at the prospect of a quiet read in the hammock or a round of golf.

Two hours later, the kids return, sweaty and dusty from riding, ready to hop into the pool. Two parents play lifeguard as the other parents assemble lunch, which is eaten on the porch.

12:30 Lunch

Like breakfast, it's self-serve. Most of it is finger

Family photo albums provide food for thought during quiet time after lunch.

food and kid friendly: There are raw vegetables and cut-up fruit, a plate of string cheese, bowls of buttered pasta, two jars of peanut butter, raisins, and stacks of sliced bread. The variety of

Lunch break on the porch of the Highpoint homestead.

choices ensures that even the pickiest eater can find something to eat.

1:00—2:00 Quiet Hour

The younger kids nap while the older ones engage in quiet play: cards, Lego,

drawing, reading. The drowsy summer sounds—buzz of flies, birdsongs, the crunch of gravel beneath a faraway car, water running, muted voices, leaves rustling in a light breeze—give the large house a sleepy, peaceful aura.

2:00 Swim

2:45—4:00 Crafts

Batteries recharged, the kids head for the crafts center set up in the barn. Each afternoon, one of the parents sets up and oversees a crafts project. One time they made boats. The kids found discarded pieces of wood at the lumberyard and nailed, glued, and painted them before turning them over to adults to be sealed with polyurethane. They then attached sails made of

Cousins proudly display their just-completed family trees.

cut-up old sheets, and named their boats. The next day they took the boats down to the river for a launch.

Another time each child drew a map of the house and grounds. First they walked around the house and its surroundings trying to conceptualize the place, then returned to the barn to re-create the house, various landmarks, and outbuildings on paper. The maps were then "laminated" with clear contact paper and used as place mats for the rest of camp.

One mother likes to lead the kids down a trail through the woods near the riverbank for a nature walk, encouraging them to look closely at nature.

Today the kids work in a light breeze on the porch, making family trees, understanding how a family fits together.

5:30 Kids' Dinner

A simple dinner for the kids is served at a table just outside the kitchen door. Like breakfast and lunch, it is self-serve. Dessert means ice cream cones on the lawn, or on this special occasion, a family tree cake marked with everybody's name.

7:00—8:00 Bath and Bedtime

Twilight throws long shadows across the lawn, and the sky over the river takes on the deep azure of evening as baths are run. Clean-faced, barefoot kids appear in nightshirts and pjs on the porch for a last gasp of family time before bed.

8:00 Parents' Time Each

evening, one set of parents takes a turn cooking simple grilled meats for dinner. "The kids may still be awake," says one parent, "but unless they're sick, we ignore 'em. This is grown-up time. Our time."

Tonight, the fathers are away on business and the mothers eat lightly. Soon, a yoga instructor will lead them through stretches in what's become a ritual whenever the men are away. Later, while sipping wine on the porch, they talk quietly about family, kids, schools, husbands, career decisions. The women of the family share their lives in the soft summer night.

The women in the family share dinner, wine, and thoughts in the early evening.

TODDLER CORNER

Toddlers are not good at games that involve rules, competition, and right and wrong ways of doing things. Attempting to involve them in races is similar to running mice through mazes—they get to the end, but they're not sure how or why. Still, they love to be together and among older kids. Select a shady, spacious area for the toddler corner, setting out large sheets or blankets for toddlers and their parents on which to sit, change diapers, or (dream on!) nap.

Have some equipment and games appropriate for 2-to-3-year-olds.

◆ WATER PLAY: Fill up kiddy swimming pools or baby bathtubs with water. Have lots of things to sail, float, and pour from: plastic bottles with sprays and spouts, buckets, boats, bath toys, whisks and eggbeaters, funnels, sponges.

◆ BUBBLES: Use this recipe for homemade bubbles:

1 cup dishwashing liquid
3 cups water
½ cup corn syrup

Let sit for a few hours ahead of time. Pour into large, shallow pans, such as roasting pans, and blow bubbles from berry baskets, wands made of pipe cleaners, plastic six-pack holders, straws taped together (breathe *out*, kids!).

◆ BEACH BALLS and other big, lightweight balls

◆ CORNSTARCH GLOP: If mess is no problem and the kids can be hosed off easily, mix cornstarch and water for a mesmerizing tactile sensation—is it a fluid? A solid? Wet? Or dry?

2 cups cornstarch
1 cup water

Mix in cake or roasting pans and supply kids with spoons and whisks.

◆ BOARD BOOKS for quiet time

be happy to bring their own existing supplies as their contribution. For a weekend-long reunion, where kids will be running around outside most of the time, it makes sense to make do with what can be scared up at home. A longer reunion might justify a greater financial investment.

Basic Crafts Supplies
• Washable markers
• Crayons
• Old newspapers (for covering tables and floors)
• Glue in small containers
• Colored felt
• Pom-poms

- Googly eyes
- Popsicle sticks
- Stickers
- Lanyards
- Doilies
- Big pads of recycled newsprint (or other inexpensive large, blank paper)
- Construction paper
- Kids' scissors
- Watercolors
- Play-Doh and plastic knives, little rolling pins, cookie cutters. Play-Doh is a known therapeutic agent: It calms the nerves better than Valium.
- Age-appropriate jigsaw puzzles
- Mad Libs
- Two decks of cards
- Coloring, follow-the-dot, and maze books
- Board games

One structured crafts project should be enough each day of the reunion. Two of the most engaging crafts projects, a Kid's Family Tree and Kid's Family Books, are described on pages 109 and 226–227.

Your Family's United States

Trace a good-sized map of the United States onto tracing paper and make enough copies for all the kids. Bring a real map and ask kids to find where they live and mark it on the map with a pushpin. Have a list of where all the family members have come from, as well as other significant family places: original family home in the United States, location of Grand- mother May's farm. On their blank maps, kids mark all the significant locations with a star (or other symbol) and the family's name. Have them give their maps titles, then laminate the maps with clear contact paper and use them for place mats.

Kids' Own Name Tags

Take a 2-by-2-inch square of oak tag or thin wood with a hole drilled through. Have the kids write their names and draw designs around them and color. Take a lanyard and lead it through the punched hole twice. String beads on each side of the lanyard. Tie, and wear.

Family Coat of Arms

Encourage adults to contribute to this project, talking about heraldic symbols and exploring what qualities your family is proud of. Then have the kids make up their own heraldic symbol. Cut the shields from oak tag, then string the completed shields along silver ribbon and hang them up as decorations.

EXTRACURRICULAR OUTINGS

A weekend reunion needs a relief valve: a morning or afternoon kept free for individuals to cut loose from the herd for a couple of hours. In an era when "dysfunctional" is the first adjective that springs to mind when the word "family" is spoken, a little steam released from the pressure cooker cannot possibly go amiss.

The reunion organizers should have on hand a few suggested activities families can pursue in groups, independently, or not at all. A profusion of activities will act as a lure to those wary relatives who are worried they'll be stuck too much with family. Never mind that they'll probably enjoy being stuck—they won't realize that beforehand. The person who chooses to spend the afternoon lying down with a good book should do so without even a soupçon of guilt—and return later in fighting shape.

Make it easy for reunion goers to plan independent jaunts. Get maps, brochures, and listings of tourist attractions from the chamber of commerce, tourist board, or resort management. Photocopy those you can't get copies of, and include them in registration packets, at the welcome station, or on a central family bulletin board. Much of this information might be alluded to in the reunion letters.

Track down less-publicized commercial destinations and activities such as tubing, whitewater rafting, great hikes or walks, fishing spots—and where to go for a fishing license and rental equipment—caves and waterfalls, boat, ski, and life preserver rentals for waterskiing, and pontoon boat rental.

Other popular destinations for group or individual trips include: factory tours, vineyard tours and wine tastings, unique architectural sites (Frank Lloyd Wright house, for example), museums, and baseball games—both major and minor league.

If the reunion is being held in a place with family history, include caravan-style tours (packs of cars) of significant family spots.

HOMESTEAD TOUR

Joan Sparrow led a tour of historical Rumely family sites, zooming around La Porte, Indiana, showing family members "the great brick monstrosities from the 1800s where my grandparents lived" and the more modest houses where she and other Rumely cousins grew up, ending up at the cemetery where many Rumelys are buried. She had planned to give only one tour, but due to overwhelming demand, she gave three.

In narrating the tour, Joan included as many vivid physical details as she could. "To humanize it for the younger ones, I showed them the ice pond where we used to skate and described walking home bundled up in my woolen clothes, desperately having to go to the bathroom. The look in the eyes of the little girls told me that they had mentally followed me there, onto the pond and into the past. The human details are what capture the imagination."

THE TEENAGER QUESTION

The fact is, for a weekend reunion you might do well to feature one off-campus, wallet-soaking activity directed strictly toward teenagers. No, not a trip to the Boston Pops, a planetarium, or a science museum, no matter how interactive and inventive those might be. Don't think "good for you," think "fun for you"—somewhere they can pay too much money to shriek, flirt, see and be seen, and eat french fries. Some awesome venues might be:

- Theme park
- Water park
- Roller rink that rents Rollerblades
- Virtual-reality entertainment center
- Theme restaurant with $12 hamburgers

And tubing, whitewater rafting, waterskiing or sailboarding, and a trip to a beach with really good surf are universal favorites (and ideal for shrieking, flirting, seeing and being seen—and you can stop for fries on the way back).

Sad but true, a sacrificial adult must accompany them—to drive, hold money at the water park, glare down the grown men ogling the nieces, find lost souls, prohibit smoking, and (metaphorically, at least) hold the hand of the shy 13-year-old cousin from Baton Rouge. Each kid should write down the family name of the reunion and the name, address, and phone number of the place where the reunion is being held. (If they're all in bathing suits at a water park, have them commit to memory the name and place where the reunion is being held.) Set a time and spot for everyone to meet, and mention it again and again, fiercely. The time-honored technique of "putting the fear of the Lord" in the kids still works—most of the time.

EVENING EVENTS

If during the day the family was engaged in classic entertainment activities, by night it turns inward, action gives way to reflection, and the family gathers around in an even tighter, more cohesive circle. The games played now by the family are games about the family.

Here are a few games that might be played over dinner or after dinner.

WHO HE?
Baby pictures are posted with a sheet of paper below each one. Everyone writes in a guess as to who the baby in the picture is, and the person with the most correct guesses wins.

FAVORITE THINGS
When Priscilla Dunhill convened her family for a reunion, she knew one thing—"that we wanted to get to know each other below the surface," she says. "So I asked each family

member to bring an object that really meant something to them, that they valued and loved, and to explain what it was, and why and how it was special." A niece brought a flute, while Priscilla herself brought her "hotpot," a box of recipes she's been collecting most of her life—a rich, textured, aromatic connection with her own and her family's past. The beauty of Favorite Things is that for a time the focus shifts off the family identity as a whole and onto each individual, and how she or he is different and unique in the family.

FAMILY TIME CAPSULE

Ask family members to bring small items that are somehow representative of their families. Have them explain what they've brought and

---

AWARDS NIGHT

In addition to awards for competitive games, which are usually given out at the evening event, award prizes for other categories. These can be opened to nominations before dinner, with voting conducted by secret ballot or by a select group of judges. Feel free to tamper with results in order to ensure that the awards are spread around. And create categories with specific winners in mind: greatest freckles, nicest smile of anyone missing more than three teeth. Categories should be as far-reaching and ridiculous as possible, and winners might be requested to make a short acceptance speech. Some other categories might be:

◆ Best sense of humor

◆ Best hair

◆ Reddest hair

◆ Thickest southern accent

◆ Most closely resembling a surfer dude

◆ Loudest sneeze

◆ Longest and shortest hair, boy and girl division

◆ Greatest number of children

◆ Ms./Mr. Congeniality

◆ Most coordinated

◆ Best teeth

◆ Best French accent

◆ Sweetest pair of eyes, male and female (ties are permitted)

◆ Best laugh

◆ Best whistler

◆ Longest married

◆ Most newly wed

◆ Greatest number of descendants

◆ Family member we wouldn't mind being trapped in an elevator with

"My cousins and I all grew up in the same neighborhood. When we went back home for a wedding, we realized how much we missed one another. Cousins are so great. When I was going through my most awkward teenage phase, cousins always made me feel like I belonged. And it's still true. I never have to explain myself—they just accept me as I am. That's why we had to get this reunion together—I really needed to 'play' with my cousins again.**"**

—Mary Brockmyre
Cambridge, Massachusetts

why, and, one at a time, drop their items into a decorated shoe box (or some other archivally suspect but easily accessible container). Include a message indicating what this time capsule is, and where and when it was assembled, in the not unlikely event that it gets put into an attic and forgotten for decades. Seal ceremoniously with sealing wax after closing.

FAMILY TRIVIA GAME

Pass out index cards before dinner, and ask everyone to submit one question about a family member—a question they themselves can answer. Those who answer the most questions (not submitted by themselves, of course) win.

Talent Shows and Fun Nights

Talent shows are a staple of reunion schedules, and for good reason. They offer a significant way for families to celebrate not only the broad family identity but individual talent as well. Of course, a family talent show would not be complete without those moments of pure silliness when family members venture to put onstage their complete *lack* of talent, emboldened only by an uninhibited sense of fun. But there should also be moments when the young violinist or yellow-belt-karate-sensei-to-be can put the results of long hours of practice to the test before an attentive and sympathetic audience.

Talent shows can be highly structured, with printed programs and rehearsed acts, or loosey-goosey affairs with family members hopping up spontaneously to perform. Some families call them fun nights—you don't need talent, but you do need a sense of fun. Talent shows can be a salmagundi of talent, jokes, family stories, toddlers singing along to a Barney tape, 5-year-olds acting out fairy tales, adults demonstrating ballroom dancing, and skits put on by teenagers imitating the behavior of their uncles, aunts, and parents. (Having kids act the parts of adult family members, imitating their idiosyncrasies and speaking voices, is guaranteed hilarity.)

The talent show coordinator

can tack a note onto the reunion correspondence or send out a separate letter, giving a sense of what kind of performances the talent show is looking for. A theme might be suggested as a jumping off point—a reenactment of some family event in the past, perhaps.

The coordinator can also encourage skits from the young cousins—the benefit of which is that the kids spend the afternoon writing and rehearsing their skits in secret, the ultimate in bonding activities. Kids can be divided into four groups—girls aged 6 through 12, boys aged 6 through 12, teenage girls and teenage boys—so that nobody is left out in the cold. Each group can then spend the afternoon spying on the others, which is always exciting.

The night of the talent show, the coordinator should put the acts into some kind of order—alternating young with old, serious with silly. Any special requests by the performers—lighting needs, a tape deck—should be made well in advance of the performance time.

Dance

For some families, no party is complete without dancing. The Robinson Roots annual banquet has a keynote speaker and is fairly formal, so the family holds a *disco-style dance* afterward so that the younger people can get down. "You have to give them their time,

too," Doretha Davis, one of the organizers, points out. "You want them to come back next year."

Or hold a *multigenerational dance,* with a deejay spinning tunes from the Big Bands days and the Beatles to the disco era and the Macarena. Recommendations for deejays can come from the manager of the reunion site, the chamber of commerce, or the local Yellow Pages—they're not cheap, though.

Square dancing, contra dancing, and *line dancing* are great for all generations, if you have the space and people, and a family reunion is a nonthreatening place for beginners to step out and have a few foolish-looking moments before getting the hang of it all. For square dancing, calculate that four couples form one square, and at least two or three squares are needed for a good dance. Callers can be found through the International Caller's Association Caller-lab (see Appendix, page 262) or through Western-wear and square dance attire shops. Check with the country music bars in the area for teachers and music—or there might be a ready, willing, and able family member who can lead everyone through the steps.

Family Campfire

Because beaches and forests have recently become more tightly regulated than in the past, campfires have become almost exotic to today's kids.

Families holding reunions in rural areas shouldn't pass up the chance to hold at least one campfire if they're legally allowed to. But parents who fondly recall nights spent singing around the campfire shouldn't count on that aspect of their memories materializing again. Kids don't sing as much in school as they used to, and they aren't as familiar with the old standards. So if you are planning a campfire songfest, have someone bring copies of the lyrics to get less-than-enthusiastic family members to join in. These days, trading jokes works better as a group activity—each family can come prepared with a handful.

Then there are the essential marshmallows. Collect sticks for roasting when it's still light and stock up with marshmallows—at least eight per person; grown-ups eat far more than they will ever own up to.

And have the makings for s'mores: marshmallows roasted over the fire and squished between chocolate bars and graham crackers for a sandwich so good you'll want s'more.

While kids may feel too sophisticated for singing around the fire, they are still susceptible to ghost stories. They're so unused to being outdoors at night that even those raised on action movies will be easily creeped out. If there's a great adult storyteller in your midst, have him make up a spooky tale. Or get the kids into the act by telling progressive ghost stories. An adult can kick off the story by setting the premise in a quiet, spooky voice. "One dark and stormy night, long ago . . ." Then each kid, holding a flashlight under his chin, picks up the tale, stopping at a suitably cliffhanging moment for his neighbor to continue.

8

THE MAIN EVENT

Openers
Evening Banquet
Family Worship
Business Meeting

Like a wedding, a great movie, or a symphony, a reunion requires some orchestration and a bit of stagecraft to produce those unforgettable moments that seem to have arisen spontaneously. With just the right amount of planning, those moments will blossom naturally, allowing the family spirit to soar. A reunion should open on a warm, welcoming note and close on a major chord, the strings swelling to a crescendo. If the family ends up laughing and crying at the same time, the reunion can be considered a success. The truth is, stagecraft works. It ensures that the players are all on stage at the proper time, that the doors to the noisy street are shut, and that the plaintive rendering of "Amazing Grace"—or any other tune that can produce tears in 20 seconds or less—is summoned up at the critical juncture.

But how much of a production should a reunion be? You don't want the family marching lockstep in overscheduled pursuit of fun, but there should be enough structured activities to provide ways for newcomers to feel at home, for young and old to bond, and for those who used to know each other well to revive their intimacy. The best family reunion blueprint builds on the sense of belonging that comes with shared activity, while also providing for unscheduled time in which families and individuals can drift off for a while on their own.

Sample Timetable

As for any big party, the day's events should be set out chronologically in a timetable, noting what needs to be done when (and by whom) both behind the scenes and center stage, in those activities involving all the reunion goers. Post the timetable on the first reunion day to remind reunion goers and volunteers what's ahead. Here's a sample timetable for a one-day backyard barbecue reunion:

8:00 A.M. Get ice (Rob)

9:00 A.M. Set out basket with bug spray, sunscreen, next to sign-in guest book on table under tent (Sara)

9:30 A.M. Put beverages on ice in coolers and buckets (Rob, Mark)
Put up sign pointing to parking area (Rob)

10:00 A.M. Family arrives

11:00 A.M. Relay races (Jim, Patty)

11:30 A.M. Fire up grill (Mark)
Put out lunch things (Ellis, Sara, Jonathan)

12:00 P.M. Serve lunch

12:30 P.M. Toasts (Mark leads)

1:00 P.M. Clean up after lunch (Jonathan and family)

1:00 P.M. Set up make-your-own sundaes (Sara, Ellis)

2:00 P.M. Group photo (photographer Alex Martin 555-1212). Everyone attends!

3:00 P.M. Hike to swimming hole (Jim and Ellis)

3:00 P.M. Set up cards and games, photo albums (Sara)

5:00 P.M. Business meeting (Uncle Dan)

6:00 P.M. Set up make-your-own sandwiches (Ellis, Sara, Maggie)

7:00 P.M. Cleanup and goodbyes —or lingering on

Troubleshooting

Whether you've reserved a block of rooms at a hotel, worked out a discount rate for a hospitality suite, or hired a professional caterer, if you've followed the fundamental financial rule of reunion planning—*underestimate attendance when there's financial risk, overestimate attendance when there's not*—many anxieties can be avoided.

But say, despite your best efforts, the number of attendees falls short. If your party is close to the agreed-on minimum, the sales manager may let you squeak by and qualify for the discount.

Similarly, if the reunion has ordered 40 dinners at a discounted rate and only 35 people show up, it may be less expensive to pay for five additional discounted dinners than to pay for 35 dinners at standard rate.

The family should be told from the start that the discount rate is contingent on an agreed-on minimum,

SAMPLE REUNION PROGRAMS

Here is how a few families whose reunions are profiled in this book structured their reunions.

Hubbard Cousins Day

FRIDAY NIGHT: Nephews and cousins set up tents
and tables on the lawn

SATURDAY: Family arrives 11:00 A.M.
Lunch
Swimming
Group photo
Daiquiris
Dinner

Austin-Kenney Family Triathlon

FRIDAY NIGHT: Carbo-loading training meal
(a.k.a. spaghetti supper)

SATURDAY: Triathlon in the morning
Lunch—in a collapsed heap
Attendance at minor-league baseball game
Awards dinner
Flashlight tag (kids under 14 only)

Raspberry Family Reunion

FRIDAY NIGHT: Arrival: Fish fry and storytelling by the elders

SATURDAY: Enactment of "Along the Trail"
Cemetery visit
Picnic and barbecue
Talent show

SUNDAY: Sunday worship
Business meeting

Chien Family Reunion

FRIDAY:	**Social time:** Find a partner (each person assigned a partner to get to know)
	Dinner
	Welcome gathering: Partner introductions
	Icebreakers
	Family tree presentation
SATURDAY:	Breakfast
	Beach time: 3-legged and 4-legged races
	Tug-of-war
	Hula
	Egg toss
	Kites and Frisbees
	Lunch
	Talent afternoon: Girls' performance
	Under 10 riddles circle
	Family talent show
	Free time: Pickup games, board games, chess, mahjong, walk on the beach, nap
	Dinner
	Tribute to the family: Stories about grandmother, video by Li-Shin
	More games
	Meeting of the next family reunion organizing committee
SUNDAY:	Breakfast
	Family spiritual time
	Sunday prayers
	Group pictures
	Reflections
	Announcements
	Lunch
	Golf, tennis, or tea
	Farewell dinner at Chinese restaurant
	Thoughts and wrap-up

and the risk of paying the full rate will be shared by the entire group.

But in the event that luck, the weather, flu season, or the hotel manager has not been on your side, there is a place to turn—the contingency fund. To bolster the fund and make up the shortfall, hold a raffle with a 50/50 pot (get kids to help with the raffle by selling tickets, picking numbers, and announcing the winner) or an auction with prizes donated by the group (time-shares in condos, computer expertise). (See page 27 for other fund-raising events.)

THE SET-UP

DECORATING WITH FAMILY BANNERS

Use an old sheet or canvas and regular housepaints. Keep the letters and decorations simple, but the bigger and brighter, the better. Poke holes in all four corners of the banner, leaving at least 6 inches of border, and stitch around the holes so they won't tear. Put clothesline or twine through each hole and hang your banner from two trees or on the wall of the banquet room.

Make a paper banner. Get a roll of butcher paper, poster paints, and old T-shirts for the kids to paint in, and hold a prereunion painting party for nearby relatives. The adults can outline the lettering of the family name while the kids paint inside the letters and decorate around the words.

FAMILY TREES

This symbol is as much a familiar and beloved emblem at reunions as a turkey is at Thanksgiving. Before the event, have the reunion artist paint a family tree and pin name tags on branches where the names belong. As people arrive and pick up their name tags, they can locate themselves in the family at the same time. Or have someone at the ready with a Polaroid camera, taking photos of the family members as they arrive. Glue the pictures onto the family tree in the appropriate spots—a great point of reference for the rest of the reunion.

FLAGS

If your relatives come from different countries, get inexpensive flags of all the countries of origin and string them along the site's perimeter. If you're celebrating one nationality in particular, that country's consulate may lend you a large flag for the occasion. (See Appendix, page 262, for a company that supplies flags.)

PHOTOS OF ANCESTORS

Photocopy or computer scan photos of the old family home or the great-grandparents who first came to America; cut them out and glue them each to a piece of poster board or thin cardboard. Use squares of foam board as stands for the photos, and put one on each dinner table. Or enlarge photographs to poster size, glue to cardboard, and prop up at the welcome table.

ORGANIZER TIPS

For the reunion organizer, the day before the reunion is like the day before any big party, with much rushing around to organize the final details. But that kind of headless-chicken activity doesn't really get a lot done. Careful planning can mean the difference between a cheerful, relaxed reunion host and a frazzled wreck. Here are some ways to make sure you can join in the activities and have fun at the reunion.

• Assemble reunion packets at home, or at the reunion site, a day or morning before the reunion (see pages 184–185).

• If the reunion is being held at a hotel, arrive a day early to oversee setting up the hospitality suite and decorations. Ask for bulletin boards on which to post photographs or easels to display the reunion schedule, and set up these displays. Give reunion packets to the registration desk for distribution to family members as they check in.

• Get the cash box and change ready for the T-shirt table.

• Schedule time to coddle yourself in the morning. If the reunion is being held at your home and the house is filled with people, you may need a quiet tea and toast in your bedroom before going out to join the fray.

• Abandon thoughts of perfection; they are not compatible with life in general and family life in particular. Perfection may be achieved at weddings, but only at huge financial expense for unsustainably brief photogenic periods of time.

• Never refuse an offer of help. Even if it's faint or halfhearted, act as though it were made in good faith, and accept it.

• Set aside specific blocks of time to mingle and hang out like everyone else and specific blocks of "working" time. From 5:00 to 6:00 P.M., for example, spend time making sure the grills are being lit and the tables are set for dinner.

• Remember that family relationships come first. Sure, it's important to try to keep the reunion on schedule and on track. But if you're having an important heart-to-heart with an elderly aunt and your watch tells you it's time to bring out the strawberry shortcake, stay and talk. The family can have dessert anytime, but you can't always have this conversation with your great-aunt.

"With regular holidays, in addition to exhausting preparation, we're all struggling with huge expectations of how it ought to be. But with a family reunion, we're not struggling toward an end product. The reunion itself is the product. There's no timetable, for example, for getting all the presents unwrapped. At a reunion, from the moment we enter the door, the way it is is the way it's supposed to be."

—Mary Guterson
Bainbridge Island, Washington

PHOTO DISPLAYS

Pictures of ancestors draw family like magnets. Ask everyone to bring *copies* of favorite old photos. Post the photographs on the wall, a bulletin board brought to the site, or a piece of foam board. (Check with your hotel or resort for guidelines about posting items.) Set apart an "Identity Crisis" corner, posting photos of people whose identities are, for the moment, unknown. Keep pen and paper nearby on which folks can write any clues to the identity of the subjects. (For a game involving old photographs, see page 172.)

FLOWERS

A few bouquets always boost the sense of occasion up a notch. If the reunion is being held outdoors, cut flowers from the garden or pick lovely but short-lived wildflowers, steering clear of Queen Anne's lace, goldenrod, and other pollen bombs. Vases aren't necessary: little bottles, creamers, and gravy boats all work fine. If the reunion is held at a hotel or conference center, buy cut flowers at a nearby florist or supermarket, bring your own vases, and arrange bouquets yourselves, saving money on the cost of a florist.

BALLOONS

If there are lots of kids—or grown-ups with a kid's idea of partying—balloons start the festivities off on just the right note. You can enlist kids to blow up and tie balloons on the day of the reunion. Better yet, rent a helium gas canister, which an adult should man. No Donald Duck imitations, please.

Reunion Packets

Printed materials are a family reunion's goody bag—what people take away with them, tangible memories of the time spent together, not to mention a reward for having made it through. But the packet should also be the on-site road map of the reunion itself, particularly for a weekend-long affair. The reunion packets, one to a family, can be picked up on registering at the reunion site. The packets might include the following items.

• Reunion schedule that lists the time and place of events that everyone should attend—for example, the group photo

• Reminder to volunteers of what activity they've volunteered for and when and where they should go beforehand

• Family directory (see pages 84–87)

• List of where all the family members are staying

• Map of the area and information about nearby tourist attractions

• List of nearby places of worship (provided by the resort, chamber of commerce, or visitors' bureau) and times of services

• Family group sheet to update

• Request for family news to be announced at the reunion

• T-shirts ordered and paid for

The reunion packet might take the form of folders with pockets, manila envelopes, tote or shopping bags (ask the convention or visitors' bureau if it can supply them).

Welcome Station

Whether it's a folding table in a public park or a hospitality suite at a resort hotel, every reunion needs a welcome station. Post two or three family members there exclusively to greet the family, as well as to let everyone know what's coming up next and which direction they should go in.

At a hotel or resort, the registration desk should direct reunion goers to the welcome station, but all essential reunion information should also be left at the desk.

The welcome station might be furnished with a guest book to be signed by each family and including addresses and children's names; a family memorabilia table, where family photos and genealogical information can be displayed; a schedule of reunion events; directories and family books; a family tree; any items to be sold as keepsakes, such as T-shirts, mugs, umbrellas, or cookbooks. If folks have come a long way, it's nice to greet them with cold drinks, coffee, cookies, or other refreshments.

NAME TAGS

Innocuous as they may seem, name tags can be a matter of controversy. After all, family members are *supposed* to know one another. But if you have more than 50 people in one place, chances are half won't know the other half. And the fact that family members tend to look alike makes it all the trickier. But there are ways to make the name tag game a little easier.

• Let people fill out their own name tags so they can let others know what they want to be called.

• If your reunion is being held at a site where other gatherings are also in progress, print the family surname on all tags so family members can introduce themselves in the elevators or on the grounds.

• Encase name tags in plastic so that they can be used the second day.

• If a lot of family members have the same name, ask people to include their hometowns on their name tags: Jim Miller, Austin, Texas; Jim Miller, Cedar Rapids, Iowa.

ICEBREAKERS

A family reunion has a unique social landscape. It includes total strangers, faces that seem faintly familiar, and faces that belong to your all-too-familiar brothers. You're supposed to be at ease and at home with all of them, but in fact it's sometimes harder to talk with relatives than with strangers at a cocktail party; after all, you're supposed to *remember* what they do.

Of course, a hard-core group will know everyone, and for them the landscape is easy to navigate. But why should everyone know everyone else? Families change all the time. People die or marry, kids grow up, and distant relatives are—well, distant. At a successful reunion, even the shiest member should end up feeling that

EMERGENCY ESSENTIALS

Wherever the reunion is held, keep on hand a first-aid kit with these basic supplies:

Antihistamine
Nonaspirin pain reliever
  (children's and adults')
Antacid
Digital thermometer
Tweezers (for tick and bee-stinger
  removal)
Antibiotic ointment with analgesic
  capability
Moist towelettes
2- and 3-inch gauze bandages
Adhesive tape
Scissors
Assorted Band-Aids
Itch-relief gel or lotion
Sunscreen
Sunburn spray
Insect repellent
Ace bandages
Syrup of ipecac (use only as directed by poison control center)
Small sewing kit with safety pins

Keep clear, typed instructions near every phone on how to call for emergency. The instructions should also be kept in a zip-lock bag in the first-aid kit. The instructions should be labeled FOR EMERGENCY HELP and should include:

• Name of house's owner or name of facility, address, and telephone number

• Local emergency numbers, in areas where 911 service is not available

• Name and number of nearest hospital, with driving instructions

• Name and number of local physician and pediatrician

• Name and number of 24-hour pharmacy

• Poison control center number

Renting a house for the reunion? Ask your rental agent or landlord for this information.

the reunion, and the whole family, belongs as much to her as to the most well-known cousin in the bunch.

Icebreakers are well named. They break up the frozen social landscape, so that shy types are sent toward big, solid clusters of relatives, cousins spin off into new formations, and old familiar groups are broken up and re-formed. Following are some icebreakers that are known to work.

THE KNOT

The Knot is a great icebreaker. Form groups of six to eight people. Each person takes the hands of two other people. It doesn't matter if the other people are nearby or across the circle, as long as the hands belong to two different people. Once everyone has done this, the group will be in a complete tangle. The goal is to disentangle the knot without releasing any hands. "Our family got disentangled in 30 seconds," says Mark Pryor, "but when I did this with a group of people I didn't know, it took us 15 minutes. The game says a lot about how we all work together, how we operate on a subconscious level and fall into roles, delegating and taking charge—and we realize that roles are not always so bad."

Consider forming new groups once all the groups are disentangled, to see if the next unknotting will be improved by wisdom gained from the first experience.

BIRTH ORDER

Ask everyone to group themselves with others who are the oldest, youngest, middle, or only child in their immediate family. Once the groups are formed, ask each one to settle on the best advantage and worst disadvantage of being that person in the birth order. Each group should send a spokesperson to the microphone with their answers. (The 8-year-olds will discover that they have plenty in common with the 48-year-olds and the 88-year-olds on these matters.)

LIMERICKS

Have people break into small groups —by birthdays, astrological signs, favorite colors, or any other grouping category. But don't let people group themselves or you'll have favorite cousins drawn together by gravitational familiarity. Each group gets pads, pencils, and an index card with the first line of a limerick about the family: "There once was a family named Dolan..." The group has to complete the limerick. Kids are as good as grown-ups at limerick writing, and unlikely teams produce the best results. When all the limericks are completed, each group sends one person to the microphone to read theirs. If a group is prolific enough to write more than one, all the better.

LIFE STORIES

For groups numbering fewer than 50, ask everyone, kids too, to walk around the room until the leader tells them to stop. Have people form pairs with the person nearest to them (but only if that person isn't already well known to them). The pairs have one minute to tell each other enough about themselves for one to be able to introduce the other to the group at large: "This is Jim Miller, from Lubbock, Texas. He owns a grain-feed business and has a son and a daughter. His wife is named Sarah, and they are both active in Boy Scouts." The pairs create an unlikely but real bond that lasts for the rest of the reunion.

THE EVENING BANQUET

For a weekend reunion, Friday evening's events should be low-key. After the stresses of long-distance travel, family members have to absorb the culture shock of being with the extended family. It takes a while to process the welcome sensation of being treated by masses of people as though you're a kid again, and accept the unbelievable reality that your youngest cousin is looking downright matronly. Friday is all about orienting oneself to the fact of the reunion. Nobody will be in the mood to dress up or be especially eloquent. Save all that for Saturday night.

Many families hold banquets or semiformal dinners on Saturday. In deciding whether your family should go that route or not, the organizers might canvass the relatives. Does the family want to spend more for a somewhat formal event? If so, do people want to include the kids—or hire baby-sitters for a parallel kids'

dinner and pajama party? Some families find that having one event that excludes kids gives parents a breather, as well as a chance to bond with their cousins—not to mention with each other. But other families want the kids to be involved in a formal affair to see how it's done; the reunion serves as role model.

The family banquet night, whether held in a hotel, at a restaurant, or on the reunion grounds, is the time to stop and reflect on family changes. In other words, taking stock of the family stock. Now's the time for the master of ceremonies to take the mike and set the tone of the event. With his natural sensitivity and grace, he communicates the rites of passage news. Obviously, it takes more than a simple announcement to bring a newcomer into the family or acknowledge a major life change. But you have to start somewhere, and formal announcements—formal in the sense of commanding a climate both structured and calm enough that family members can listen appreciatively and respectfully to family news—is a good place to start.

What's worth announcing? Births and weddings, graduations and new jobs, paid-off mortgages and quitting smoking. Obviously, as long as everyone is together, make all the reunion announcements now, as well—where the fishing trip will meet and when, what time the worship service will be held. But announce the mundane stuff before the deep, rich stuff of life. You want to finish the announcements on a spirited high note.

• Most families announce their news at the banquet, where there is the greatest chance of everyone being present.

• Don't believe teenagers who claim to be indifferent or opposed to the prospect of their news being broadcast to the family at large. To teenagers, fame is close to godliness.

• You may want to acknowledge family members who have died since the last reunion (or in the past few years). Have other family members vet the list to make sure no names have been left out.

• Introduce those who've recently joined the family: babies, stepkids and their parents, spouses.

• And absolutely introduce and cheer the oldest family member at the reunion. Here's your future and your past all in one person. Celebrate him or her—this dear, fragile person who is at the same time demonstrably the toughest of the lot.

Once the ritual of the evening banquet is over, the family often adjourns for fun and games—talent shows, memory nights, dancing, or family campfire. (See Chapter Seven.)

SPIRITUAL ROOTS: FAMILY WORSHIP

By its very nature, a family reunion is a natural venue for spiritual expression. Reunions often come about when a family begins to acknowledge an awareness of life's transience and wants to celebrate the continuity of the human spirit through the generations. We attend reunions to be with our elders while we still can, and there comes a time during any reunion when we sit back and scan the group, and realize—suddenly—whom we have lost since the last time we were all together.

Reunions are about keeping spirit alive and thinking about what we value most, and transferring those values to our children. At some reunions a time is set aside when everyone gathers together and reaches way down, spiritually. It can be during a family meal when the whole family pauses to say grace or to honor the ancestors who made our lives (and this gathering) possible.

Many families share deep spiritual bonds. Attending a special religious service during the reunion strengthens that bond as the family prays together and commemorates those loved ones who have recently passed away.

In other families there may be a wide range of spiritual practices, and any structured religious event should bear in mind the varying beliefs of all the members. Here are some ways families have acknowledged their spiritual feelings at reunions:

The reunion is opened and closed with a family prayer—sometimes while the family is standing, clasping hands. Grace is said at each meal by a different family member.

An informal memorial service is held to honor family members who have recently passed away. Everyone

SPIRITUAL ROOTS

THE ROBINSON FAMILY

What: *Weekend classic*

Who: *Members of Robinson Roots, a family organization, originally from South Carolina*

Where: *Conference center in the Northeast*

Number of Participants: *85*

Unofficial Motto: *"The family that prays together stays together."*

Family Trait: *Rising to the occasion.*

It's hard to believe that the family members stiffly descending from the chartered bus in rumpled sweatsuits and jeans, after a 16-hour trip up the Eastern Seaboard, will emerge an hour later in formal evening dress, ready for the family banquet. But nobody in this family is fazed by the schedule. "We rise to the occasion," one older woman assures a newcomer. "That's what sets this family apart."

The banquet room in the conference center is set with floral centerpieces created by this year's host committee. Young cousins distribute a program of the evening's events as cousins, aunts, and uncles sweep in, sporting gold spangles, beadwork, patent leather shoes, and crisp shirts. This is billed as "an elegant affair," with a purpose. "Our reunions show our young people what kind of people we are," Doretha Davis says. "We're an organized family. We always have a formal banquet on Saturday night. We want our children to know that sometimes there are events worth getting out of jeans for."

Robinsons arrive by chartered buses, car, and train.

Preachers in the Robinson family embrace.

It's a musical family, too. Before the banquet, there is a blessing, a prayer, and the singing of the anthem "Lift Every Voice and Sing." Doretha Davis exhorts the group to sing louder: "We sing this only once a year as a family, and I can't *hear* you!"

An 11-year-old cousin delivers a pledge similar to the Black Family Reunion Pledge, found on page 193, as a way of focusing the intentions and priorities underlying the family reunion.

And then it's time to stop and honor the seniors in the family, and the eldest steps up to the mike. "Not a lot of the people who grew up with me are still around.

But I say, I'm 85 years old, and I can still put my hands on my hips and—" She breaks off to swivel her hips energetically, and the family cheers. She leans into the microphone and tells her juniors in a strong, good-humored voice, "If you don't think you're going to get old, keep living!"

Waiting for worship in their Sunday best.

"Look who just fell through the door!" says one cousin, greeting another. "Let the party begin!" The young cousins peel off for the disco, a meeting room transformed into a dance hall, while the older family members form small clusters and talk late into the night.

The next morning, sleepy-looking folks appear at the breakfast buffet in sneakers and reunion T-shirts, load up plates with heaping servings of eggs and pancakes, and quietly vanish. An hour later, they

reappear, once again transformed. It's time for the family prayer service, and everyone shows their respect by appearing in their Sunday best.

The Sunday worship is the culmination of the reunion, its spiritual heart. "The first time we had a worship service at the reunion, 20 years ago, I felt a depth of feeling I'd rarely experienced," Doretha Davis recalls. "I can't explain how moving it was, kneeling to take communion with the entire family. Many of us belong to different churches,

21st Reunion Program

but we decided that since the Robinson patriarchs and matriarchs had all been African Methodist Episcopal, all future reunion services would be AME, too. After all, we're honoring our ancestors in our worship."

The family choir sings hymns and spirituals at Sunday morning service.

Rising for a blessing from the Reverend Becoates.

At the heart of the service is the family choir. Months in advance of the reunion, volunteers are requested for both a children's choir and an adult choir. (The choir is one reunion activity that never goes begging for members.) Copies of favorite hymns and one or two of the great Negro spirituals are distributed beforehand, and on the first day of the reunion each choir rehearses for an hour.

Now they are ready. The choir members, all dressed in white, walk single-file down the aisle as a cousin plays the electric organ. "What a friend we have in

Rising to the occasion at the family banquet.

Jesus," they sing, as the family rises together. There are seven preachers in this family, and the one leading the worship, the Rev. Becoates of New York, invites the others to the front of the room. The air is electric as family members are blessed by their relatives.

A woman whispers, "It's wonderful when the whole family worships together."

"Make a joyful noise unto the Lord," her husband murmurs. "Amen," they say together.

At their 21st annual gathering, The Robinson Roots Reunion makes a joyful noise unto the Lord.

Oldest family member (2nd from right) and seniors are honored with plaques at the evening banquet.

Black Family Pledge
by Maya Angelou

———

BECAUSE we have forgotten our ancestors,
     our children no longer give us honor.

BECAUSE we have lost the path our ancestors cleared,
     kneeling in perilous undergrowth,
     our children cannot find their way.

BECAUSE we have banished the God of our ancestors,
     our children cannot pray.

BECAUSE the old wails of our ancestors have faded beyond our hearing,
     our children cannot hear us crying.

BECAUSE we have abandoned our wisdom of mothering and fathering,
     our befuddled children give birth to children
     they neither want nor understand.

BECAUSE we have forgotten how to love, the adversary is within our
     gates, and holds us up to the mirror of the world, shouting,
     "Regard the loveless."

Therefore we pledge to bind ourselves to one another, to embrace our
lowliest, to keep company with our loneliest, to educate our illiterate,
     to feed our starving, to clothe our ragged, to do all good things,
     knowing that we are more than keepers of our brothers and
     sisters. We ARE our brothers and sisters.

IN HONOR of those who toiled and implored God with golden tongues,
and in gratitude to the same God who brought us out of hopeless
desolation, we make this pledge.

"My sister-in-law had lost her husband six months before the reunion, and she asked that we hold an informal ceremony for his family to remember him and the impact he had on our lives. We planned a time when the kids were busy. My sister-in-law had brought candles, which we lit one by one, and the ceremony expanded to commemorate other relatives who had died, as we all shared memories of our deceased loved ones. It was a very meaningful time and something that would not have been successful in our family when I was growing up; we do not show emotion easily. I'm so glad my sister-in-law was assertive enough to make the memorial service happen."

—Susanne Oberhauser
Caroline, Wisconsin

is invited to share memories and offer prayers in an individually determined format that fits the family. "The reunion was wonderful, but there was a great gaping hole where my father should have been," says one young woman. "The memorial service helped find a place for him, bring him into the group again."

A worship service may be held at the reunion site, with a family member leading. Sometimes the family member is a clergyman. At the Rumely reunion, a young priest in the family performs Mass every day in a chapel on the reunion premises, the altar decorated with wildflowers picked each morning by the children. But more often the leader is just a family member speaking on what the family means to her or him.

Other families hold their services at a church or temple away from the reunion site. The pastor or rabbi is usually prepared in advance to make special mention of the family in the service and prayers. Family members may act as readers or soloists at the service. The Raspberry family attends an Episcopal church, "but since not all our family are Episcopal, the rector makes the service a bit more ecumenical for us," says Winifred Raspberry Coleman.

Ecumenical Prayers

Most of us sense that prayers of all religions are similar—an expression of reverence, awe, and thanks, an appeal for spiritual strength and worthiness. At the same time, few of us can bring ourselves to speak words exclusive and particular only to another belief system. Here are a few prayers that can suit a wide range of religious beliefs.

Make a joyful noise unto the Lord,
    all ye lands.
Serve the Lord with gladness: Come
    before his presence with singing.
Know ye that the Lord he is God: It
    is he that hath made us, and not
    we ourselves; we are his people,
    and the sheep of his pasture.
Enter into his gates with thanks-

giving, and into his courts with praise: Be thankful unto him, and bless his name.

For the Lord is good; his mercy is everlasting; and his truth endureth to all generations.

Psalm 100

Waking up this morning, I smile.
Twenty-four brand-new hours are before me.
I vow to live fully in each moment and to look at
all beings with eyes of compassion.

Thich Nhat Hanh

Lord, we brought in the harvest.
The rain watered the earth, the sun drew cassava and corn out of the clay. Your mercy showered blessing after blessing over our country.
Creeks grew into rivers; swamps became lakes. Healthy fat cows graze on the green sea of the savanna. The rain smoothed out the clay walls, the mosquitoes drowned in the high waters. Lord, the yam is fat like meat, the cassava melts on the tongue, oranges burst in their peels, dazzling and bright.

Lord, nature gives thanks,
    Your creatures give thanks.
    Your praise rises in us like the great river.

West African prayer

O God, give me, I pray Thee,
light on my right hand
and light on my left hand
and light above me
and light beneath me,
O Lord, increase light within me
and give me light
and illuminate me.

Ascribed to Muhammad

I come before thee as one of thy many children. See, I am small and weak; I need thy strength and wisdom.

Grant me to walk in beauty and that my eyes may ever behold the crimson sunset. May my hands treat with respect the things which thou hast created, may my ears hear thy voice!

Make me wise, that I may understand the things which thou hast taught my people, which thou hast hidden in every leaf and every rock.

I long for strength, not in order that I may overreach my brother but to fight my greatest enemy—myself.

Make me ever ready to come to thee with pure hands and candid eyes, so that my spirit, when life disappears like the setting sun, may stand unashamed before thee.

Sioux

"At our reunions, we all go to Sunday Mass, even those of us who don't go very often at home. But when you're sitting there and each pew is filled with members of your family, pew after pew, it's such an emotional experience—it's hard to explain why."

—Nancy Kenney Hays
Cambridge, Massachusetts

BUSINESS MEETING

Every family gives it a different name—the family meeting, the business meeting, the postmeeting. But whatever it's called, the business meeting is usually held at the end of the reunion to summarize what the reunion has accomplished, explain the costs, open the floor to comments about this year's location, accommodations, food, and events, and set the early planning stages for the next family gathering.

Very organized families use business meetings to elect officers. One family always votes an uncle into the role of president; he forgets about being president until the next reunion, when he's voted in again. If this is your first reunion, you'll need to decide if the business meeting is open to all. At some reunions only adult blood relations are allowed to attend. Even if your family isn't organized into officers, it's a good idea for one person to chair the meeting and another to act as secretary. Minutes of the business meetings will make a wonderful archive of family information.

At the business meeting the members may do any or all of the following:

• Read the minutes of the previous reunion.

• Elect officers for the next reunion committee.

• The treasurer or chief reunion officer reports on expenses. All cost overruns are detailed and explained, and any use of contingency funds itemized. If the reunion didn't require a large registration fee, and printing and mailing costs need to be covered, now's the time to pass the hat.

• Talk about the costs of this year's reunion and make suggestions for possible fund-raisers to help those who did not have the means to attend.

• Entertain comments about the current reunion site: What did the family like about the place? What did not work out so well?

• Note family rites of passage for the record: births, marriages, and deaths, and the oldest and youngest attendees.

• Read letters from those who could not attend the reunion.

• Discuss the attendance level: How many came? Is attendance up or down? What factors affected attendance?

• Decide if there will be any follow-up communiqués—a reunion album, for example, or a newsletter.

• Make a decision about when to hold the next reunion (see pages 232–233.)

• Name a host family for the next reunion, and take suggestions for a new site.

• Discuss the possibility of a mini reunion—held in the winter or the following year if the next reunion is planned for two or three years later.

Use a Family Reunion Record Sheet (see Appendix, page 265) to record some or all of the information.

TAKING LEAVE

"God, I hate the last day!" mutters Chris Coleman, at the Grange reunion. "I just hate it!"

All passages out, transitions, and separations can be hard going, the end of a reunion especially so. You feel teary, vulnerable. Some family members can't, won't, and don't say good-bye. They simply leave, sending word that they had to catch an early flight or were needed back at work by afternoon. After all, good-byes are difficult and complicated. There are the sisters you spent too little time with. The promises to visit that you know you can't keep, as much as you might want to. The shared thought when hugging an older aunt that this may be the last good-bye. The pang of having reconnected with a cousin from whom you now have to part.

After a reunion, as we slam the car door and move onto the highway, we leave the shelter, support, and warmth of extended family. We're back in the world now as single people or members of a nuclear family, and we may feel isolated, fragile, and small.

"This country was formed by the process of leaving home," says anthropologist Dr. Gwen Kennedy Neville. Part of what makes reunions so emotionally compelling, she believes, is the way they enact that leave-taking again and again. An extended family may be nurturing and supporting, but in the end we Americans push out from it,

"We left Asilomar elated, spirits soaring, and promised each other we'd write and visit more often. Somehow, that didn't happen. The burdens and demands of life intervened, months passed, and pledges made with the sincerest of intentions went unfulfilled. Even so, we will always harbor in our hearts the memories of Asilomar. The game of "big wind blows." The morning walks along the windy beach. The talent show. The radiant glow of the twilight bonfire. The storytelling session of the senior generation. The late-night bonding sessions. The emotional speeches at the close of the conference. Above all, the warmth and the love blossoming among an eclectic group of people traversing very different paths in life, but bearing a common ancestry.

We came to Asilomar as relatives. We left as friends, with hearts full of love."

—Michael Wang
Columbia, Missouri

moving forward in pursuit of our individual destinies. And that melancholy ambivalence is something we actually need to feel, whether we want to or not. It goes with the territory.

But kids lift the spirits. When they yell out to their newfound cousins, "Y'all come see us in Texas!" they mean it. They believe it.

Still, it helps to have an outlet for those overwhelming emotions of love and loss. It helps to have some rite of closure.

At a worship service, usually held on the reunion's last day, the emotional vulnerability and shakiness of family members is released, expressed, and accepted. Some families hold hands in a family prayer circle, to feel the warmth of the unbroken connection one last time.

Remember the function high school yearbooks used to serve? They were indispensable third parties through which to filter raw adolescent emotions. That's one function of a family reunion guest book. Even if it's only a composition book, pass around a guest book in which everyone signs and writes a comment.

Just as people often walk out of a play studying the program, so it is with printed material from the reunion. In fact, the more printed material you have for your family to take with them, the better. Reading about the family and having mementos of the event can help ease the separation.

Build into the reunion the option of staying another day. Ask the sales manager to extend the reunion rates an extra day. For those who have to leave, the image of a core group of family members staying on offers a reassuring image of continuity.

Fortunately, despite the melancholy of a reunion's end, most people bounce back with a sense of revived family connection and confidence. Some are even relieved to have been there and gotten out alive—alive with an afterglow. A few days with family can be emotionally exhausting, and many are glad to return to their regular lives. "The postmortem after Family Day is the best time," says Julie Ades. "You've seen all the cousins, you've eaten all that food, then you kick back in the car with your sisters and talk about everyone. It's sheer bliss." Planning to spend one more day with your sisters or brothers, gossiping easily at a less frenetic pace, taking a slower, more gradual leave, may be the way to say good-bye to the family reunion— until next time.

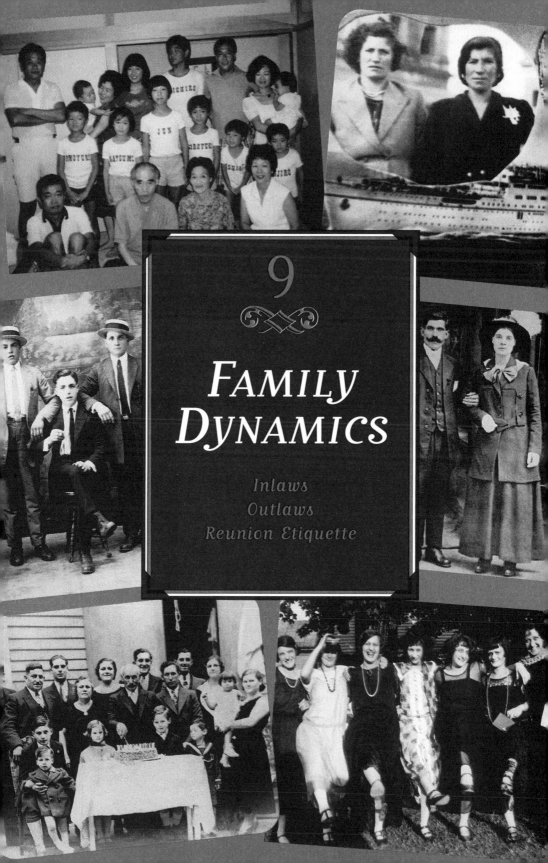

9

FAMILY DYNAMICS

Inlaws
Outlaws
Reunion Etiquette

A Chinese proverb says, "No family can hang out the sign, 'Nothing the matter here.'" Every family has its issues, its patches of unresolved conflict, its difficult personalities who will most likely remain difficult until death relieves them of all difficulty. Few of us view family members with unalloyed adoration. The good news is that anxieties and ambivalences, regrets and doubts, are not incompatible with love. And families—even those that are slightly nuts—are not incompatible with growth and change. Reunions can be a time and place where relationships out of kilter can be put back on track again. Where what has been left dangling can be connected. Where those most prone to being outside looking in can be drawn across the threshold and into the heart of the family.

For some, the prospect of a family reunion can raise uncomfortable feelings bordering on dread, as memories of less-than-perfect relationships with family surface. But with a bit of thoughtful effort, relationships *can* improve, and reunions are just the place to strengthen what's right and valuable in them. Below are common family problems and tactical responses for coping with them. (Some responses were suggested by family therapists Drs. Evan Imber-Black and Janine Roberts.)

"My family is big on labeling: My younger sister is the cute one, my older sister is the athlete, I'm the academic one. What can I do to break free of an identity that no longer fits—and perhaps never did?"

To break free of a family label, first consider the role itself. How do you live up to it? In what ways isn't it true? How can you behave differently to put the label to rest? Before the reunion, plan small, deliberate actions to step out of the family-designated role; these work better than grand, dramatic gestures. The point is not to shock your family, but to present yourself in all your many facets. Volunteer for reunion activities that might be viewed as out of character: the "cute" sister might report on family history, the athlete can bake a family reunion cake. Eventually, family members who continue to attach outgrown labels to you will be in the minority.

"Should we invite my uncle, the family black sheep, to the reunion?"

Unless a relative has committed a heinous, unforgivable crime (failing to call Grandmother at Christmas is not in this category), he should be invited to the reunion. It's just as helpful to analyze the labels we apply to others as the labels that are applied to us. In what way is your uncle a black sheep? What do you, as an independent adult, feel about his behavior? What would you think of him if you didn't know much about his past? The label "black sheep" emphasizes, in a strongly negative way, another family member's differences. Perhaps your family—or at least you—are now prepared to cope with, even enjoy, what makes other family members different. And perhaps the black sheep was not all that radically different to start with.

"How can those who feel outside the family loop—single people, middle-aged people who haven't had kids, gays, or freewheeling artist types—take their place in the family circle at a reunion?"

If possible, those who feel like outsiders should try to get involved in the reunion planning. By doing so, they help create the reunion in their own image, they bond with other family members in a shared effort, and as a result, they're viewed by those attending as family insiders. Those who don't meet certain family expectations should try before the reunion to figure out what common ground they *do* have with other family members and build on that: an interest in family history, for example, or being terrific with young children. They can then sponsor a genealogical workshop at the reunion, for instance, or help in the crafts cabin, emphasizing aspects—other than lifestyle choices or circumstances—that they share with other family members.

"My relationship with my cousin always winds up more competitive than friendly. How can I change that?"

Before the reunion, think about which relationships have been problematic over the years and in what ways. Then work out a strategy for breaking out of the old patterns: Resolve to keep a clear head, for instance, so that you won't get pulled in when your cousin starts a game of one-upmanship. Step back and observe what's going on in the relationship with an almost anthropological interest: "Isn't it interesting that when

THE FAMILY CHARACTER

There probably is a family without a family "character" out there somewhere, but if it gets lucky, an infusion of character will inject itself into its conventional world. Family characters are the uncles and aunts who break the mold, defy family definition, and find the whole concept of social conventions and cultural expectations just plain ridiculous. But they're charming about it—nonconformist but not misanthropic, as though their personalities are too buoyant to be confined by predictable behavior.

Sure, labeling family members can be a limiting game. But how can we resist celebrating the family character? The one who wears the striped shirt and polka-dot tie to the wedding and bellows, "Of course they match!" The one who is the first to embrace the outsiders, the one the kids gather around to inhale a contagious sense of fun and a shrugging off of stiff formality, the one we always forgive for holding forth in a corner while everyone else is dutifully cleaning up, because his stories are just so wonderful. The cheek pincher and the back slapper. Raise a glass to the family character. You know who he or she is. Everybody does.

she says this, I feel like that?" Once you fail to produce the predicted response, the competitive dynamic stalls, so the game can't continue. Now try changing the subject to something that interests you both equally.

"I have a hard time liking some of my relatives. But I do want to stay connected to them."

Figure out which relatives you have the most ambivalent feelings about. Then view each one as he or she would be seen by a good friend. As you step into the shoes of someone who actually likes the person, the good points come into sharper focus, and you may find yourself moving in the direction of affection—or at least tolerance and understanding.

"What if I have a major issue I want to settle with a family member—or a big family secret that has been unconfessed for years?"

Reunions should not be used as a forum in which to work through long-standing issues before a large, live audience. If you have a bone of contention with a relative, deal with it person to person. Plan in advance to take an hour or two out of the reunion and go off by yourselves to talk things over. What this approach lacks in drama, it makes up for in effectiveness.

"What do I say to relatives who've gone through hard times— fighting cancer or losing their job or getting divorced? Maybe I shouldn't say anything at all."

Keeping silent isn't the answer. Better to make some kind of supportive remark than simply ignore the situation. The person who's been going through a difficult time can pick up on your expression of concern or shut down conversation. Take the cue, and respect it. But often they *will* welcome the reaching out, and a reunion is a good time for it. As one recently divorced woman said shortly after her family reunion, "I was dreading the reunion. I felt like such a failure. The divorce was so raw, like an open wound. But at the reunion, I felt such acceptance from the family that I could let down my defenses."

Reluctant Spouses

They're our next of kin, but not blood relations. They shape us, define us, and help shape and define our extended family as well. They are the fresh blood and new genes that evolutionary diversity requires for the survival of our tribe. So let's toast the spouses at the reunion. True, the archetypal in-law at a reunion is a reluctant (usually male) person who would rather break rocks in the hot sun than struggle through an exchange of small talk with Great-Aunt Dorothy. But handled with care, a spouse can be brought into the fold, more or less painlessly. Here are a few guidelines:

• **Respect his differences.** Every family has its set point of distance regulation—a sort of emotional temperature dictating the levels of closeness and distance in family members'

"*T**hank God for the ones who marry in. They save us from ourselves.***"**
—*Michael Brody*
Chatham, New York

relationships. Some families thrive on surface chatter but don't delve deeper, while other families argue heatedly about minor points as a way of connecting emotionally. If an in-law comes from a background with a different way of handling closeness, he can have a hard time adjusting to the rhythm of his new family's comfort level. That alone can cause stress. Which is why the next point is so critical.

• **Request only one command performance a day.** Then let him go his own way—out, away, wherever: fishing, golfing, to the mall, or back to bed.

• **Limit dwelling in the past.** "My husband can't take another reunion," one informant tells us. "He hates it when everyone sits around the campfire and talks about the good old days, when he wasn't even in the picture." Sure, a reunion can bring in-laws into the family culture by imparting family stories, history, and Uncle Ed's really bad jokes, but few spouses can cope with a nonstop immersion into a family's past.

• **Suggest reunion activities that your spouse actually likes.** If the reunion features his kind of fun—fishing, golf, sailing—he'll be happy and want to return the next time.

OPEN CAMPFIRE

THE SANDBERG FAMILY

What: *Weekend camping reunion*

Who: *The descendants of a couple who emigrated from Sweden in the early 1900s*

Where: *Lakeside campground in the Catskill Mountains*

Number of Participants: *49*

Family Traits: *Schmoozing, openness, unaffectedness*

A state park offers bucolic settings and affordable lodging.

Diana Bruu, a thin blonde woman wearing a baseball cap with a Swedish flag emblem, sits back in a lawn chair, watching the hikers troop by. Every year she comes to this picturesque campground in the Catskills, less for the bracing delights of the mountain life than to immerse herself in the warm comforts of being among her three siblings, her own three children, and assorted grandnieces and nephews.

"Our family is like an updated version of the Waltons," says her daughter Lois. "We have modern-day issues, but we handle them the old-fashioned way: with acceptance, love, and good humor."

On Saturday, while most of the family repair to the beach, Lois's husband Greg leads an afternoon hike. This year he's collected about 10 hearty Sandbergs and Bruus. Diana

Diana Bruu enjoys the great outdoors her way.

smiles encouragingly and waves them off with a touch of impatience. As the last one disappears into the trees, she calls out to her daughter Alyson, "All clear! The healthies are gone!" Diana and Alyson light up cigarettes.

Diana had been explaining how her family came to have the name Wedell—hardly a Swedish name, and the family is very Swedish. "When my father came over from Sweden in 1900 with his young bride, his name was Haakinsen."

"Spelled with two a's, right?" pipes up her son

Peter, as if on cue.

"Two a's. They came through Ellis Island and they had to sit in that great hall—have you been there? They gave their name to be called and waited. Waited. Waited! Hours went by, the room began to clear. No call for Haakinsen. The day came to an end, the sky darkened. Still no call for Haakinsen. You can only imagine what they were thinking. They were the only people left in that big hall. Then the name 'Wedell' was called. My grandfather looked at his young bride, she looked at him, and he said, 'OK, that's it, we are Mr. and Mrs. Wedell.' They bounded up to the Ellis Island officials and said, 'Mr. and Mrs. Wedell are here.' All their lives, you know what my grandparents wondered? Whatever happened to the real Mr. and Mrs. Wedell?"

"Did we ever find out what kind of name Wedell is?" Alyson asks.

"German," Diana answers. "We're on the wrong family tree."

Every year the Wedell family—the four grandchildren of the original Mr. and

Greg introduces the youngest hiker to rock climbing.

Mrs. Haakinsen, their grown children and grandchildren, and a few extended family members, gather at this

Hikers head off up the mountain, catching up on each other's year between huffs and puffs.

lakeside camp on the wedding anniversary of the Haakinsen's only child, Mildred Wedell Sandberg.

"You know, this place is right near the camp for policemen's kids we used to go to," Peter said. "We have

to take that same windy road with no guardrails to get here. I used to have nightmares about that road as a kid."

"Weird that we end up here every summer," Alyson says. She and Peter are both quiet for a moment. Their father, a policeman, died when they were young. There's pain in the subject.

"I hate that damned windy road," Diana says.

Alyson and her partner Kristine begin to haul in loads of wood, preparing for when the Bruu family gathers around its campfire and talks, talks deep into the night. "I'm getting ready for my barn burner," says Alyson, dropping the wood near the fire ring. "That's my favorite time."

"Mine, too," says Kristine.

Sandberg hikers celebrate reaching the peak of Sunset Rock with a swig of spring water.

Alyson and Kristine were married on Cape Cod last summer. "To tell you the truth, I had no idea how the rest of the family would take it," Alyson recalls. "At best I thought they'd be sort of polite and maybe send a gift. But no. They all came. ALL of them."

"They wanted to see you happy," Diana says mildly. "And they knew Kris was making you happy."

"I like the campfire game we played last year," Alyson says. "The one where we all sat around the fire and said in one word what we admired about each other."

"Plenty of 'ooooooh' moments there," says Diana, patting her heart. "You don't know what a daughter-in-law thinks about you until it's actually spoken."

"Remember when we said in one word what most annoyed us about each other?" Kristine recalls.

"What was the word you used to describe me?" Diana asks Alyson. "Overbearing?"

"No, not that," says Alyson. "Maybe 'opinionated.' Let's forget it."

"We won't repeat that exercise again."

"Let's do the positives again this year," Kristine says. "My own family won't talk about real things. They're the masters of small talk."

"We're the masters of big talk here," Alyson says.

"I don't know how to small talk," Diana says.

A nephew stops by the campsite as his parents

Reunion downtime means "doing your own thing."

cruise past in their car en route to the bed-and-breakfast where they're staying. The camping life is not for them. "There go your parents," Diana points, "if you want to find them."

"I'm here to escape, not to find," the nephew replies. "I love them but . . ."

The hikers troop back in. "Where's that beer?"

grandchild so much as *born*. Why is that?"

None of her children answers, as some head for the lake and others to the showers, praying the erratic campground shower is pumping hot this evening. Later they'll gather at the pavilion for a potluck dinner.

"After dinner, my oldest uncle, Kenneth, always

Poring over family albums in the lakeside pavilion.

An evening tribute to a beloved Uncle Kenneth.

they shout, collapsing into lawn chairs, exchanging "war stories" about how hard the walk was, although they wouldn't have been happy had it been any easier. Eight-year-old Eileen had led the hike the whole way.

"Look at that child," Diana observes to no one in particular. "What this family needs are more children. All my friends' grandchildren are getting married now. I don't have a single

makes a speech noting family milestones. This year one of my aunts graduated college after 10 years of night school," says Lois Bruu. "Another uncle surprised everyone with songs on the guitar, having quietly taken lessons in his retirement a few months ago."

Then it's time for the surprise event honoring Kenneth. His nephews and nieces stand on a bench, each holding and calling out a letter to spell his name.

When the last nephew shouts, "H—plain and simple, for he's a hell of an uncle!," cheers break out, confetti and bubbles fill the air—and someone yells, "We love you—in spite of you, we love you!"

As photos are taken in the golden evening light, Diana stands back and surveys the family while the in-laws (the outlaws, they call themselves) gather for their own portrait. Not a Swede among them.

"Why is it that a bunch of Swedish Lutherans like ourselves end up marrying Irish and Italian Catholics?" Diana squints, mulling over the topic. Nobody answers, as the family scatters and re-forms itself in the last light of the day.

Encourage the in-laws to make up a skit for the talent show, lovingly (and otherwise) showcasing family characteristics.

- **Don't expect him to remember names or relationships.** He won't.
- **Don't expect him to mingle without you.** He won't do that, either.
- **Don't sign him up for activities or volunteer him for duty without asking him first.** If he does get involved in the organizing of the reunion, he may find his way into the family and really belong. But like everything else, it's got to be consensual.
- **Give him the family he's always wanted.** More father figures, brothers, sisters, mother figures—a chance to form adult friendships. If you cajole your significant other into attending the reunion, and lay off his case once he's there, he might discover for himself what the reunion has to offer: more people to love and be loved by. Not a bad deal at all.

Bringing in the In-laws and Outlaws

When family members come together, they often revel in their intimacy by speaking in family code, the secret language of shared memories and references alluded to in shorthand. That's part of the beauty of family. And a reunion is one of the few times you have to indulge in it. But a steady diet of in-jokes and catchphrases will succeed in making newcomers feel out of it at a time when the point is to feel in the thick of it.

THE PRODIGAL CHILD

It's called individuation, when young adults go off and create their own identities apart from their families' vision of them. When, as Joyce Little of New Brunswick puts it, "you feel as if you've got too many relatives." Reunions are in tough competition for time, attention, and funds of young people who have internships, summer jobs, or first-time jobs with little vacation time, college loans to pay off, and the boyfriends and girlfriends who are, to put it mildly, more of a draw than Uncle Ed and Aunt Fran. (Evolution demands that the urgencies of courtship take priority over schmoozing with relatives.)

Don't lose contact with these young adults, but don't force the issue either. History has taught that, like the prodigal son, they will be back.

The family should not be a private club: There will always be new members coming in and members going out. And charting membership changes—people moving and divorcing and dying, children being born and being adopted, folks marrying in—is one of the central reasons for holding a reunion in the first place. When people come to a reunion as family members for the first time, they should feel that they belong, not as if they aren't yet worthy of the

Ten Commandments of Reunion Etiquette

❖ ❖ ❖

A reunion isn't controlled by protocol, as a wedding is. And each family cultivates its own idiosyncrasies. Still, a few laws do govern reunions—natural, underlying laws that must be followed lest the world be thrown into chaos and confusion. And we don't want that. So, with the help of Judith Martin, also known as Miss Manners, we've drawn up the following Commandments.

1. Thou shalt not forget thine ordinary manners nor thy common civility, just because thou art amongst thy brothers and sisters.

2. Thou shalt tolerate the tiresome relative (at least for a little while).

3. Thou shalt not play footsie with a distant cousin or thy cousin's spouse.

4. Sniping and carping about a reunion's lack of organization is an abomination.

5. Thou shalt orchestrate spontaneous praise unto the reunion organizer.

6. Thou shalt not talk about everything under the sun. Agree to disagree, and steer clear of such topics as the Vietnam War (now and forever), abortion rights, gay marriage, gun control, Waco.

7. Parents shall not use intimate details of their kids' lives as conversational fodder. (Boasts of children's accomplishments are acceptable, but parents shall be discreet in their phrasing and timing.)

8. Thou shalt not reveal devastating family secrets about thyself or others unless thou hast arranged therapeutic support systems.

9. Thou shalt not publicly criticize the bad manners or poor behavior of any child not thine own.

10. Thou shalt flatter thy kinfolk—falsely or not. All nieces tap dance divinely, all babies are beautiful, and all aunts look as wonderful as ever.

family secret code ring. Here are some suggestions to bring outsiders into the inner circle.

• **Everyone should introduce themselves (and be introduced) by their first and last names.** At an extended family reunion, it's rare that any one person is so well known to the teenagers, second cousins from out of town, and new in-laws that they require no introduction. If there's a master of ceremonies, he can make this point at the start, and remind folks at memory nights and meetings to give their full names.

• **Assign seats at the first dinner to shake up family cliques.** Put quiet types with talkers, and balance the generations and family branches. Or draw the names of the reunion attendees and form tables randomly. Kids old enough to manipulate a fork and stay upright in an adult chair can occupy a children's table or two. Setting a bunch of 7- to 10-year-olds to work making place cards is a good bonding activity, too.

• **Let everyone in on the joke.** When it doesn't destroy a story's momentum, try to give a bit of background and some identifying detail.

• **Reach out to the widows and widowers of family members.** When spouses die, in-laws often feel that their relationship with the extended family has ended, too, at a time when the connection may be more vital than ever. Have someone call and urge them to attend the reunion —or coax them into serving on one

---

A SIBLING HIKE

Brothers and sisters, especially if they live far from one another and only see each other at reunions, may find it hard to separate long enough to connect with other relatives. Janine Roberts' family solved that problem by scheduling a sibling hike, without kids, spouses, or cousins, at the reunion's start. On the hike the siblings talk freely, easily, unself-consciously, and exhaustively, so that on their return, they feel they've shared time in a meaningful way and are ready to reach out to others.

---

of the reunion committees so that they feel right in the heart of things.

• **Help stepchildren blend in.** Introduce stepchildren without hemming and hawing; "stepchildren" and "stepmother" may not be felicitous terms, but they are accurate. When announcing new family members in any rites-of-passage announcements, don't single out stepkids. Since their parent is probably also new to the family, have them all introduced at the same time. Don't pretend that there's more history than there is between the family and the stepkids in a well-meaning attempt to help them belong. It's a pretense that gives the impression that the reality is not acceptable. In time, there will be more and more shared history, but for now, accept the stepkids for who they are.

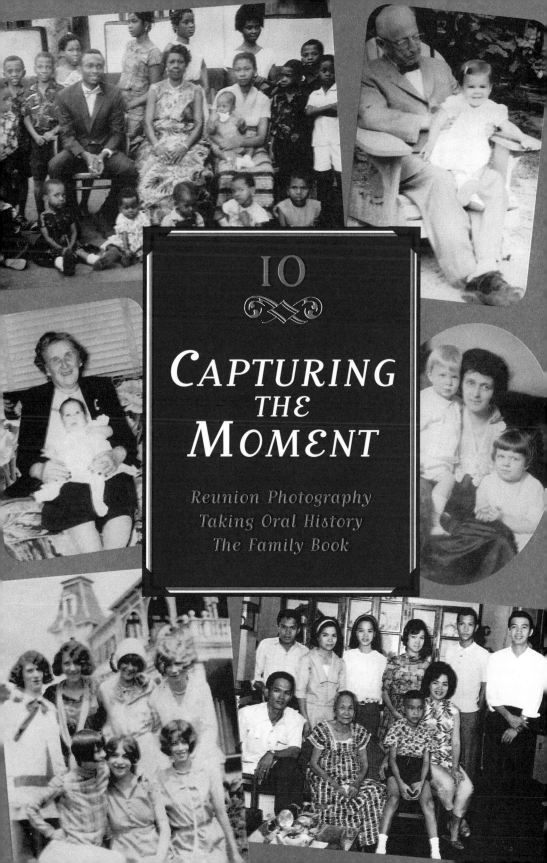

10

CAPTURING THE MOMENT

Reunion Photography
Taking Oral History
The Family Book

The very nature of a family reunion directs our thoughts to the passage of time, to recovering lost times, and especially to preserving the present for future generations. When we pause and look around at a reunion and see so many family members gathered in one place, we realize poignantly that this moment will never occur exactly like this again, that family membership will change in the next few years in ways we can't anticipate, and that it's essential to record this moment for other generations. This is how we once were, and thanks to photography, how we will always be: a frozen shadow of a richer time. You may never have thought of your family photos as pieces of American folklore, but they are.

"Snapshots are hardly random visions of a family's life," says folklorist Steve Zeitlin. "They're part of a family's self-expression. Someone has chosen what is to be captured on film, and decided how the subject is to be presented. Once the photos are printed, there's selecting, discarding, and organizing. Snapshots show what is viewed as important in a family, and worth preserving. And of course, where there's a photo, there's a story to go with it."

Photography: Freezing Time

Reunions, of course, are family folklore extravaganzas, and if ten families are coming, chances are there'll be ten cameras in attendance as well. To make sure that the work of all those shutterbugs gets put to use, encourage someone to volunteer as family archivist to put together a "reunion album." Everyone should send the archivist copies of their reunion prints, labeled with the names of everyone in each picture and the year. The archivist prepares the album, with captions, for display at the next reunion.

Set a time at the reunion for the family photo shoot. Don't leave it to chance; put it on the schedule, then announce it again at a meal. And ask everyone to wear the reunion T-shirts.

Appoint the best photographer in the family to take the "great American reunion" group portrait, where the entire family gathers for the record. For this shot consider renting a wide-lens camera; salespeople at the camera store can instruct you in its use. The prints are not very expensive, and you can have the print cropped to your specs in one of the better photo developing shops.

Hiring a professional photographer for a group photo can take the pressure off the reunion organizers. Let him deal with the hassle of mailing the photos and collecting payment—and let him figure out how to squeeze 65 amateur models into one photograph. The downside is how much a professional can cost. Consider including the price of one group photo per family in the reunion registration fee, with all other photos optional and ordered directly from the photographer himself.

The resort or hotel where you're holding the reunion may be able to suggest a photographer. Or call the local newspaper and ask for the photography staff. Newspaper photographers often work freelance and are adept at getting in-motion candids.

Videography: The Moving Image

Video cameras and family reunions may seem the perfect marriage. But whoever uses a video camera should bear a few things in mind.

Ask permission to shoot before you begin. A reunion shouldn't be a video ambush, with people ducking out of camera range.

Ask people to identify themselves by first and last names. *You* may know them well enough, but what about those watching this tape 30 years from now?

Tape family members when they're least aware of the camera, but most prepared to face the public. When they're exchanging anecdotes, for instance, or speaking at a memories night or performing in the talent show. But don't tape when people are eating—you risk capturing too many unflattering moments.

Pan slowly. It's hard to go too slowly when videotaping. You don't want to give the viewer whiplash. Consider giving a quiet voice-over explaining what's happening to the viewer.

ORAL HISTORY: BEARING WITNESS

A reunion connects family members whose lives have been rich and varied, and an oral history is one way to preserve those lives for all time. A historical document, an oral

Say Cheese: Photo Ops 101

The entire Chien family with their banner gathers for the classic reunion shot.

Take the great American reunion group portrait. If your group is fewer than 25 people, find a gentle hillside and form three or four rows. Better to form more rows that are less wide than to have two long rows—the shorter rows enable you to see the faces better. Consider painting a banner to be used as backdrop in the family photo. Include the family name and year of the reunion, and have the folks in the front row hold it. Years from now, there'll be no debate about when the photo was taken.

Caption the reunion portrait with the names of everyone in it. When there are more than 50 folks in the photograph, pass out

For every 10 people at a reunion, 9 will have a camera. Here, the youngest photographer.

sheets of paper with boldly printed numbers on them. Have everyone write their names on the back of the paper and hold up the numbers for one or two of the first shots, creating a reference photo. Then collect the numbers (make sure nobody decides to change seats suddenly), and take the formal portrait. Use the names and numbers to create a caption, and send it out with the family photo.

Don't take too many group shots at the picnic table. Yes, that's a classic photo technique at weddings. But not-so-small fortunes go into making wedding tables look beautiful enough to live up to the camera's pitiless gaze. Your reunion tables are more likely to feature soda bottles, paper plates, splotches of ketchup, and blotches of coleslaw.

Compose your shots. A little styling goes a long way. We know life is no Martha Stewart vision—but 30 years from now you'll be glad you removed that bag of potato chips when snapping the kids building a sand castle on the beach. And pay attention to where you pose family members: What's that to the left of Aunt Kitty? Oh, a crate of plates and a garbage can.

Create family photo ops. Ambitious family members can make a backdrop to pose against—an ancestor painted on plywood with his face cut out so that each reunion goer can grin through the hole. Or use a prop that has meaning for the family. For example, the Rumely family made their name in the world through Rumely tractors, so a cousin brought a Rumely tractor to

A style director isn't a bad idea for a large, boisterous group.

the reunion site, and everyone had his or her picture taken seated on the great machine.

Don't forget candid shots. They evoke the spirit of the event and are often the most fun to look at later.

The golden light of sunset bathes the family in a warm glow.

Get some classic combinations: left, the oldest and youngest; right, five sisters and mother.

Cool dudes in two generations.

Tighten your shots. When in doubt, step in a little. You don't really need to see your cousins' feet—it's the look in their eyes you want to capture. And bend down to be at eye level with your younger subjects.

Take at least one roll of black-and-white shots. Color pictures are lovely, but black-and-white prints last about 30 years longer.

Make sure to get the classic reunion shots. The oldest family member with the youngest, the tallest brother with the shortest, all the kids, all the teenagers, all the babies lined up (however briefly), the individual families, the individual branches, the oldest set of brothers and sisters, three or four generations of sisters, and so on.

Getting down to your subjects' level gives you the shots you want.

Years later, other generations will pore over your photos.

history is the gathering of a world view, a firsthand account of how life was lived by one person, as he or she recalls it. When you take an oral history, you produce a selective history of a life that will not be lived in just that way, ever again.

Oral history is something more and something less than telling family stories. Here are the stories less easily told: the ones without a beginning, middle, and end, without a happy ending or a clear resolution. Oral history is not about dusting off family lore. You have to take the road less traveled, recording the stories with the ambivalent air, and life as it is truly lived.

In a sense, all personal history is public history. All American families embody the history of our country in their lives, and none of this experience should disappear with those who lived it. All should be recalled and preserved for the future.

Taking an oral history requires a purposeful interviewer. Shape your interview by preparing questions in advance. (See page 219 for suggestions.) Create a structure flexible enough to permit digressions to places you'd never think to go and detours away from areas that are too sensitive or private. But be firm enough to keep the interview on course.

When you take an oral history, you want more than just dates and place names to show how one person's choices and struggles shaped her life. And more than that: How do you elicit a picture of how the world

"Interviewing my father was a revelation. It was the only time I'd ever really talked about so many issues with him. He claimed it was just because I'd never asked him. But it was more that he was ready to talk and I was ready to listen. Becoming the interviewer vested me with a kind of authority I had never had in the family. I became something more than just a daughter—but I was more of a daughter than ever."

—Lynn Martin
Baltimore, Maryland

and its history, sheer luck, or a sense of providence, shaped her? Never ask a yes-or-no question. Keep questions personal, close to the texture of life as it was really lived. Ask for vivid sensory details. And don't argue about dates. This is your interviewee's point of view, mistakes and all.

Record in a quiet room with few competing noises. You don't want your interviewee wearing herself out straining to hear and be heard. If possible, use an omnidirectional microphone that stands up rather than the built-in mike found in most tape recorders. Sit face to face in comfortable chairs with a table between you, so that neither has to turn and twist to see the other. Keep a pitcher of water or iced tea and a few cookies on hand for a boost.

Identify participants and the circumstances of the taping. At the start of each side of a cassette, give your

"The true history of this country is written in the minds of older people. Every year 2 million people over the age of 64 die. It's imperatively important that their oral histories be gathered. Each family's history is a tiny piece of the mosaic of the country's history. We've lost so much already."
—Alex Haley
author

name, interviewee's name, the date and place of interview, and number of the cassette: "Cassette 2, side B."

Bring a pen and pad with you. You'll want to jot down follow-up questions without interrupting the interview subject. Tell her you can stop the tape any time she wants.

Plan on a two-hour block of time. That should be enough to warm up to the topic, delve in detail, and wind things up for a satisfying sense of closure—neither exhausted nor left with the sense of leaving too much unsaid.

Videotaping is not necessarily better than audiotaping. A videotaped oral history—two people sitting still and talking—is pretty static, and the presence of a video camera may make your interviewee self-conscious. Because the interviewer needs to concentrate on asking and listening, not taping, a third party would have to be present to videotape.

Use photographs to trigger memories. Bring along, and ask the interviewee to bring along, a few choice photographs to jog the memory, and inquire about the people and places featured in them.

Don't forget the vital statistics. You'll want to get your interviewee's date and place of birth and marriage, as well as the full names of her parents, siblings, spouse, children and stepchildren.

End the interview on a high note. Frame the last questions positively, letting the interviewee think of accomplishments with pride.

Take good care of the cassettes. Store them away from radiators and the electromagnetic waves that come from major appliances. Label and number the cassette boxes as well as the cassettes themselves with the full names of the interviewer and interviewee, plus date and location of the interview. Rewind the cassettes every few years to help prevent "print through"—when the signals from one side of a tape bleed through to the other side. Duplicate the tapes and give one to your interviewee, the others to family members important to the interviewee. If you're transcribing the tapes, don't use the master tape for transcription: all that starting and stopping may wear it out.

THE FAMILY BOOK: GENERATION TO GENERATION

Books are a thing apart. They're valued more than other household goods and treated more respect-

Taking Oral History

**Here are some questions
you can ask:**

◆ Describe the house you grew up in,
room by room. How many slept in your
bedroom? What possessions did you call
your own? What clothes did you wear to
school—describe the shoes, what kinds of
socks? Did you have hired help around the
house?

◆ What other relatives were around on
an everyday basis?

◆ Did anyone else live in your house with
you, apart from your nuclear family?

◆ What was your first day of school like?
How did you get there? What did you
have for lunch? How many kids were in
the class?

◆ How was Sunday spent in your family?

◆ What book or poem that you read in
school meant the most to you?

◆ What were you afraid of as a kid?

◆ What was a typical punishment in your
household?

◆ What was a typical summer's day for
you when you were 8? What were your
favorite games? Who did you play with?

◆ How were birthdays observed when you
were a kid?

◆ What were the typical contents of a
Christmas stocking?

◆ What children's story, fairy tale, or biblical story was most memorable?

◆ How did you and your husband or wife
meet? What was your first date like?
What was courtship like in those days?

What was the family's reaction to your
spouse?

◆ What lessons did your parents teach you
that stuck with you and shaped your life?

Ask questions about major historical
events and how they affected your interviewee personally: the Great Depression,
the polio epidemic, World War II,
McCarthyism, etc. How did he or she first
become aware of them? Newspaper, radio,
family? Were they discussed at the dinner
table?

◆ Were there instances when you faced
racial, ethnic, or religious bigotry? What
was your response and how do you wish
you had responded? Do you ever think of
those instances now?

◆ What was your first job? How old were
you? What did you wear to work?

◆ What was your first home away from
your family like? What did you eat for
dinner? Who cooked it?

**Close the interview on
a major chord:**

◆ What was something you did right in
your life that you would advise others
to do?

◆ What did you learn late in life (but better late than never) that you would like to
impart to others?

◆ What would you have done differently,
if you could?

◆ What are you most proud of having
done?

fully, and they occupy an honored place in the home. A family book is doubly special. Tracking a family's movement through space and time, a family book can explain in words and photos who we were, how we got from there to here, and how that movement made us who we are today.

A family book doesn't have to be a footnoted narrative or even bound. Assembling a family book shouldn't be intimidating: To a large degree, the photos, photocopied documents, and unadorned facts can speak for themselves. An entirely satisfying version can be compiled like a scrapbook, with photos, newspaper clips, wedding announcements, and genealogical family trees and notes.

The lucky one is the person who pulls the family book together. Like a singer who comes to "own" a song after she's sung it enough times, the compiler of a family history takes possession of it. The story becomes hers to tell, and she becomes the expert and authority whom others approach for answers.

A reunion provides a useful deadline for completing a family book—or launching one. At the reunion you have all your resources pooled together: Now's the time to ask Aunt Marie to tell you more about Aunt Helena who lived in Milwaukee in the 1940s and ran a successful tavern—or so they say. Now's the time to take pictures of family members who haven't yet contributed pictures for the book. And a family book makes a fantastic follow-up to a reunion, just the thing to arrive in the mailbox six months afterward, as the memories begin to dim.

To begin a family book, decide where you want to start in the history of the family. One ambitious but viable project may be a brief history of your family since its arrival in America. Begin by telling where your family emigrated from, what kind of work they did in the Old Country, and what kind of work they found when they first arrived here. Give the address or town where they first lived, and where they moved to.

Then break down the family story into manageable chunks. Have a chapter for each branch of the family—the descendants of each of five brothers who came to America in 1899, for example. Interview people from each branch of the family, or create a short questionnaire for family representatives to fill out. You can't be sure of all the facts. Hedge your bets by prefacing your assumptions with "we believe" or "possibly," for example, "We believe that the family continued to live in Fall River until they moved to Woonsocket in 1924."

You may want to include photocopies of original documents: immigration papers, baptismal certificates, passports, report cards, diary entries, business ledgers, personal letters. Maps of where the family came from, photocopied from a historical atlas that shows the national borders that existed at that time, put the movement of the family into graphic

BEWARE OF SCAMS

Once your name gets onto the mailing list of genealogical societies or commercial concerns, you may get offers from companies trying to sell you histories or family books that supposedly contain your family's exclusive history. A legitimate book with information about your real family would cost hundreds, if not thousands, of dollars: That's what genuine research and writing by real professionals would add up to. What these scams are usually selling are bound phone directories listing strangers who happen to share your last name.

There are reputable (if costly) outfits that can help you prepare a bound history of your family, assisting you with every step of the process. (See Appendix, page 263, for a suggestion.)

Favorite recipes, with anecdotes attached, and descriptions of family meals also bring a family to life. Consider simply listing the events in a typical day in the life of your grandmother. Write down favorite family sayings and words of advice from your grandparents and great-grandparents before they vanish into the ether of time. And if oral histories of other relatives have been taken, extract a few select excerpts from transcripts to include in the family book.

Remember as you write to presume that your reader has little background knowledge about the family. This book should be a resource for a great-great-grandchild who happens upon it a hundred years from now and has no idea who Aunt Maggie is. Caption, date, and label all photos and newspaper clippings as well.

You'll need to decide how you want the family book bound. A three-ring binder costs about the same as plastic spiral binding (available at most copy shops), but it has the advantage of permitting additions and updated family trees, and it includes plastic sleeves to hold photos and photocopies, tabbed dividers to separate each chapter, and pockets to hold family memorabilia. Office supply companies sell binders with clear plastic overlays that allow you to insert a cover page onto the front of the binder. The disadvantage of a ring binder is that it feels more like a photo album and less like a book than a spiral binder does.

relief. Ask family members to submit one or two old photographs, accompanied by anecdotes giving a picture of life as it used to be. Don't focus exclusively on photographs of people. Pictures of old family houses are evocative as well. If no photographs exist of a particular grandmother's house, ask your subject to draw the layout from memory. When you describe the homes of your ancestors, you give a reality and texture to their lives otherwise hard to attain.

A FAMILY REUNION BOOK

THE CHIEN FAMILY

What: *Weekend classic*

Who: *Five siblings and their cousins, raised together as one family in Szechuan Province, who gathered for their first reunion since leaving China.*

Where: *Asilomar Conference Center, near Monterey, California*

Number of Participants: *80*

Family Traits: *High activity and enthusiasm levels, a focus on higher education*

Chin-Yi Chien, the family's guiding light.

The facts of the Chien family are easily told. The family's prosperous, cultured way of life in China was destroyed first by the Communist Revolution, then by the viciously anti-intellectual Cultural Revolution that followed. Most of the five brothers and sisters—and cousins raised so closely with them that they considered themselves siblings—left for the United States, where almost all of them distinguished themselves academically or professionally. What this story doesn't tell is how a family who undergoes all this deals with so much loss, discontinuity, and dislocation. And no one outside the family can comprehend the emotional price of having to rebuild, restore, and start anew in a country not one's own.

The Chiens' story never really came together, even for its members, until their first reunion. Here, on the California coastline, a sense of family wholeness and strength was restored, the power of which took many family members by surprise. The reunion made clear what they had been missing. Frank Yin grew up in Denver "with an acute sense of being different." His nuclear family, he felt, "was an incredibly small speck in an

A family portrait taken in Szechuan province in the early 1920s.

ocean of humanity, and not only that, we were somehow a speck that had been misplaced. This was a feeling I did not very much like." Frank wrote in the Chien Family Reunion Book. This combination album, yearbook, and family directory is an evocative encapsulation of the power of

past of the extended family helping them to feel more at home in their new world. "That first reunion was extremely moving," says Stephen Teng, who worked on the Chien Family Reunion Book with his nephew's wife, Jeanne Spencer, for almost three years, completing it and

Chin-Yi Chien, known to her children and grandchildren as Popo. A sepia print of her looks out from the opening page: beautiful, dignified, graceful, the reunion book's—and the family's—guiding spirit. For many years, she had no home of her own, but moved among the houses of

Carrying on: The Chung generation of Chiens poses for the camera.

unity the family experienced at the reunion.

For Frank, discovering extended family helped alleviate his feeling of isolation; the dense network of people and memories to which he belonged gave him a new source of confidence and pride, a sense that he was no longer adrift.

Many Chiens found enrichment in the reunion, the familiarity and shared

having it printed only the day before the family's second reunion.

"I finally got to meet this *da gia tin* (big family) my mother had always told us about, and I wanted to find out more about the older generation. I also wanted to create something to show my children what their roots are."

The book is dedicated to the family matriarch (Hsu),

her five children. Her offspring write tributes to her in the book: She "never raised her temper," Stephen Teng recalls; Popo was "my everlasting playmate on countless afternoons," writes Stephen's sister Shiree. "Popo will live forever inside all our hearts, and she will smile at the thought that she taught us well to always care, and protect each other."

Taking a page from the family book.

The Chien Family Reunion Book celebrates the family Popo brought up and their descendants. It includes the following:

♦ Page for each nuclear family, with each Chien family member giving date of birth, educational background, current profession, address, name and profession of spouse, names of children and their dates of birth, lists of hobbies and family traits, and a cluster of handpicked photos.

♦ Page of wedding photos from past as well as current generations.

♦ Chien family database with addresses, phone numbers, E-mail addresses, birth dates, and Chinese zodiac signs.

♦ Collage of photographs from the reunion—the tug-of-war, walks on the beach, the crazy-awards ceremony—as well as a copy of the reunion program to help jog memories.

♦ Deeply moving memories of the beloved Popo written by family members.

♦ Essays on family history, some written in Chinese and English, such as Robert Chien's "A Chien Family History," which goes all the way back to A.D. 950.

The Chien trait of high cheekbones gets passed down through the generations.

♦ Frank Yin's essay on the complexity of Chinese-American identity today.

♦ Reunion statistics listing total numbers of family members, those who attended the reunion, and those absent.

♦ Family trees for each branch of the family.

♦ Family medical information—on gout, twins, colon cancer, written by physicians in the family.

Looking at the book, one feels the reunion's energy created by the sense of belonging, of finding traits in common, of sharing a family history that personalizes the devastating effects of the Communist Revolution in China and the Cultural Revolution that followed. The Reunion Book provided something the reunion could not: It brought together, in pictures and stories, the family members who had stayed behind in China with those who had left for America.

The first reunion had been a hive of planned activity, as the family discovered one another within the safety of a structured schedule. The second reunion, also held at Asilomar, was less frenetic, more thoughtful. And this time, a Chien sister who had remained in China was able to attend. When most of the family left to go sightseeing one afternoon, the sister sat down to tell those who remained how her father, Popo's husband, had actually died. The American branch knew he had died in prison, but none knew the full details.

"Because it was so painful, my aunt had never told the story before," says Li-Shin Yu, a New York–based film editor. Almost 40 years had passed, but the time had from the first one. Not so much fun-and-games, but a meaningful and moving time."

The sweep of history and human emotion is contained in the Chien Book. The cost of printing and binding it was high, almost $100 a copy. "Between the cost and the pressure to complete the questionnaires, sometimes we wondered whether it was really worth it," says Li-Shin. "Now I have to essays like that of Michael Wang, who writes, "When the children were safely in their slumber, the 'adults' converged on various cabins. First the wine flowed freely, then did the tête-à-têtes. We poured out our souls regarding our personal relationships, both good and bad, our secret hopes, our silly fears. It was both comforting and exhilarating knowing that everybody around was

A three-legged race on the mile-long Asilomar State Beach includes all generations.

come. A cousin asked for and was granted permission to videotape. With a small group around her, Li-Shin's aunt began to talk. She spoke of the nightmare of her father's imprisonment, of how hard it was to go through it alone. The group was overwhelmed by emotion. When the rest of the family returned, they watched the video after dinner. "The intensity stayed with us for the rest of the reunion," Li-Shin recalls. "It was a very different reunion admit that the result is truly priceless."

The book sums up the reunion's power through connected to everyone else somehow, all of us in our lime-green T-shirts. We were all family."

The girl cousins perform a dance for the evening festivities.

"Insecurity as much as arrogance causes many of us to spurn our family histories until we feel we have defined ourselves."
—Edward Hoagland
author

A great cover will give the family book presence. Many copy shops will color photocopy a full page of slides: A montage of slides from the family reunion or family archives makes a stunning cover.

Before printing, enlist a sharp-eyed cousin to proofread, catching spelling and grammatical mistakes. When you photocopy, use archive-quality paper that will outlive you (order from an archival company—see Appendix, page 244) and take the paper with you or have it shipped to the copy store. Since you're supplying your own paper, your printing charges should be reduced.

You should determine in advance how you want to pay for the printing of the family book. You can sell it at cost, or at a slight profit in order to afford to give copies free of charge to relatives on fixed incomes. Or, if the family book is ready in time for the reunion, its price may be included as an optional charge on the registration form or folded into the registration fee. Perhaps the family book can be sold at the reunion—or you may want to create one as a gift for the family. However you pay for it, be sure to give yourself credit on the title page and include a page of thanks naming all those who contributed.

When your family book is finished, consider donating a copy to the Mormon Family History Center, an appropriate historical society, or your library's genealogical collection. Then sit back in your favorite reading chair to savor the deep pleasure of having created a treasure that family members will refer to for years.

KIDS' FAMILY BOOKS

Why should the family historian have all the fun? Have the kids write and publish their own books about the family—it might even be a reunion craft project on a rainy day. Since kids are fairly egocentric, these books will be mostly about Me and My Family. You can use standard composition books, covering them at home with bright fabrics. Write out a list of questions for the kids to answer in their book, as well as the autobiographical information that comes naturally to them. Some questions might be:

• How many cousins do you have?
• What is your favorite thing to do with your cousins?
• What do you like best about your grandparents?
• When did your family first come to America? Where did they come from? Where in America did they first live?
• One interesting thing about my family is...

Kids should have a fairly free-wheeling time with their books—after all, school's out. Kids who don't know how to write can draw pictures and dictate the captions to an older person (10-year-olds are ideal for taking dictation from 4-year-olds).

THE FAMILY COOKBOOK

For families whose very spirit seems to lie in their love of food, a family cookbook may be the best way of preserving the family soul as well as what nourished it. A cookbook can serve as the family book—evocative and useful, producing a smile of recognition every time it's taken from the kitchen shelf and put to practical use. And it's a way of maintaining a very sensuous link to the past: Distributing family recipes is one way to ensure that your children will end up eating what your grandmother ate.

Food is the sensory evidence of how life was once lived, and family cooking is proof that not everything changes with time. Ethnic cooking is often the last part of the heritage to go. Long after the accents and the home decorations have been thoroughly Americanized, pockets of pure ethnic cooking will remain. They are yours to preserve.

As with directories and family books, cookbooks can be developed in a range of ways.

• **Put out a call for recipes.** Create eight categories: Appetizers, Soups, Salads, Meat and Fowl, Fish, Pasta, Desserts, and Cocktails. Ask for families to send in at least one recipe for one category—even better, one for *each* category. It will work best if each recipe is for a set number—for eight, say—to keep the recipes more or less uniform.

• **Ask for a short anecdote with each recipe,** such as its origin, who first made it, a time the contributor remembers eating it as a child, or other associations the contributor might have with the food. Ask your contributors to recall a typical meal from their childhood, and scatter these stories throughout the cookbook as windows into the past. Let people know that they don't need to romanticize their past; eventually, it will be romanticized by the patina of time. After all, memories of growing up in the spanking-new suburbs of 1950s Cleveland are just as much a part of the American experience as recollections of homesteading in the arid fields of North Dakota. What was their favorite meal? Their favorite dessert? (The contributors might also reminisce about favorite ethnic or old-time meals made by their grandparents or great-grandparents—meals they don't have recipes for.)

Give the cookbook a silly name. The Dargan family from South Carolina called theirs *The Dargan Cook-Kin Book*. If ever there is a time for a corny pun, this is it.

Solicit ideas for the cookbook title, too—the competition will draw the menfolk into the process.

If there aren't many contributors, stapling the cookbook might serve as the means to bind it. But a cookbook will be treasured if it can live upright on a shelf, spiral-bound at the copy shop, rather than sitting in a drawer with all the other odd printouts. Have the cover laminated to protect the book from kitchen spatters.

The cost of the cookbook could be folded into the registration fee, and the cookbooks made available for everyone at the reunion—one copy per family. Or the book could be sold at cost. Order enough copies for each family at the reunion, plus 5 percent more—you never know, it could be the reunion best-seller.

Companies exist to help you compile and then bind family recipes into a professional-looking cookbook, designed to be sold as much to friendly strangers at flea markets as to family (see Appendix, page 263).

FAMILY SOUVENIRS: WE REMEMBER

What genealogists have found as they assemble their family on paper, and what most of us know from pulling together albums from a shoe box of snapshots, is that tangible mementos of family togetherness fulfill the desire to hold the present, fasten it down, keep the moments of our lives from disappearing with the passage of time.

Once you've done what you can to preserve the past for the future, you feel free to enjoy the present while it lasts, rather than anxiously holding onto it as time moves forward. And putting our mark and shape on the past means that it becomes more manageable, more defined, more *us*—giving us a sense of continuity that flows from the past to the present and into the future, despite the enormous changes wrought by time, and those that will eventually change us, and our families, forever.

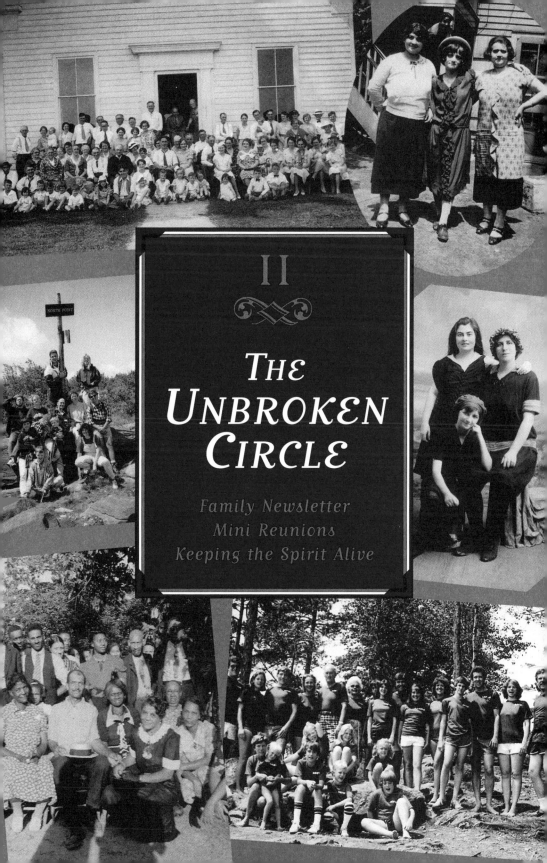

II

THE UNBROKEN CIRCLE

Family Newsletter
Mini Reunions
Keeping the Spirit Alive

If the reunion has gone well, a kind of high stays with you afterward. Perhaps it's that unexpected and moving sense of belonging. Or maybe you come away with a renewed sense of what really matters, and can shuck off the rest. Sometimes it's the deep satisfaction of having really connected with a loved one, and what has needed to be said has finally been said. After a great reunion, there's a feeling of having been part of a larger fabric, where young and old managed to interweave with kindred spirits to form a whole. Now, as family members take off in different directions to return home, the question, "How can we stay connected even as we separate?" is posed in a hundred different ways.

As their last official act, the reunion organizers might want to write a follow-up letter to keep the embers burning and the reunion spirit alive. (The letter also boosts the spirits of reunion organizers in the grip of post-reunion letdown.) A follow-up letter might include the reunion's vital statistics: how many people attended, who they were and from where, how much money remains in the treasury. And it might also briefly recap the reunion events for those who couldn't attend and thank by name the stalwart volunteers who made everything happen. Send out the reunion photograph with the letter. And if the photo came out well, consider having a photo calendar made as a keepsake for everyone (see Appendix, page 263).

FAMILY NEWSLETTER

Many reunions inspire family members other than the reunion organizers to become more involved and family-oriented—and to start a newsletter. With a newsletter, those on the sidelines get to feel like insiders, and the insiders get to know those outside the loop. A newsletter showcases family talent and achievement, boosts the sense of community, and gives the satisfying sense that you belong to a lively, active club.

If it's your first attempt at desktop publishing, follow this rule of thumb: Getting a newsletter ready for publication takes twice as long as you imagine. So be realistic about the newsletter's production schedule and don't announce the number of issues you'll bring out each year. But do set a deadline for yourself to help you focus and budget your time.

If possible, work on a computer. If you don't have one, maybe a family member can donate one he considers obsolete.

Create a "mission statement, even if it's just a sentence or two," advises Jenny Lund, curator of education at the Museum of Church History and Art for the Latter-Day Saints, who edited her family newsletter for nine years. Her newsletter's purpose was "to teach about the family heritage and create connections." Yours might be "to help the family think of itself as a unit" or "to stimulate interest in our historical past." Even if the mission shifts as time goes on, you'll still have a focus for each issue. And give your newsletter a name—names with historical significance work well.

"The content should focus on what all the readers have in common," says Jenny Lund. So know your audience. But don't assume that because you know everybody, everybody else does, too. Watch out for insider jokes and references that not all readers will get.

Create a loose "formula" for your newsletter, balancing, for example, articles about the past and present. Each issue might include:

- historical article, with remembrances of family life in the past or a profile of an ancestor
- profile of a young contemporary family branch, with photos
- obituaries of family members, written for the newsletter or reprinted from newspapers
- news of graduations, honor roll achievements, college enrollments, weddings, birthdays, and births
- calendar of upcoming events, and news of an upcoming reunion
- contribution from a child (one per issue is about right). Involvement of kids will bring in the parents.

Since open pleas for contributions usually go unheeded, pick up the phone and ask someone to write something specific: "We'd like you to write a profile of your mother." Assure your contributors that they don't have to create a perfect piece of literature, and that you will clean up the spelling, grammar, and syntax. But handle the editorial cudgel tactfully. Few contributors will be familiar with the editorial process in which cuts are made for space and clarity. Prepare all contributors for that probability, and clear all changes with them before publication.

Don't use only photos of the best-known family members: spread the attention around. Convert photos to halftones, which reproduce well. Computer scanners that digitize photos do this, as do print shops. Finally, enlist a proofreader before going to press.

To defray the costs of the newsletter, you can: include the subscription price as an optional payment on the reunion registration form, or sell the subscriptions at the reunion and through the mail. And be prepared to absorb some of the newsletter's cost yourself.

PLANNING AHEAD: THE NEXT REUNION

Deciding when to hold the next reunion, or whether to make a regular timetable for holding reunions, is as much a question of intuition as practical consideration. The end of a reunion is the ideal time to decide, when a family is in the throes of warm family feeling tempered by the reality that for some, returning home entails a long, tedious, expensive journey.

Some families swear by their annual reunions. The continuity and reliability of the yearly event gives a sense of security—family members know they can count on the gathering, even if they aren't able to attend each year. But for other families, holding a reunion every year might erode its sense of specialness and lose its luster as an event. A sense of

*"**S**ince the Mendozas fled Cuba, we hold a reunion only every 15 years because the family is scattered in Miami, Spain, Venezuela, and New Jersey. But everybody comes. Everybody. We take over a country club, no expense is spared... and hire a fantastic Latin band. To the ones coming over from Spain and Venezuela, the reunion is like coming home. But 15 years is too long. I understand that everyone needs time to make financial arrangements and travel plans. But 10 years would be reasonable. And it would still be a blast."*

—Nikki Mendoza
Miami, Florida

fatigue can set in, for those attending as well as for those organizing. And for families who have to travel far, attending a reunion each year may monopolize vacation time and money.

"We arrived at holding our reunion every three years by the feel of it," says Nancy Kenney Hays. "It was like the three bears, with the beds that were too hard, too soft, and just right. We used to have reunions every five years, but that felt too long. And we felt that two years was too short in terms of organizing and building up a head of steam. Three years was just right."

Each family has to weigh the benefits of continuity over the sense of repetition, and the boon of reliability over the possible loss of enthusiasm.

REVIVING THE REUNION SPIRIT

Once a reunion is brought to life, and new ones are planned for the future, a family shouldn't expect the enthusiasm for the event to continue without a little tweaking. For a tradition of a reunion to survive, the reunion organizers must be adaptable in their vision of how the event should be held. The ideal is to strike a balance between continuity and change, rather than assuming that what has always worked in the past will always work in the future. When a reunion falters, and the numbers of attendees dwindle, it's usually because the balance has fallen too much on the side of continuity—holding the reunion as it's always been held. The beauty of a reunion is that there are no rules, and the reunion doesn't need to follow the same liturgy year after year. The flexible family adapts to changing circumstances—and you should expect your reunion to shift accordingly too.

The reunion organizers should also bear in mind what forces are competing with reunions for the time, attention, and financial resources of family members. In the old days, reunions were welcome holidays from the hard lives on the farm; simply taking a day off for a home-cooked feast was enough of a lure for a long drive.

"The only time my cousins and I saw each other anymore was at funerals. Finally we said, 'We've got to stop meeting like this. Whenever we get together, we're crying our eyes out.' So now we have a hell of a good time when we see each other at the reunion. And any tears are tears of laughter."

—Joan McKenna
Queens, New York

But families today are used to cruises, resorts, Disney World. Can reunions even compete? Absolutely, because they have it all over Disney when it comes to genuine emotional connections and because families are searching for ways of spending time together meaningfully and actively. Reunions that don't supply those connections and don't recognize where the competition for the family's time and money lies are the ones in trouble. If your family reunion seems to suffer from a case of the "dwindles" or "growing pains," consult the reunion diagnostic chart on the next page for where to go from here.

Mini Reunions

At its best, a reunion isn't an end in itself but the beginning and strengthening of connections. If you emerge from a reunion having found two or three cousins to enter your life as real connections, you are immeasurably

CAN THIS REUNION BE SAVED? DIAGNOSTIC CHART

Here are some symptoms of waning enthusiasm for the family reunion and prescriptions for saving it.

PROBLEM	PRESCRIPTION
Refusal to change: Insistence on holding every reunion the third weekend in July, at the same park, with the same horseshoe stakes, even though nobody likes horseshoes anymore	Enlist new blood to adjust to real changes in family: new organizer, new program, new location
The dwindles: Third cousins gather in honor of ancestors they never knew to share memories they never had, because that's what their parents did	Dissolve and re-form, with more personal connection, or reinvent as a purely historical event
Lack of organization: Reunion organizers know that family members adore each other so much, they can just hang out happily for days at a stretch with no planned activities	Plan activities that connect people so that they feel a sense of emotional satisfaction
Overpricing: Reunion organizers feel that everyone will love going on a cruise together, with all those activities	Contact other family members as "reality check" about what is affordable, and renew sensitivity to the financial situations of the extended family
Overfrequency: Reunion organizers are so thrilled by reunion's success, they persuade everyone to make it an annual event	Reduce frequency of reunions, increase enthusiasm

enriched. While holding a full-blown reunion every year or two may be overly ambitious, you can still hold a mini reunion—a small gathering that reminds you for a short time how it feels to belong to something bigger and gives you the chance to pursue relationships in more intimate, relaxed situations. Organized families, like the Spear-Hurdman-Shy Reunion Club, have chapters in different cities that work as ongoing social clubs through the year, holding events that function as mini reunions: theater-going parties, dinners, and so on.

Nuclear families, too, hold mini reunions as opportunities for connecting beyond the pressured confines of the traditional holidays. "I wanted to see my siblings and parents away from my mother's house," says one young adult, "without all of us regressing into the way we were as teenagers—sulking on the couch and rolling our eyes." Her mini reunions rotate among all the siblings' homes, studiously avoid any connection to holidays, and focus on a game created by the host family—to bring the family together as well as create memories to laugh about later.

PASSING THE TORCH

Most reunion organizers worry about the succession issue. Who will take over when they're gone? Will the reunion survive them?

If Susanne Oberhauser achieves what she wants to achieve, the reunion will take care of itself: "I have three goals in going to the effort of holding these reunions. One is to become closer to my siblings, closer to them now than I was 20 years ago, when we were all caught in the hustle and bustle of raising kids and making a living. Another is to see my three daughters stay connected. And the third is to see that my grandkids become close and stay close."

Reunions are the purposeful creation of memories that bind families as they move into the future, memories that become stories that become links between generations and branches of family. That one event can touch so many people so deeply makes it hard to imagine that most reunions begin from the focused efforts of a single person. A reunion can't happen without a committee and the delegation of chores—but most of all, it can't happen without the human engine that fires up the whole machinery. A reunion is one of those areas in life—less rare than people imagine—where one single person makes a difference.

Each generation has a handful of people who can pick up the torch and make that difference. Tribes have always identified and nurtured leadership potential early on, to insure the tribe's continuity and strength. Just telling someone that he or she has what it takes to be a great reunion organizer is a way of preparing them, honoring them, endowing them with

"**At** our reunions, our kids see themselves as a link in an endless chain—it didn't all start in our house and it won't end there. The reunion gives them a sense of possibilities and the role of luck in life—the good, decent people in our family, intelligent and fun to be around, didn't always get all the breaks, even if they should have. But our family respects them all the same. And reunions remind us that we're more than individuals. Our culture places an emphasis on the individual, on self-actualization. But our lives are more than our personal history. They're infinite, with no discernible beginning and no foreordained end. Our family is like a stream, always flowing, always changing."

—William Raspberry
Washington, D.C.

a larger sense of themselves. Preparing to pass the torch is a way a family can tell its individuals that they're special.

Shining On

You might think that the less you see of your family, the stronger your desire to see them. But it doesn't work that way. As with any relationship, the more involved you are, the more emotionally invested you become. Each contact strengthens, not loosens, the family ties, and makes them all the more compelling. What a reunion can do is connect the family and pivot the perspective so that the family is facing the future together.

Honoring the past and celebrating the present are a reunion's most clear objectives. But a reunion's secret weapon is the way it turns a family into a forward-looking entity. As the group anticipates and plans a next reunion, it projects itself into the future. As we imagine the family converging at a single place at some not-so-distant date, we mentally pitch ourselves forward. Connecting with family becomes a date, a promise, a common purpose, as the pages of a calendar are scrolled forward and a day or two are circled for the family's next reunion. Suddenly, we're not just moving on. We're moving ahead.

Appendix

CHAPTER TWO

Timetables for Family Reunions

Even if a family can't organize a reunion that works like a well-oiled machine, it can use the timetables that follow with the knowledge that most dates (with the exception of those right before the event) can be delayed by a week or so without disastrous results. What you don't want to dillydally about is reserving the reunion location—even if it's just a pavilion in a state park. Nail that down, and the rest will follow. Without it, nothing can happen.

Distribute copies of these countdowns (you can adjust the details for your own family's idiosyncrasies) to all members of the reunion committee.

BACKYARD BARBECUE TIMETABLE

◆ **6–4 MONTHS AHEAD**
Get family consensus to go ahead
Scope out backyard's logistics or find park with shelter
Draw up mailing/phone list
Set date
Reserve park shelter (if necessary)
Mail invitations or make calls

◆ **4 MONTHS AHEAD**
Determine rental or loaner needs: tables and chairs, coolers, etc.
Reserve tent (if using one)
Design and order T-shirts

◆ **2 MONTHS AHEAD**
Make final attendance list; make follow-up calls
Determine purchasing needs: charcoal, paper plates, etc.
Enlist set-up and other volunteers

◆ **1 MONTH AHEAD**
Make potluck assignments

Draw up menu
Make parking arrangements
Reserve rental equipment
Buy nonperishable items: paper plates and cups, plastic cutlery, etc.

◆ **2 WEEKS AHEAD**
Make reunion day checklist

◆ **5 TO 2 DAYS AHEAD**
Buy perishable food
Check cameras for batteries and film
Start food preparation
Pick up or have "loaners" delivered: coolers, chairs, etc.

◆ **DAY BEFORE**
Pick up rental supplies
Put up tent

◆ **REUNION DAY**
See reunion day checklist
Reserve time for enjoyment
Abandon dreams of perfection and embrace the moment!

HOMECOMING TIMETABLE

♦ **1** YEAR AHEAD
Get family consensus to go
  ahead
Scope out backyard's logistics
  or find park with shelter
Compile mailing/phone list
Set date
Mail exploratory letter
Reserve park shelter
  (if necessary)

♦ **9** MONTHS AHEAD
Create reunion committee and
  decide what reunion
  activities will be held and
  whether reunion will be
  catered or potluck
Arrive at budget

♦ **6** MONTHS AHEAD
Mail explanatory letter
Assemble directory or family
  book (if desired)
Engage caterer (if using one)

♦ **4** MONTHS AHEAD
Determine rental and loaner
  needs: tables and chairs,
  coolers, etc.
Reserve tent (if using one)
Design and order T-shirts

♦ **2** MONTHS AHEAD
Make final attendance list;
  make follow-up calls
Determine purchasing needs:
  charcoal, paper plates, etc.
Determine decorations

♦ **6** WEEKS AHEAD:
Potluck coordinator makes
  assignments

♦ **1** MONTH AHEAD
Make parking arrangements
  (if necessary)
Buy nonperishable items: paper
  plates and cups, plastic
  cutlery, etc.
Confirm park reservation

♦ **2** WEEKS AHEAD
Make reunion day checklist
Confirm potluck assignments
Check in with all volunteers

♦ **5** TO **2** DAYS AHEAD
Buy perishable food
Check cameras for batteries
  and film
Start food preparation
Pick up or have "loaners"
  delivered: coolers, chairs, etc.

♦ DAY BEFORE
Decorate the site
Pick up rental supplies
Put up tent (if using one)

♦ REUNION DAY
See reunion day checklist
Reserve time for enjoyment
Abandon dreams of perfection
  and embrace the moment!

♦ DAY AFTER
Kick back and enjoy the
  leftovers.

WEEKEND CLASSIC TIMETABLE

◆ **2 YEARS TO 18 MONTHS AHEAD**
Get family consensus to
  go ahead
Form reunion committee
  to arrive at general dates
  and locations
Scout possible sites
Compile mailing list

◆ **18–12 MONTHS AHEAD**
Mail exploratory letter
Determine budget—arrive
  at family "mean"
Find location
Set date

◆ **12–9 MONTHS AHEAD**
Reserve location or block of
  rooms
Assemble active committees
Send explanatory letter
Assemble directory or family
  book (if desired)

◆ **6 MONTHS AHEAD**
Set reunion schedule and
  activities
Send out invitations and
  registration forms
Make banquet or other
  catering arrangements

◆ **4 MONTHS AHEAD**
Design and order T-shirts

◆ **2 MONTHS AHEAD**
Send out follow-up postcard
Prepare printed materials:
  programs, schedules
Determine decoration scheme

◆ **1 MONTH AHEAD**
Buy nonperishable goods:
  name tags, raffle tickets,
  crafts supplies
Mail psych-up letter

◆ **2 WEEKS AHEAD**
Make reunion running-order
  checklist: who is responsible
  for what when
Check in with reunion
  volunteers
Confirm reunion arrangements
  with facility

◆ **1 WEEK AHEAD**
Check cameras for batteries
  and film
Assemble welcome packets

◆ **REUNION WEEKEND**
See running-order checklist
Reserve time for enjoyment
Abandon dreams of perfection
  and embrace the moment!

◆ **DAY AFTER**
Kick back and enjoy the leftovers
Call or write volunteers to
  thank them for their help
Write thank-you letter to
  location manager, if happy
  with service

◆ **1 WEEK AFTER**
Write afterglow letter to all
  family members—those who
  attended and those who
  didn't—and bask in the
  afterglow

FAMILY CAMP TIMETABLE

◆ **18** MONTHS TO **1** YEAR AHEAD
Get family consensus for go
ahead
Determine general locales and
dates for family camp
Compile mailing/phone list
Determine budget—arrive at
family "mean"

◆ **1** YEAR AHEAD
Find and reserve site; raise
funds to make early deposit
Request vacation time from
employer!

◆ **6** MONTHS AHEAD
Scout dinner locations for
special night out
Determine interest in activities
and schedule
Distribute information on area
where family camp is held

◆ **4** MONTHS AHEAD
Design and order T-shirts
Plan rainy-day alternatives

◆ **2** MONTHS AHEAD
Plan off-site excursions
Determine household chore
distribution
Engage hired help for reunion
period
Determine what needs to
be brought and who
brings what

◆ **2** WEEKS AHEAD
Make room assignments
Make cooking assignments
Finalize arrangements with
rental agent
Print schedule in calendar
form

◆ AT THE REUNION
Determine and set up "kitty"
Shop for basic supplies
Get to know one another
as you once knew one
another and as you've
never known one another

BUDGET FOR BACKYARD BARBECUE OR HOMECOMING

Per person fee = grand total divided by lowest realistic estimate of possible attendees: _____

	Estimated cost	Actual cost
Printing: letters, programs, directories, postcards		
Postage		
Tablecloths, napkins, utensils, bought or rented		
Table and chair rentals		
Tent rental		
P.A. system rental		
Charcoal		
Rented grill, if needed		
Rented coffee urns		
Beverages: soda, beer, wine, coffee, tea		
Food		
Facility rental		
T-shirts		
Professional photographer or camera rental for group photo		
Special entertainment: bagpiper, ethnic dancers, line dance teacher, pony rides		
Other		
Total		
10% to 15% contingency fee		

BUDGET FOR WEEKEND CLASSIC

Per person fee = grand total divided by lowest realistic estimate of possible attendees: _____

	Estimated cost	Actual cost
Printing: letters, programs, directories, postcards	_____	_____
Postage	_____	_____
Baby-sitters	_____	_____
Hospitality suite or meeting room rental	_____	_____
P.A. system rental	_____	_____
Audio-visual rental	_____	_____
Extra group activities: tennis court time, pavilion rental	_____	_____
T-shirts	_____	_____
Professional photographer or camera rental for group photo	_____	_____
Entertainment: bagpiper, ethnic dancers, line dance teacher, DJ, band	_____	_____

If lodging and meals are being paid for by reunion organizers rather than individual families:

	Estimated cost	Actual cost
Lodging	_____	_____
Meals	_____	_____
Other	_____	_____
Total	_____	_____
10% to 15% contingency fee	_____	_____
GRAND TOTAL	_____	_____

Archival-Quality Materials

You'll want to print and store materials that you hope will survive for generations to come—family histories, genealogies—on acid-free paper. Following are highly regarded companies that supply archival products to museums, universities, and conservators. Their catalogues are lessons in how to maintain archives:

Light Impressions (800) 828-6216
Gaylord Brothers (800) 448-6160
The Archival Company
(800) 442-7576

The following organization offers leaflets on preserving documents, textiles, and family collections:

**Northeast Document
Conservation Center**
24 School Street
Andover, MA 01810
Phone: (508) 470-1010

Professional conservators can restore or recommend sophisticated treatments to protect your aging valuables. But no standards exist by which conservators are measured, so be careful in choosing one. For a brochure on how to choose a conservator and a list of conservators in your area, contact:

**American Institute for Conservation
of Historic and Artistic Works (AIC)**
1717 K Street NW, Suite 301
Washington, DC 20006
Phone: (202) 452-9545
Fax: (202) 452-9328

Press Releases and Special Citations

PUTTING TOGETHER A PRESS RELEASE

Most of us love to see our names in print, and when our family is honored by being mentioned in print, we love it even more. In American life, nothing ratifies our specialness as much as media attention. And what would our family scrapbooks be without yellowing newspaper clippings crumbling behind the glaze of an album's plastic page covers? How can you garner this recognition? Feed the hungry media press releases.

Target the newspapers that might be interested in your reunion. Small-town newspapers, ethnic newspapers, and religious community newspapers are best bets. Small newspapers faced with slow news days may be grateful for an article they can slug in with few editorial changes.

Send the press release to the newspaper two to three weeks before the reunion. Call the newspaper to ask whom to send it to—the society editor, the local news editor—and direct the press release to that editor. Be sure to spell the name right.

Format: Put the words "Press Release" in the upper left-hand corner, with the name, address, and phone number (and fax number) of the contact person. In the upper right-hand corner, put "For immediate release" or "Release date: _____."

Write a headline that describes what makes your family reunion special and worth notice: "Schultz Family Celebrates 100th Anniversary in USA."

Put the four W's in the first paragraph: who, what, when, and where. This is a people story, so concentrate on the "who": who's hosting the reunion and who's coming to it. Give background on the family: notable accomplishments, what effect the family has had on the town ("The Martin family has run Martin Insurance on Bond Street for over 100 years, and Lionel Martin served as mayor from 1948–1963").

SPECIAL CITATIONS: LETTER OF COMMENDATION OR KEYS TO THE CITY

Reading a letter of commendation or producing the keys to the city from the mayor of the town where the reunion will be held (or possibly the governor of the state) is a great way—a modern version of a clarion call—to start off a family reunion's most formal gathering. Even when half the reunion goers live out of state and have never heard of the elected official, a letter of commendation brings an air of importance to the gathering.

Letters of commendation cost a mayor, state senator, congressperson, or governor little in terms of effort while generating a great deal of voter goodwill, so your family may discover that an elected official is quite forthcoming. Write the elected official six months before the reunion, and follow up with a second letter a few months later if you haven't received a reply. In the letter, mention points that the official can use in his own letter in paying tribute to the family.

T-Shirt Biz

A T-shirt shop needs at least three months notice before the reunion—a time when probably not all reunion goers have ordered or paid. But go ahead and order enough T-shirts for all those who might attend; sometimes relatives feel too strapped to send in a registration fee and money for the T-shirt at the same time, but almost everyone will want a T-shirt once they arrive—especially the kids. It's always a good idea to order most T-shirts in the extra large size; family members have a way of growing into them.

Since T-shirt costs go down the greater the quantity (25 T-shirts cost about $10), it may be just as economical to overestimate by five or ten anyway. Each T-shirt should be marked up by a few dollars to cover the cost of unsold T-shirts. Any money left over can be moved into the contingency fund.

CHAPTER THREE
Backyard Logistics

THINK ABOUT PARKING

Get a rough count of how many families are coming, and how many cars with them. If you're squeezed for space and there's no street parking, ask a neighbor a week or more in advance if he can accommodate extra cars. No luck? Scope out a public parking lot with a public phone and plan to run a shuttle to and from the lot; consider borrowing or renting a minivan to accommodate the crowd. If families are staying at motels or bed-and-breakfasts, run a shuttle to and from them.

Expecting a disabled relative who needs his own "handicapped" parking space at your house? Reserve a parking spot with a sawhorse or other bulky object such as lawn furniture, and mark it with a large sign reading RESERVED PARKING.

SPRUCE UP THE HOUSE

A day or two before the reunion, clear the living room of fragile knick-knacks, antique vases, and light-colored or fragile rugs. Presume the worst: 15 cousins, muddy sneakers, freeze tag—your living room.

Tidy up all the bathrooms, not just the guest bathroom. When that one is occupied, family members will pad around the premises in quest of a free one. In addition to corralling stray underwear:

- Replace old toothbrushes.
- Empty wastepaper baskets.
- Replace towels in the guest bathroom with good-quality paper hand towels, and plenty of them.
- Replace bar soap with liquid soap.
- Keep spare rolls of toilet paper in plain view.
- Put out a clean comb or brush, mouthwash, hand cream, sunscreen.
- A few flowers in a bud vase go a long way.
- Put away all personal items (unless you revel in the scrutiny).
- Put out fresh boxes of tissues.

Lodging: Listings and Resources

JEWISH CAMPS

Most Jewish camps are in the Northeast, many near the Berkshires. Often they are rustic camps intended for city kids rather than all-age retreats, and they are usually in session during the summer months. But fall might be an ideal time in the Berkshires anyway, with the lure of the foliage, the Berkshires' cultural sites, and a profusion of outlet shopping nearby. Eisner Camp, in Great Barrington, Massachusetts, is especially welcoming to families from September through mid-June, and fully winterized. Phone (212) 650-4130 for information. For a directory of Jewish camps:

Association of Jewish
Sponsored Camps
130 East 59th Street
Room 632
New York, NY 10022

CHRISTIAN CAMPS

Christian camps are less likely to be booked the entire summer with regular summer camp programs for kids and may have a weekend available here or there for family groups. Christian Camp International/USA can supply you with a directory of camps. It is not a complete listing of church camps in the United States, though; check with your own church staff and friends.

Christian Camp International/USA
Box 62189
Colorado Springs, CO 80962-2189
Phone: (719) 260-9400
Web site: www.gospel.com

The camp where the Grange family stayed, described in this chapter, is in the Black Hills National Forest. For more information:

Storm Mountain Center
Steve Foss, Director/Manager
23740 Storm Mountain Road
Rapid City, SD 57702-06540
Phone: (605) 343-4391
Fax: (605) 343-0154

NONDENOMINATIONAL SUMMER CAMPS

Most camps are listed in *Guide to ACA-Accredited Camps* published by the American Camping Association. A camp that has been accredited by the ACA meets its health and safety standards. The guide also lists day camps (often available on weekends) and includes separate lists for rental facilities and Christian camps.

The guide is published annually and can be bought at bookstores or ordered directly from:

American Camping Association, Inc.
5000 State Road 67 North
Martinsville, IN 46151-7902
Phone: (800) 428-CAMP
E-mail: aca@aca-camps.org
Web site with a database of ACA-accredited camps: www.aca-camps.org

But don't limit your search to these lists. Owners and directors of camps might be interested in the extra income your reunion will bring in the off months of June and September.

YMCA CONFERENCE CENTERS

There are seven YMCA conference centers, and they book years in advance:

YMCA Blue Ridge Assembly
84 Blue Ridge Circle
Black Mountain, NC 28711
Phone: (704) 669-8422
Fax: (704) 669-8497

YMCA of the Rockies
Estes Park Center
2515 Tunnel Road
Estes Park, CO 80511-2550
Phone: (970) 586-3341
        (303) 623-9215
Fax: (970) 586-6078

YMCA of the Rockies
Snow Mountain Ranch
P.O. Box 169
Winter Park, CO 80482
Phone: (970) 887-2152
        (303) 443-4743
Fax: (303) 449-6781

YMCA of the Ozarks
Route 2, Box 94
Potosi, MO 63664
Phone: (314) 438-2154
Fax: (314) 438-5752

Frost Valley YMCA
2000 Frost Valley Road
Claryville, NY 12725-9600
Phone: (914) 985-2291
Fax: (914) 985-0056

Holiday Hills YMCA
Conference Center
2 Lakeside Drive
Pawling, NY 12564
Phone: (914) 855-1550
Fax: (914) 855-9535

Silver Bay Association
Silver Bay, NY 12874
Phone: (518) 543-8833
Fax: (518) 543-6733

STATE RESORT PARKS

State resort parks are so well priced
and such good values that many
book up to two years in advance.

Gulf State Park
Gulf Shores, AL 36452
(334) 948-7275

DeGray Lake Resort State Park
Bismarck, AR 71929
(800) 737-8355

F.D. Roosevelt State Park
2970 Highway 190 East
Pine Mountain, GA 31822
(404) 663-4858

Cumberland Falls State
Resort Park
Corbin, KY 40701
(606) 528-4121

Lake Barkley State Resort Park
Cadiz, KY 42211
(800) 325-1708

Lake Cumberland State
Resort Park
Jamestown, KY 42629
(800) 325-1709

Eugene T. Mahoney State Park
Ashland, NE 68003
(402) 944-2523

Letchworth State Park
Castile, NY 14427
(716) 493-3600

Lake Murray Resort and State Park
Ardmore, OK 73401
(800) 654-8240

Roman Nose Resort Park
Watonga, OK 73772
(800) 654-8240

Quartz Mountain Resort
and State Park
Altus, OK 73655
(800) 654-8240

Western Hills Guest Ranch
Wagoner, OK 74477
(800) 654-8240

Hickory Knob State Resort Park
Route 1, Box 199-B
McCormick, SC
(864) 391-2450

Canaan Valley Resort State Park
Davis, WV 26260
(304) 866-4121

Pipestem Resort State Park
Pipestem, WV 25979
(304) 466-1800

HOUSEBOATS

For a listing of houseboat rental companies in the United States and Canada:

Houseboat Association of America
4940 N. Rhett Avenue
N. Charleston, SC 29405
Phone: (803) 744-6581

Houseboat Magazine publishes an annual vacation guide filled with details on the different companies and the areas they service:

Houseboat Magazine
520 Park Avenue
Idaho Falls, ID 83402
(800) 638-0135

Fodor's Family Adventures by Christine Loomis features a useful roundup of reliable locations.

CONDOMINIUMS

For a referral to a condo travel agent:

Condominium Travel Associates (CTA)
2001 West Main Street, Suite 140
Stamford, CT 06902
(800) 492-6636

Also check out *The Complete Guide to Condo Vacations,* Lanier Publishing.

GUIDEBOOKS

State and National Parks
The Complete Guide to America's National Parks, edited by Jane Bangley McQueen, National Park Foundation. Fodor's Travel.

America's 100 Best-Loved State Parks by Robert Rafferty, Macmillan. For more information, check out the Web site at www.nationalparks.org and/or use a search engine such as Yahoo!

Sports Resources
The Best Public Golf Courses in the U.S., Canada, the Caribbean and Mexico by Robert McCord, Random House.

Golf Digest's 4,200 Best Places to Play, Fodor's Travel.

Ballpark Vacations by Bruce Adams and Margaret Engel, Fodor's Travel. Lists all the minor and major league stadiums across the country. Also check out minor league baseball's Web site, which lists most teams and schedules around the country: www.minorleaguebaseball.com.

Ethnic and Historical Guides
African-American Historic Places. Preservation Press, National Park Service, National Register of Historic Places.

Hippocrene USA Guide to Historic Hispanic America by Oscar Jones and Joy Jones, Hippocrene Books. Focuses on Texas and the Southwest.

Historic Black Landmarks: A Traveler's Guide by George Cantor, Visible Ink Press, Gale.

Irish-American Landmarks: A Traveler's Guide by John A. Barnes, Visible Ink Press, Gale.

Plantations & Outdoor Museums in America's Historic South by Gerald Gutek and Patricia Gutek, University of South Carolina Press.

Smithsonian Guide to Historic America, edited by Roger G. Kennedy, Stewart, Tabori & Chang.

Factory Tours
Watch It Made in the U.S.A. by Bruce Brumberg and Karen Axelrod, John Muir Publishing. Free visits to such sites as the Vermont Teddy Bear factory, Hershey in Pennsylvania, and Corning Glass.

Family Vacations
The Best Bargain Family Vacations in the U.S.A. by Laura Sutherland and Valerie Wolf Deutsch, St. Martin's Press.

Fifty Great Family Vacations: Western North America by Candyce H. Stapen, Globe Pequot Press.

Fodor's Great American Vacations, edited by Chelsea S. Mauldin, Fodor's Travel.

Great Family Vacations series by Candyce H. Stapen, Globe Pequot Press.

Gene Kilgore's Ranch Vacations, John Muir Publishing. This guidebook also includes sites with great fly fishing and cross-country skiing.

CHAPTER FOUR

DIRECTORY FORM

____ If you do not want to be included in the directory, check here and return.

Name: _____
        (include nickname and maiden name)

Address: _____

Phone: _____ Fax: _____

E-mail address: _____

Birth date (optional): _____

Occupation: _____

Hobbies, volunteer activities, special interests: _____

_____

Spouse's name: _____

Spouse's occupation: _____

Spouse's hobbies, volunteer activities, special interests: _____

_____

Branch of family: _____

Children   Birth date   Hobbies and Interests

_____

_____

_____

_____

Any special events or thoughts about your life or the family you'd like to share? Please limit to 100 words: _____

_____

_____

_____

_____

Please send one photo of you and your family with the names of everyone affixed on the back with a sticky note. Sorry—these cannot be returned.

CHAPTER FIVE

Genealogy Resources

A good starting point is the catalogue of the National Genealogical Society, 4527 17th Street North, Arlington, VA, 22207. Its offerings range from an inexpensive Beginner's Kit with information on getting started to blank pedigree charts and family group sheets to the more arcane problems of investigating the genealogies of different nationalities and ethnic groups.

Other basic texts available at the bookstore:

Unpuzzling Your Past by Emily Anne Croom (Better Ways Books) is a comprehensive introductory survey of this detail-rich field.

A Guidebook of American Genealogy, edited by Arlene Eakle and Johni Cerny (Ancestry Publishing), is *the* bible of genealogists. It lists sources for everything from employment records to ships' passenger lists to land tax records. If it's not here, you probably don't need it.

International Vital Records Handbook by Thomas J. Kemp (Genealogical Publishing Company) provides sample forms with which to request vital records from different states. You photocopy the forms, fill them out, and send them to the appropriate state, saving you the time-consuming steps of writing for the appropriate form and then waiting for it to arrive.

Latter-Day Saints Genealogical Library and Family History Centers

The Church of Jesus Christ of Latter-Day Saints runs the world's largest genealogical library in Salt Lake City, which has become a mecca for amateur and professional genealogists. The library has information on more than 2 billion names, with 2 million reels of microfilmed genealogical records—most of which circulate, so you can get them on loan from a local family history center. Write the library for more information at 35 North West Temple, Salt Lake City, UT 84150, or call (801) 240-2331.

The LDS Family History Centers, with extensive microfilmed documents available, are open to everyone and can be found in virtually all metropolitan areas. The centers are listed in the yellow pages in various ways: Latter-Day Saints Family History Center, LDS Family History Center, and Church of Jesus Christ of Latter-Day Saints Family History Center. (Occasionally, there may also be a listing for a Family History Center. Call and check that it is run by the Latter-Day Saints.)

These centers exist to try to create as diverse and vast a body of genealogical information as possible; workers at the centers are as helpful to non-Mormons as they are to their fellow church members. You may find that information on your family has already been recorded by a distant cousin or two and maintained in the LDS archives. Visit a center, and

NUTSHELL FAMILY HISTORY

The first member of the _____ family to arrive

in the United States was _____ in _____.

He/she came from _____.

He/she settled in _____.

Other relatives living with him/her:

_____

_____

_____

_____

_____

_____

_____

_____

_____

_____

Occupations held by these first-generation family members:

_____

_____

_____

_____

_____

_____

_____

_____

_____

_____

FAMILY GROUP SHEET

Prepared By _____   Date _____

Husband

Occupation(s) _____

	Date — Day, Month, Year	City	County	State or Country	Religion
Born					
Christened					Name of church
Bar Mitzvahed					Name of temple
Married					Name of church/temple
Died					Cause of death
Buried	Cem/Place				Date will written/proved

Father _____
Mother _____   Other wives _____

Wife

Occupation(s) _____

					Religion
Born					
Christened					Name of church
Bat Mitzvahed					Name of temple
Married					Cause of death
Died					Date will written/proved
Buried	Cem/Place				

Father _____
Mother _____   Other husbands _____

Children (given names)	Sex M/F	Birth			Birthplace			Date of first marriage/Place	Date of death/Cause		
		Day	Month	Year	City	County	St./Cty.	Name of spouse	City	County	State/Country
1											
2											
3											
4											
5											
6											
7											
8											
9											
10											
11											
12											

the librarians will walk you through many steps of the process.

Genealogy Librarians

The genealogy librarians of the larger public libraries are wonderful resources as well, and need your "business" to justify their existence. Use them. They can usually refer you to local genealogical societies, with whom you can work as a group to receive support and advice, and share your enthusiasm and frustrations.

Medical Family Tree

A medical family tree assembles family medical histories to give you a clear picture of what your health risk factors may be. When you know which diseases you may be at genetic or environmental risk for, you and your doctors can be on the lookout for the first detectable signs of those diseases, and you may be able to take steps to help prevent their occurrence. Family reunions are not the time and place to work the room in search of details on how your relatives died or what medical battles they're now fighting. But you *can* announce that you're putting together a family medical tree and would like to speak with any interested people who wish to share information after the reunion. When you've finished with your research, offer a copy to everyone, but send copies only to those who have requested one.

For a medical family tree, get information on your siblings, parents, grandparents, aunts, and uncles (even those not related by blood, because of the possible environmental factors that apply equally to in-laws and blood relations), great-aunts and great-uncles, and first and second cousins. Speaking to older members of the family may not be the best way to take a family medical history, cautions Carol Krause, author of *How Healthy Is Your Family Tree?* Talking about illness may have been taboo in the "old days," particularly diseases affecting "private parts": breast, ovarian or uterine, or prostate cancers—all of which have strong hereditary implications. Ovarian cancer, for instance, may have been euphemistically referred to as stomach cancer. But anecdotal reports from family members *can* be useful, especially in helping to identify health risk factors such as smoking, alcoholism, and obesity.

For an accurate picture of how and why a relative died, death certificates can be good sources of medical information. Typically, they record primary and secondary causes of death; the secondary cause is often the "real" cause. A primary cause may be noted as pneumonia, but the secondary cause—a heart attack, for instance—may be the underlying fatal condition and the one of most interest to you. Death certificates often give the age at death as well as the length of illness, associated surgeries, and the hospital where the surgeries were performed (helpful if you want to acquire the medical records themselves). For a copy of a death certificate, write to the office of vital statistics or comparable bureaucracy in the state where your relative died and ask how you can get a copy. If your relative lived and died in another country, contact that country's consulate for information on how to obtain a copy of the death certificate.

Be sure to find out the onset age for the diseases affecting your family. Diabetes and arthritis, for instance, are different diseases depending on whether they begin in childhood or adulthood, as is breast cancer, depending on whether it appears in early adulthood or late middle age.

What to do with the information once you get it? You can mark it down on a family tree or put it into narrative form, allowing yourself more room to expand on the anecdotal evidence and the questions that remain unanswered.

How do you interpret your medical findings once your results are in? Siblings, parents, and children are *first-degree relatives.* Aunts, uncles, and grandparents are

GENETIC INHERITANCE

According to Carol Krause, we share:

50% of our parents' genes

50% of our siblings' genes

25% of our aunts' and uncles' genes

25% of our grandparents' genes

Identical twins share 100% of each other's genes.

second-degree relatives. Carol Krause believes you should consult a specialist (with medical history in hand) if:

• Two first-degree relatives have been diagnosed with the same cancer (cancer of the breast, uterus, ovaries, and colon are part of a cancer syndrome; these cancers should be considered "the same")

• One first-degree relative under the age of 50 has been diagnosed with cancer or serious heart disease

What kind of specialist should you see? A medical geneticist at a major university medical center—the genetics field is evolving so rapidly that only the major centers are up on the latest developments.

COUSINS CHART (FAMILY STRUCTURE WHO'S WHO)

Second cousin twice removed. Sounds mathematical, as though establishing a family relationship required the use of trigonometric algorithms. But like so many apparently daunting areas of expertise, it's really just a matter of learning the lingo. In the definitions below, "you" serve as the frame of reference, around which all the other relations revolve.

Uncle and aunt	Your parents' brothers and sisters, and their spouses. You don't need any blood connection to be a full-fledged aunt or uncle. Your mother's sister's husband is not your uncle by marriage. He's your uncle, fair and square.
Niece and nephew	Son and daughter of your siblings and siblings-in-law. As with uncle and aunt, they're not your nieces and nephews by marriage, they're your nieces and nephews, plain and simple, even if they're your spouse's siblings' kids and don't have a single drop of blood in common with you.
First cousin, full cousin, cousin-german	Children of your parents' brothers and sisters. You and your first cousins share one set of grandparents.
Double first cousins	If a pair of brothers marries a pair of sisters, their kids are not only first cousins, they're double first cousins: They have both sets of grandparents in common.
Second cousins	You and the children of your parents' cousins are second cousins and share at least one great-grandparent. Your child and your cousin's child are second cousins.
Third cousins	You and the children of your parents' second cousins are third cousins and share at least one great-great-grandparent. And so on with the fourth, fifth, and sixth cousins.
First cousin once removed	A relationship that is *removed* is one that exists in two different genealogical generations. *Generation* refers to the order of birth, a genealogical level.
(cont'd on next page)	Your aunt and your mother may have been born 20

COUSINS CHART (FAMILY STRUCTURE WHO'S WHO)

First cousin once removed (continued)	years apart, but they are still of the same generation. Your parent's first cousin is your first cousin once removed. The child of your first cousin is also your first cousin once removed: your grandparent is that child's great-grandparent. You can do the whole "removed" thing for every category of cousins—second cousin once removed, and so on. But by then you'll probably drive everyone completely crazy.
Grandaunt and granduncle	We always called grandpa's sister "great-aunt." But the experts say that terminology is incorrect. These terms are. (Which doesn't mean we have any intention of using them.)
Great-grandaunts, great-granduncles	Your great-grandparents' brothers and sisters.
In-laws	Family by marriage: Your spouse's parents, spouses of your siblings, and spouses of your spouse's siblings. That is, your brother's wife is an in-law, but none of her siblings are. And your husband's sister's husband is your in-law, but none of his brothers are. And in-laws pretty much stop with your parents-in-law and your siblings-in-law. You are not in-laws with the parents of your sister-in-law's husband. And the two sets of parents of a couple are not in-laws to each other either; they are the competitive grandparents—an entirely different category.
Affinity relatives	Your husband or wife's blood relatives—the in-laws that are biologically related to your spouse.
Birth mother, biological mother, natural mother	Terms for the biological mother of a child who has (usually) been adopted by other parents.
Adoptive mother	Mother of a child who is not biologically her own.

CHAPTER SIX

What to Rent

TENTS AND TABLES

For every 25 people, you'll need:
- Three 8-person (5-foot-round tables or 8-foot-long) tables for eating (the little cousins can squeeze in here and there)
- One 6-foot or 8-foot table for food service
- One 8-foot table for beverages
- One 8-foot table for dessert and coffee (this can serve as a family display table at the start of the reunion)
- 25 chairs

To save on space consumption and rental costs, consolidate the desserts, beverages, and coffee on the same table, eliminating one table.

Tents typically come in three sizes:
20 ft. × 20 ft. = 400 sq. ft.
20 ft. × 30 ft. = 600 sq. ft.
30 ft. × 30 ft. = 900 sq. ft.

When figuring out the size you'll need, give little heed to the rental company's estimates; they usually don't include the room people need to move around comfortably. Factoring in the area of the dining tables and chairs, as well as free space in which to move, each person needs 16 square feet of tent space. In figuring out the size tent you'll need, don't forget to add the area of the serving tables—and the area around the serving tables people need to move comfortably. Take each serving table's square footage and multiply it by three.

Here's the formula for figuring out how big a tent a reunion of 25 will require:

25 people = 400 sq. ft.
3 8-foot serving tables = 180 sq. ft.
Total area needed: 580 sq. ft.
Always round up the number:
600 sq. ft. = 20 ft. × 30 ft. tent

Whenever possible, size up to a larger tent—in this case, up to a 30 ft. × 30 ft. tent. A larger tent gives room for family displays or performances and offers everyone a buffer zone around them.

Rental companies typically put up tents on a Thursday and take them down on a Monday, charging you a one-time fee. Ask for the dates of the company's scheduled assembly and takedown: You'll want the tent, tables, and chairs in place the morning *before* the reunion. Reserve the tent as soon as you know the reunion's date. If you have able-bodied relatives who can follow ambiguous mechanical instructions, you may be able to pick up and set up the tent yourselves, saving on half the rental costs.

Standard we-rent-everything agencies usually offer better rates than party rental agencies, although the stock is generally not as elegant. Many churches and community centers (lodges and VFW halls, for example) rent out folding chairs (and sometimes folding tables) at fees lower than rental company rates. And a table made of plywood and sawhorses, covered with a tablecloth, is a farmhouse staple that still does the trick.

CHECKLIST FOR BACKYARD BARBECUE OR HOMECOMING

Item	Quantity needed	Have on hand	To be supplied and by whom	To be rented
Coolers				
Folding tables (you'll need one by the grill)				
Dining and serving tables				
Folding chairs				
Grills				
Portable P.A. system				
Coffee urns: 55-cup or 100-cup size				
Cold beverage cups				
Coffee cups				
Forks, spoons, and knives				
Napkins				
Dinner plates				
Dessert plates				
Tablecloths				
Ice				
Extension cords				
Guest book and pen				

ASSORTED RENTABLES

• Portable P.A. system: With a combined microphone and amplifier, a P.A. system turns a reunion into an Event. Kids love to gab into a microphone, old folks can hear and be heard, and a speaker can seize the attention of the whole family, creating a cohesive group experience.

• Coffee urns: 55-cup or 100-cup size. Note: Rented coffee urns draw a great deal of electricity. Two urns in one plug = one blown fuse.

• 2 ft. × 5 ft. rectangular grill

• Linen tablecloths and/or napkins: Sure, you can use paper, but renting linen really raises the tone—it doesn't rip, make a crunchy noise, or flap so much the breeze.

• Flatware, glasses, and plates: Another splurge that gives the reunion a boost.

What to Buy

Consider using a restaurant supplier for best prices—some do sell retail. Check with a friendly deli owner or restaurant owner for a name—or they may agree to sell to you directly. Here are the quantities you'll need:

• Cups for cold beverages, preferably 10 ounces: 4 per person, if reunion lasts all day

• Paper coffee cups: 2 per person

• Plastic forks, spoons, and knives: 3 times the number of people attending (preferably the higher-quality utensils that don't bend when you apply pressure and can be washed and used again)

• Napkins: 5 times the number of people attending—better to have too many than too few

• Paper dinner plates: $1\frac{1}{2}$ times the number of people attending

• Dessert plates: $1\frac{1}{2}$ times the number of people attending

---

KITCHEN CHECKLIST

❑ Ajax or other cleanser
❑ Aluminum foil
❑ Aprons: two or three clean ones for people who want to pitch in
❑ Dish towels: clean and bright
❑ Dishwashing liquid
❑ Dishwasher detergent
❑ Garbage bags: twice as many as you imagine you'll need

❑ Liquid hand soap
❑ Matches
❑ Paper towels
❑ Plastic wrap
❑ Pot holders: clean and bright
❑ Sponges and scouring pads
❑ Zip-lock bags, all sizes

CHAPTER SEVEN

Storytellers

The National Storytelling Association publishes a regularly updated directory of storytellers. The directory is broken down by state, and the storytellers briefly describe the kind of stories they tell.

> **National Storytelling Association**
> P.O. Box 309
> Jonesborough, TN 37659
> (800) 525-4514

Square Dance Callers

To find a caller, contact local square dance clubs, western wear or square dance attire shops, or you may contact:

> **The International Caller's Association Callerlab**
> 829 3rd Ave., SE
> Suite 285
> Rochester, MN 55904
> (507) 288-5121

The *National Square Dance Directory* may be obtained for about $10.00 each from:

> **National Square Dance Directory**
> P.O. Box 880
> Brandon, MO 39043
> (800) 542-5575

CHAPTER EIGHT

Flags

The following companies sell flags of various nations:

> **A. Thompson Flags & Banners**
> (800) 426-1350

> **Ace Banner & Flag Co.**
> In NY: (212) 620-9111
> Out of NY state: (800) 675-9112

CHAPTER TEN

Bound Family Histories

Stitching the binding of your family history is an expensive proposition—but you'll have a real *book,* and it will last and last. One company that will help you prepare your manuscript for publication (and, for additional fees, help with the editing and copyediting) is Family History Publishers. A typical family history, 200 pages long with 30 photos, costs almost $1900 for 100 copies.

Family History Publishers
845 South Main
Bountiful, UT 84010
(801) 295-7490

Cookbooks

While it is cheaper for a family to compile its own cookbook and print and bind it at a print shop, some families may look for a more professional appearance. The following companies supply everything from blank recipe cards to spiral-bound, laminated, professional-looking volumes.

G & R Publishing Co.
507 Industrial Street
Waverly, IA 50677-1679
Phone: (800) 383-1679
E-mail: gandr@gandrpublishing.
com

Cookbook Publishers
2101 Kansas City Road
Olathe, KS 66061
Phone: (800) 227-7282

CHAPTER ELEVEN

Photo Calendars

This company makes up good-quality one-year calendars from a single photo, and it offers free shipping and handling.

Mystic Color Lab
Masons Island Road
P.O. Box 144
Mystic, Connecticut 06355-0144
(800) 367-6061
Web site: www.mysticcolorlab.
com

ATTENDANCE LIST

Name of family	Number attending	Hometown

OUR FAMILY REUNION RECORD

The _____ Family Reunion was

held on_____ at _____

_____

Descendants of: _____

Number of attendees: _____

Oldest: _____ Youngest: _____

Family members who traveled farthest: _____

Most newly wed couple: _____

REUNION COMMITTEE

Chief Organizer(s): _____

<u>Name</u>   <u>Responsibility</u>

_____

_____

_____

_____

_____

_____

_____

_____

_____

Next reunion to be held _____

and hosted by _____

_____

NOTES

NOTES

INDEX

A

Activities, 150-76
  awards nights, 173
  banquets, 54, 188-89
  beauty shop, 164
  birth order, 187
  business meetings, 195-96
  campfire, 176
  crafts cabin, 165-70
  dancing, 163-64, 175, 262
  ethnic roots and, 91-92
  evening events, 172-76
  extracurricular outings, 170-71
  family coat of arms, 170
  family time capsule, 173-74
  favorite things, 172-73
  flexibility and, 160
  genealogy workshops, 105
  hired entertainment, 165
  homestead tours, 171
  icebreakers, 186-88
  for in-laws, 203-8
  in-laws' question night, 76
  kids' own name tags, 170
  life stories, 187-88
  limericks, 187
  magic shows, 165
  rainy-day, 162-65
  scheduling, 150-51, 179
  sibling hikes, 210
  skits, 92, 175
  spiritual expression, 189-95,
    197-98
  sports gear for, 152
  structured, for kids, 150, 159-70
  talent shows and fun nights,
    174-75
  for teenagers, 172
  for toddlers, 169
  unstructured, 152

  water play, 161-62, 169
  whole-family, coordinator for,
    31
  your family's United States, 170
  see also Games, for kids; Games,
    intergenerational
Affordability checklist, 26
African American families:
  Alex Haley on oral history, 218
  "Black Family Pledge,"
    (Angelou), 193
  family tree, 110
  genealogy and, 98
  profiles of reunions of, 14-15,
    190-92
  short history of reunions of,
    13-16
Ancestors:
  genealogical research on, 96-99
  illustrious, tales of, 74
  photos of, 92, 182, 184
  visiting gravesites of, 108-12
  see also Family trees
Angelou, Maya, 193
Archival-quality materials, printing
    and storing, 244
Artists, family, 31
Assortative kinship, 85
Attendance lists, 266
Auctions, 27, 182
Awards nights, 173
Awards persons, 31

B

Baby-sitting, 35
Backyard barbecues, 20-21
  budget for, 242
  checklist for, 260
  evaluating feasibility of, 49

F

PHOTO CREDITS

David Burnett/Contact Press Images, *pages 38* (bottom); *40* (bottom); *41* (bottom).

Katina Houvouras, *pages 204–207; 215.*

Roger McCord, *pages 214* (bottom); *216* (bottom, left and right).

Lawrence Okrent, *pages 39* (top); *40* (top, left and right).

Sheila Scully, *pages 49; 166–168; 190–192; 216* (both, top left).

Johnny Sundby/Dakota Skies Photography, *pages 64* (bottom); *65* (bottom); *66; 67.*

Thank-you to all the families who took and sent in pictures of their reunions.

Thank-you to the Workman employees who contributed pictures of their families for the chapter openings.